Endangered and Threatened Animals of Texas
Their Life History and Management
by
Linda Campbell

Resource Protection Division
Endangered Resources Branch
4200 Smith School Road
Austin, Texas 78744

1995

Front cover photographs:
Scenic of grassland near Van Horn, Texas: Glen Mills, Texas Parks and Wildlife Department
Attwater's Prairie Chicken: Ben Brown
Ocelot: Tom Smylie, U.S. Fish and Wildlife Service
Kemp's Ridley Sea Turtle: Bill Reaves, Texas Parks and Wildlife Department

Back cover photographs:
Whooping Crane: Bill Reaves, Texas Parks and Wildlife Department
Fountain Darters: Glenn Longley, Southwest Texas State University
Houston Toad: Glen Mills, Texas Parks and Wildlife Department

Project Coordinators: Lee Ann Johnson Linam and Patricia Morton
Art Director: Pris Martin
Design: Suzanne Davis
Cover Design: Suzanne Davis

©1995 Texas Parks and Wildlife Department
Endangered Resources Branch

Endangered and Threatened Animals of Texas – Their Life History and Management
was funded in part by the U.S. Fish and Wildlife Service,
under Section 6 of the Endangered Species Act.

Another "Learn about Texas" publication from
TEXAS PARKS AND WILDLIFE PRESS
ISBN: 1-885696-04-3

Endangered and Threatened Animals of Texas Their Life History and Management

Introduction

Texas possesses an incredibly rich and diverse natural heritage. Its natural assets include 5,000 species of plants, including 2,000 different wildflowers, 550 species of birds, mountains, deserts, forests, prairies, wetlands, and coastal beaches. Texans have a responsibility to protect the natural resources of the state and to maintain healthy ecosystems for future generations. State and federal agencies can provide technical guidance in managing natural resources, but the survival of ecosystems and species will depend on private landowners and other informed Texans who care and want to help protect the unique natural diversity found only in our great State.

This publication includes information on the distribution, habitat, biology and management of animals occurring in Texas that are listed as endangered or threatened by the U.S. Fish and Wildlife Service. Federally-listed endangered animals are those which are in danger of extinction throughout their range. Threatened animals are those species which could become endangered. Declining animal populations are often a barometer of ecosystem health. They can warn us of threats to the natural resources on which we depend. The decline of species high in the food web, such as the Peregrine Falcon and Bald Eagle, due to pesticide contamination, are reminders that endangered animals sometimes signal problems that can also affect people.

This publication was extensively reviewed by research scientists, agency biologists and resource management professionals familiar with each species and its habitat. The publication is a result of the cooperative efforts of the Texas Parks and Wildlife Department, U.S. Fish and Wildlife Service, U.S. Natural Resources Conservation Service (formerly known as the Soil Conservation Service), Texas Agricultural Extension Service, Texas Department of Agriculture and research scientists from across the United States, Canada, and Mexico. As the state agency responsible for the stewardship of Texas' remarkable wildlife resources, we seek to provide current, accurate, and useful information to landowners and managers, educators, and the public concerning endangered and threatened species. The Department will continue to develop practical, creative solutions to the challenges of endangered species management. Partnership with private landowners, who collectively own and manage over 97% of the land in Texas, is the key to accomplishing lasting conservation of rare resources in Texas.

The publication of this book is significant for two reasons. It brings together in one place valuable information about these species, making it easily accessible to the general public and in particular private landowners upon whose good stewardship these animals depend for their continued existence. Secondly, it has furnished the means by which the USFWS can give landowners certainty that if they follow the management guidelines provided here they will fully comply with the provisions of the Endangered Species Act. That certainty is provided for a minimum of five years. The letter providing that assurance has been reproduced in this publication. For this reason, I believe that for Texas landowners, this is the most significant book on endangered species ever published.

We have tried very hard to present the most accurate and current information concerning the biology and conservation of Texas' endangered and threatened animals. We recognize that our knowledge is incomplete for many of these species. We invite landowners, natural resource professionals, sportsmen, and outdoor enthusiasts throughout Texas to add to our knowledge of these species. Please let us know about how any of the sections can be improved with what you know about these species, their habitats, and how to manage these habitats. We must all work together so we can be proud of the Texas we will leave to future generations.

Andrew Sansom
Executive Director

United States Department of the Interior

FISH AND WILDLIFE SERVICE
P.O. Box 1306
Albuquerque, New Mexico 87103

In Reply Refer To:
Region 2/ES-SE

29 NOV 1995

Mr. Andy Sansom
Texas Parks and Wildlife Department
4200 Smith School Road
Austin, Texas 78744

Dear Mr. Sansom:

We are excited that the joint project to provide management guidelines to landowners for listed animal species is nearing completion. Hopefully, these biologically based guidelines will provide the certainty landowners have been wanting.

Our joint goal was to develop guidelines that if followed would not result in any take of listed species and thus would not require any kind of authorization under the Endangered Species Act. Based on current biological information, we believe the accepted management practices identified in the leaflets meet this goal. Therefore, landowners and other managers using these practices do not need to contact the Service or State for any approval or review. Because data and information may change as ongoing studies and demonstration projects are carried out, we believe the guidelines should be reviewed every 5 years and updated to provide current biology and management practices and ensure they continue to meet the no take goal.

If you have any questions or need assistance in getting these leaflets ready for distribution, please contact Jana Grote in our Austin office at (512) 490-0057.

Sincerely,

Nancy M. Kaufman

Regional Director

Acknowledgements

The Endangered Resources Branch of Texas Parks and Wildlife would like to thank all those who reviewed and commented on the species accounts included in this publication. Assistance from a wide variety of agency biologists, university scientists, and resource management professionals is greatly appreciated. We would also like to thank all those who shared their photos of species and habitats, allowing TPWD to minimize publication costs and to pass this savings along to the people of Texas. Special thanks go to the Graphic Arts Department of Texas Parks and Wildlife for this production. Finally, we are grateful to the U.S. Fish and Wildlife Service for providing funding through Section 6 of the Endangered Species Act.

List of Reviewers

Dr. Scott Altenbach
University of New Mexico
Department of Biology
Albuquerque, New Mexico 87131

Mr. R.E. Ambrose
U.S. Fish and Wildlife Service
1412 Airport Way
Fairbanks, Alaska 99701

Dr. Hector Arita
Centro de Ecologia
UNAM
Apartado Postal 70-275
04510 Mexico, D.F.

Mr. Bill Armstrong
Kerr Wildlife Management Area
Route 1, Box 180
Hunt, Texas 78024

Dr. John Barlow
Department of Ornithology
Royal Ontario Museum
100 Queen's Park
Toronto, Ontario
Canada M5S 2C6

Dr. Bob Barth
University of Texas
Department of Zoology
Austin, Texas 78712

Ms. Carol Beardmore
Ecological Services
U.S. Fish and Wildlife Service
10711 Burnet Road, Suite 200
Austin, Texas 78758

Dr. Robert Benson
Bioacoustics Lab
Dept. of Engineering Technology
Texas A&M University
College Station, Texas 77843

Mr. Gene Blacklock
3525 Bluebonnet
Corpus Christi, Texas 78408

Mr. David Blankinship
Realty Office
U.S. Fish and Wildlife Service
320 North Main, Room 225
McAllen, Texas 78501

Mr. Dan Boone
Texas Parks and Wildlife Dept.
1342 South Wheeler
Jasper, Texas

Ms. Angela Brooks
U.S. Fish and Wildlife Service
Corpus Christi, Texas
Rio Hondo, Texas

Mr. Kirby Brown
Private Lands Enhancement and
    Public Hunting Program
Wildlife Division
Texas Parks and Wildlife Dept.
4200 Smith School Road
Austin, Texas 78744

Dr. Richard Byles
U.S. Fish and Wildlife Service
P.O. Box 1306
Albuquerque, New Mexico
    87103-1306

Mr. Paul Chippindale
Department of Zoology
University of Texas
Austin, Texas 78712-1064

Mr. Fred Collins
Center for Avian Propagation
    and Research
Route 2, Box 625
Hearne, Texas 77859

Mr. Patrick Conner
Ecological Services
U.S. Fish and Wildlife Service
611 East 6th Street, Suite 407
Austin, Texas 78701

Mr. Terry Cook
The Nature Conservancy of Texas
P.O. Box 164255
Austin, Texas 78716-4255

Mr. Tim Cooper
U.S. Fish and Wildlife Service
c/o Corpus Christi State University
Campus Box 338
6300 Ocean Drive
Corpus Christi, Texas 78412

Mr. John Cornelius
U.S. Army, HQ III Corps & Ft. Hood
Attn: AFZF-PW-ENV-NR, Bldg. 1938
Fort Hood, Texas 76544-5057

Ms. Noreen Damude
Nongame and Urban Wildlife
    Program
Wildlife Division
Texas Parks and Wildlife Dept.
4200 Smith School Road

Austin, Texas 78744

Dr. David Diamond
Endangered Resources Branch
Resource Protection Division
Texas Parks and Wildlife Dept.
4200 Smith School Road
Austin, Texas 78744

Dr. Jim Dixon
Dept. of Wildlife and Fisheries
Texas A&M University
Nagle Hall
College Station, Texas 77843

Dr. Anthony Echelle
Zoology Department
Oklahoma State University
Stillwater, Oklahoma 74074

Dr. Robert Edwards
Department of Biology
Pan American University
Edinburg, Texas 78539

Mr. Lee Elliott
Endangered Resources Branch
Resource Protection Division
Texas Parks and Wildlife Dept.
Corpus Christi State University
6300 Ocean Drive
Box 317
Corpus Christi, Texas 78412

Dr. William R. Elliott
12102 Grimsley Drive
Austin, Texas 78759

Mr. Tom Engles
Department of Zoology
University of Texas at Austin
Patterson Bldg. No. 140
Austin, Texas 78712

Ms. Edith Erfling
U.S. Fish and Wildlife Service
17629 El Camino Real, Suite 211
Clear Lake, Texas 77058

Mr. Ted Eubanks
2701 Amherst
Houston, Texas 77005

Mr. Mike Farmer
National Audubon Society
P.O. Box 5052
Brownsville, Texas 78523

Dr. Ted Fleming
Department of Biology
University of Miami
Coral Gables, Florida 33124

Mr. Nathan Garner

Texas Parks and Wildlife Dept.
11942 FM 848
Tyler, Texas 75707

Mr. Gary Garrett
Heart of the Hills Research Station
HCR-7, Box 62
Ingram, Texas 78025

Dr. Fred Gehlbach
Department of Biology
Baylor University
Waco, Texas 76798

Mr. Rick Gilliland
USDA/APHIS
WTSU 2402 North 3rd Ave.
P.O. Box 277 WT STA
Canyon, Texas 79016

Mr. Phil Glass
U.S. Fish and Wildlife Service
17629 El Camino Real, Suite 211
Clear Lake, Texas 77058

Dr. Gary Graham
Endangered Resources Branch
Resource Protection Division
Texas Parks and Wildlife Dept.
4200 Smith School Road
Austin, Texas 78744

Dr. Brian D. Greene
819 East Guinevere
Springfield, Missouri 65807

Dr. Sue Haig
Cooperative Ecosystem Research
    Unit, NBS
Oregon State University
3200 S. W. Jefferson Way
Corvallis, Oregon 97331

Mr. Lou Hanebury
U.S. Fish and Wildlife Service
1501 14th Street West, Suite 230
Billings, Montana 59102

Mr. Tim Hayden
Construction Engineering
    Research Lab
Department of the Army
Attn: CECER - IMT
P.O. Box 9005
Champaign, Illinois 61826-9005

Ms. Ann Henry
Ecological Services
U.S. Fish and Wildlife Service
10711 Burnet Road, Suite 200
Austin, Texas 78758

Ms. Laura Hill
U.S. Fish and Wildlife Service
911 N. E. 11th Ave.
Portland, Oregon 97232

Dr. Dave Hillis
Department of Zoology
University of Texas
Austin, Texas 78712-1064

Ms. Peggy Horner
Endangered Resources Branch
Resource Protection Division
Texas Parks and Wildlife Dept.
4200 Smith School Road
Austin, Texas 78744

Dr. Clark Hubbs
Department of Zoology
University of Texas
Austin, Texas 78712-1064

Dr. Grainger Hunt
BioSystems Analysis, Inc.
303 Potrero Street, Suite 29-203
Santa Cruz, California 95060

Dr. Clyde Jones
Department of Biology
Texas Tech University
Lubbock, Texas 79409

Mr. Matt Judy
U.S. Natural Resources
    Conservation Service
7300 N. IH 35
Temple, Texas 76501

Mr. Royce Jurries
1131 Travis Street
Columbus, Texas 78934

Mr. Dean Keddy-Hector
Endangered Resources Branch
Resource Protection Division
Texas Parks and Wildlife Dept.
4200 Smith School Road
Austin, Texas 78744

Dr. Flavius Killebrew
Department of Biology and
    Geosciences
West Texas State University
Canyon, Texas 79016

Dr. Mark Kirkpatrick
Department of Zoology
University of Texas
Austin, Texas 78712-1064

Mr. Randy Kreil

Natural Resource Biologist
North Dakota Game and Fish Dept.
100 North Bismarck Expressway
Bismarck, North Dakota 58501-5095

Ms. Linda Laack
Laguna Atascosa NWR
U.S. Fish and Wildlife Service
P.O. Box 450
Rio Hondo, Texas 78583

Mr. Steve Labuda
U.S. Fish and Wildlife Service
Attwater Prairie Chicken NWR
P.O. Box 518
Eagle Lake, Texas 77434

Mr. Clifton Ladd
Espey, Huston & Assoc., Inc.
916 Capital of Texas Hwy. South
P.O. Box 519
Austin, Texas 78767

Dr. Jake Landers
Texas A&M University
Extension Range Specialist

Mr. Mike Lang
U.S. Fish and Wildlife Service
Brazoria NWR
P.O. Box 1088
Angleton, Texas 77516-1088

Mr. Rick Larkin
Texas Parks and Wildlife Dept.
1805 East Lufkin Avenue
Lufkin, Texas 75901

Mr. Greg M. Lasley
1507 Alameda
Austin, Texas 78704

Mr. Jim Lewis
Regional Office
U.S. Fish and Wildlife Service
P.O. Box 1306
Albuquerque, New Mexico
     87103-1306

Ms. Lee Ann Johnson Linam
Endangered Resources Branch
Resource Protection Division
Texas Parks and Wildlife Dept.
4200 Smith School Road
Austin, Texas 78744

Mr. Glenn Longley
Edwards Aquifer Research and
     Data Center
Southwest Texas State University
San Marcos, Texas 78666

Mr. David Mabie
Texas Parks and Wildlife Dept.
715 South Bronte
Rockport, Texas 78382

Dr. Robert MacFarlane
MacFarlane and Associates
9503 Sharpview Drive
Houston, Texas 77036

c. Dr. Rene Marquez-M.
Instituto Nacional de la Pesca
P.N.I.M.T.M.
Playa Ventanas S/N
Apartado Postal 591
Manzanillo, Colima
28200 Mexico, C.P.

Dr. Terry Maxwell
Department of Biology
Angelo State University
San Angelo, Texas 76901

Mr. Gene Miller
Texas Parks and Wildlife Dept.
3409 South Georgia, Suite 25
Amarillo, Texas 79109

Mr. Mark Mitchell
Texas Parks and Wildlife Dept.
P.O. Box 41
Lolita, Texas 77971

Ms. Pat Morton
Endangered Resources Branch
Resource Protection Division
Texas Parks and Wildlife Dept.
4200 Smith School Road
Austin, Texas 78744

Dr. Randy Moss
Freshwater Studies
Texas Parks and Wildlife Dept.
P.O. Box 947
San Marcos, Texas 78667

Mr. Steve Nelle
U.S. Natural Resources
     Conservation Service
33 East Twohig, Room 108
San Angelo, Texas 76903

Ms. Kathy Nemec
U.S. Fish and Wildlife Service
17629 El Camino Real, Suite 211
Clear Lake, Texas 77058

Mr. Patrick O'Connor
U.S. Fish and Wildlife Service
611 East 6th Street, Suite 407
Austin, Texas 78701

Ms. Lisa O'Donnell
U.S. Fish and Wildlife Service
Ecological Services
10711 Burnet Road, Suite 200
Austin, Texas 78758

Dr. David Owens
Department of Biology
Texas A&M University
College Station, Texas 77843

Ms. Melissa Parker
Endangered Resources Branch
Resource Protection Division
Texas Parks and Wildlife Dept.
P.O. Box 4655
SFA Station
Nacogdoches, Texas 75962

Dr. Andy Price
Endangered Resources Branch
Resource Protection Division
Texas Parks and Wildlife Dept.
4200 Smith School Road
Austin, Texas 78744

Dr. John Rappole
Convention and Research Center
National Zoological Park
Smithsonian Institute
Front Royal, Virginia 22630

Dr. James Reddell
Texas Memorial Museum
University of Texas
2400 Trinity
Austin, Texas 78705

Ms. Dickie Revera
NMFS Lab
4700 Ave. U
Galveston, Texas 77551

Ms. Sarah Rinkevich
U.S. Fish and Wildlife Service
Albuquerque, New Mexico

Mr. David Riskind
Public Lands Division
Texas Parks and Wildlife Dept.
4200 Smith School Road
Austin, Texas 78744

Dr. Craig Rudolph
So. Forest Experiment Station
P.O. Box 7600
SFA Station
Nacogdoches, Texas 75962

Dr. Mark Ryan
School of Natural Resources
University of Missouri
Columbia, Missouri 65211

Mr. Craig Saanes
U.S. Fish and Wildlife Service
203 West 2nd Street
Grand Island, Nebraska 68801

Dr. David Schmidly
TAMU Galveston
P.O. Box 1675
Galveston, Texas 77553

Dr. Charles Sexton
Austin Department of
    Environmental Protection
P.O. Box 1088
Austin, Texas 78767

Ms. Donna Shaver
Padre Island National Seashore
National Park Service
9405 South Padre Island Drive
Corpus Christi, Texas 78418

Ms. Judy Sheppard
Colorado Division of Wildlife
6060 Broadway
Denver, Colorado 80216

Dr. Nova Silvy
Dept. of Wildlife and
    Fisheries Sciences
Texas A&M University
Nagle Hall
College Station, Texas 77843-2258

Mr. Raymond Skiles
USDI, National Park Service
Big Bend National Park, Texas
    79834

Dr. Doug Slack
Dept. of Wildlife and Fisheries
Texas A&M University
Nagle Hall
College Station, Texas 77843-2258

Mr. Sylvestre Sorola
Texas Parks and Wildlife Dept.
106 Jodobo
Del Rio, Texas 78840

Dr. Warren Pulich, Sr.
2021 Rosebud Drive
Irving, Texas 75060

Ms. Ruth Stanford
Ecological Services
U.S. Fish and Wildlife Service
10711 Burnet Road, Suite 200
Austin, Texas 78758

Mr. Warren Starnes
U.S.D.A. Forest Service
Homer Garrison Federal Bldg.
701 N. First
Lufkin, Texas 75901

Dr. David Steed
David L. Steed & Assoc.
107 Hwy. 620 South, 8F
Austin, Texas 78734

Ms. Mary Jo Stegman
U.S. Fish and Wildlife Service
17629 El Camino Real, Suite 211
Clear Lake, Texas 77058

Dr. Don Steinbach
Texas Agricultural Extension Service
Dept. of Wildlife and Fisheries
Texas A&M University
Nagle Hall
College Station, Texas 77843-2258

Mr. David Stuart
Kickapoo Caverns State Park
P.O. Box 705
Brackettville, Texas 78832

Mr. Danny Swepston
Texas Parks and Wildlife Dept.
3409 South Georgia, Suite 25
Amarillo, Texas 79109

Dr. David Tazik
Construction Engineering
    Research Lab
Department of the Army
Attn: CECER - IMT
P.O. Box 9005
Champaign, Illinois 61826-9005

Dr. Michael Tewes
Texas A&I University
Box 218
Kingsville, Texas 78363

Dr. Bruce Thompson
NBS, Cooperative Wildlife
    Research Unit
New Mexico State University
Las Cruces, New Mexico 88003

Mr. Steve Thompson
Laguna Atascosa NWR
U.S. Fish and Wildlife Service
P.O. Box 450
Rio Hondo, Texas 78583

Mr. Okla W. Thorton, Jr.
Route 2, Box 398
Ballinger, Texas 76821

Mr. Jerry Turrentine
U.S. Natural Resources
    Conservation Service
1022 Garner Field Road, Suite 101
Uvalde, Texas 78801

Dr. Merlin Tuttle
Bat Conservation International
P.O. Box 162603
Austin, Texas 78716

Mr. Gary Valentine
U.S. Natural Resource
    Conservation Service
W.R. Poage Federal Bldg.
101 South Main
Temple, Texas 76501

Dr. George Veni
Veni and Associates
11304 Candle Park
San Antonio, Texas 78249

Mr. Gary Waggerman
Las Palomas Wildlife
    Management Area
410 North 13th
Edinburg, Texas 78539

Mr. Matt Wagner
Nongame and Urban Wildlife
    Program
Wildlife Division
Texas Parks and Wildlife Dept.
4200 Smith School Road
Austin, Texas 78744

Mr. Rex Wahl
Division of Environmental Affairs
Texas Department of Transportation
125 East 11th
Austin, Texas 78701-2483

Dr. Tommy Welch
Dept. of Rangeland Ecology and
    Management
Texas A&M University
College Station, Texas

Dr. Larry White
Dept. of Rangeland Ecology and
    Management
Texas A&M University
College Station, Texas

Dr. Bobby Whiteside
Aquatic Biology Department
Southwest Texas State University
San Marcos, Texas 78666

Ms. Kim Withers
Dept. of Wildlife and Fisheries
    Science
Texas A&M University
Nagle Hall
College Station, Texas 77843-2258

Mr. Jim Yantis
Texas Parks and Wildlife Dept.
Route 1, Box 611
Hearne, Texas 77859

Mr. Curt Zonick
School of Natural Resources
University of Missouri
Columbia, Missouri 65211

Greater Long-nosed Bat

Scientific Name: *Leptonycteris nivalis*

Federal Status: Endangered, 9/30/88 • State Status: Endangered

Description

The Greater or Mexican Long-nosed Bat is a relatively large bat compared with most U.S. bat species. It measures about 2 3/4 to 3 3/4 inches in total length, can be dark gray to "sooty" brown in color, and has a long muzzle with a prominent nose leaf at the tip. Its long tongue, an adaptation for feeding on flower nectar, can be extended up to 3 inches and has hair-like papillae on its tip. It has a minute tail that may appear to be lacking.

Greater Long-nosed Bat
© Merlin D. Tuttle

Distribution and Habitat

The Greater Long-nosed Bat has been found in southwestern New Mexico, the Big Bend area of Texas, the Chinati Mountains of Presidio County, Texas and southward to central Mexico. The species was first discovered in the United States in 1937 in a cave in the Chisos Mountains of Big Bend National Park. In Texas and northern Mexico, at the northern part of their range, these bats are found in desert scrub vegetation dotted with century plants (agaves), mesquite, creosotebush, and a variety of cacti. In Big Bend National Park, long-nosed bats are associated with five distinct vegetation types at various elevations. These include the arroyo-mesquite-acacia (1800-4000 ft.), lechuguilla-creosotebush-

cactus (1800-3500 ft.), deciduous woodland (3700-7800 ft.), pinyon-juniper-oak woodland (3700-7800 ft.), and cypress-pine-oak (5800-7200 ft.).

For day roosting sites, Greater Long-nosed Bats depend on caves, crevices, abandoned mines, tunnels, and old buildings. These highly colonial bats are frequently found near the entrances of caves and other roosts, in the twilight zones. The bats often occupy the same roosts from year to year. In the United States, thousands of individuals may roost together at a single site, although large aggregations are more uncommon today than in the past.

Life History

Although movement patterns are not well known, Greater Long-nosed Bats are thought to move from central Mexico into northern Mexico each year, with part of the population crossing the border into Texas and New Mexico. The colony of bats at Big Bend, and perhaps those in northern Mexico, occupy their northern roosts from June through August, after which they move south to winter in central Mexico.

The young are born in Mexico during April, May and early June, then move northward with their mothers. Females are believed to give birth to one or perhaps two young each year. Although not documented for the Greater Long-nosed Bat, mothers of other bat species recognize their own young by a combination of smell and distress cries made by their offspring. Young bats nurse for about one month and are generally capable of flying by five weeks of age. Few adult males have been recorded in Texas, suggesting that males and females may segregate geographically, with males rarely appearing in the most northerly part of the species' range.

The feeding ecology of the Greater Long-nosed Bat is of great importance in understanding its life

history and recent decline. These bats are nectar feeders, emerging at night to feed on the showy flowers of plants such as agave or century plants (*Agave* spp.). They are very strong, highly maneuverable fliers, and like hummingbirds, are able to hover in flight while they feed. A mutual relationship exists, with the bats depending on the plants for food, and the plants benefitting from the bats as pollinators.

Agaves flower by sending up a green stalk supporting numerous flower clusters that produce large quantities of nectar each night. Besides consuming the nectar, the bats also ingest pollen, picked up inadvertently on their fur as they feed and later ingested during grooming. The pollen provides vitamins and minerals and is rich in protein. Agave nectar is 17-22% sugar, and the pollen is about 20% protein.

The Greater Long-nosed Bat and a similar species, the Lesser Long-nosed Bat (*Leptonycteris curasoae*), are the main pollinators of several agave species, including *Agave angustifolia* (mezcal plant), *A. salmiana* (pulque plant), and *A. tequilana* (tequila plant). The Greater Long-nosed Bat prefers higher and cooler places in parts of New Mexico, Texas, and Mexico;

whereas, the Lesser Long-nosed Bat generally inhabits lower elevations in New Mexico, Arizona, Mexico, and parts of Central and South America. In some areas, the two species are found together.

Greater Long-nosed Bats, with their long muzzles and tongues, are well adapted to feeding on nectar and protein-rich pollen. Adapted for specialized feeding, they migrate to follow the bloom periods of a number of plant species. In Big Bend National Park, agaves begin blooming in mid-May at lower elevations and early June at higher altitudes. The bats arrive in Texas about one month after flowering of agaves has begun. After spending most of the summer in Big Bend, they leave the United States in late summer or early fall as the agaves go out of bloom. They follow later-blooming agaves southward through Mexico. By November, they are several hundred miles into Mexico, where they feed on the blooms of subtropical trees and cacti. They spend the winter in the lush Central Valley of Mexico, feeding on a large variety of flowers. In the spring, they work their way back north, following the bloom times of various cacti and agaves.

Threats and Reasons for Decline

Although the Greater Long-nosed Bat occurs throughout much of Mexico, there are indications of substantial population decline both in the United States and Mexico. The population at the only known roosting site in the United States, a cave in Big Bend National Park, fluctuates widely in numbers from one year to the next. Yearly estimates of population size range from zero to as many as 10,650 individuals. Reasons for these fluctuations are unknown, but some scientists believe that the colony forms in years when overpopulation or low food supply in Mexico forces the bats to move northward. However, even considering natural fluctuations and different methods of estimating numbers, there still appears to be a downward trend in the numbers of bats at the Big Bend colony.

Population declines in Mexico have also been documented. An abandoned mine in Nuevo Leon, Mexico, which had an estimated population of 10,000 Greater Long-nosed Bats in 1938, had no sign of the species in 1983. Another mine in Nuevo Leon had a ceiling covered with newborn bats in 1967, but only one bat was found in 1983. Considering this information, the U.S. Fish and Wildlife Service added this bat, along with its close relative the Lesser Long-nosed Bat, to the list of endangered species in 1988.

The reasons for these population declines are not entirely understood, but are thought to be associated with loss of roosting sites and food sources. Colonial roosting species, such as many bats, are particularly vulnerable to disturbance and destruction of roosting habitat, since this can result in the displacement of large numbers of animals at one time. Also, only a limited number of caves, mines, and other roost sites provide the proper roosting environment (temperature and humidity). While the roost site in the United States is protected within Big Bend National Park, the bats spend most of the year in Mexico, where human disturbance and destruction of roost sites is a common occurrence. In Mexico, a country with 137 species of bats, there are few laws protecting bats or their roosts. However, in May of 1991 the Mexican government listed three bat species (*Choeronycteris mexicana*, *Leptonycteris nivalis*, and *L. curasoae*) as endangered. In addition, two bat caves are proposed for protection by the State of Tamaulipas.

In tropical Mexico where vampire bats are a problem, ranchers and the public often consider all bats to be vampire bats, which sometimes spread diseases to livestock and people. Thus, destructive control practices targeted for vampire bats often kill beneficial species.

Loss of food sources may be another threat contributing to the decline of the Greater Long-nosed Bat. Agaves are an important food source, and are the primary blooming plants available in northern Mexico during their northern migration in the spring, and again in August when they move south. Harvest of agaves for the production of liquor, and in northeastern Mexico, for preparation of "quiote," a traditional sweet, may be contributing to the decline of this important food source. However, the extent to which these harvest activites affect the bats is unknown.

Agave plants are harvested just before they bloom by removing the "cabeza" or carbohydrate-rich meristem (actively growing tissue) and

Agave plants in bloom
© Merlin D. Tuttle

leaf base at the center of the plants. When agaves are harvested, not only are they removed from the bats' present food supply, but future generations of agave plants also are eliminated. This is especially critical, since a single plant grows for 30 to 40 years and flowers only once, then dies.

Finally, the loss of agave plants due to clearing of rangeland areas in northern Mexico may also reduce the food supply and thus affect bat populations. Again, the degree to which these activities affect the bats is unknown.

Recovery Efforts

Research is currently underway to better understand the life history, habitat requirements, limiting factors, and management practices affecting the Greater Long-nosed Bat and the plants which provide their food. Efforts by scientists to locate roosting sites are currently being initiated in Mexico. Periodic surveys are conducted to assess population status at the only known roosting cave in the United States, located in Big Bend National Park.

Greater Long-nosed Bat in flight
© Merlin D. Tuttle

Recovery efforts also include providing information to the general public and school children concerning the great diversity and importance of bats. Education campaigns are also underway in Mexico to provide information to the public concerning management of vampire bats.

Where To Learn More About the Greater Long-nosed Bat

Visit Big Bend National Park to learn more about the Greater Long-nosed Bat and its habitat. Read about Texas bats in *The Bats of Texas* by David Schmidly. Bat Conservation International, a non-profit organization located in Austin, can provide additional information on Texas bats.

How You Can Help

If you enter a cave or other place where bats are present, be aware that these mammals are very sensitive to human disturbances. Maternity colonies and hibernating bats should be avoided, since even slight disturbances can be harmful. It is best to leave the area immediately. Viewing of bats is best done by waiting outside the roost site until the bats emerge to feed in the evening. Also, because the Greater Long-nosed Bat depends on agave plants for its food, do not cut or otherwise disturb these plants.

You can be involved in the conservation of Texas' nongame wildlife resources by supporting the Special Nongame and Endangered Species Conservation Fund. Special nongame stamps are available at Texas Parks and Wildlife Department (TPWD) field offices, most state parks, and the License Branch of TPWD headquarters in Austin. Part of the proceeds from these sales are used to protect habitat and provide information concerning endangered species.

Visit a Texas bat emergence on a Conservation Passport tour. Conservation Passports, available from TPWD, are valid for one year and allow unlimited access to most State Parks, State Natural Areas, and Wildlife Management Areas. You can help by supporting bat conservation efforts in the United States and in Mexico. Conservation organizations in Texas also welcome your participation and support.

For More Information Contact

Texas Parks and Wildlife Department
Endangered Resources Branch
4200 Smith School Road
Austin, Texas 78744
(512) 912-7011 or (800) 792-1112
or
U.S. Fish and Wildlife Service
Ecological Services Field Office
10711 Burnet Road, Suite 200
Austin, Texas 78758
(512) 490-0057

References

Arita, H.T. 1991. "Spatial Segregation in Long-nosed Bats, *Leptonycteris nivalis* and *Leptonycteris curasoae*, in Mexico." *Journal of Mammalogy* 72(4):706-714.

Arita, H.T., and D.E. Wilson. 1987. "Long-Nosed Bats and Agaves: The Tequila Connection." *Bats* Vol.5, No. 4. Bat Conservation International. pp. 3-5.

Easterla, D.A. 1972. "Status of *Leptonycteris nivalis* in Big Bend National Park, Texas." *Southwestern Naturalist* 17:287-292.

Howell, D.J. 1988. *Report on* Leptonycteris nivalis *for Big Bend National Park*. 11 pp.

Nabhan, G.P. 1985. *Gathering the Desert*. The University of Arizona Press. Tucson, AZ. 209 pp.

Neighbor, D.S. 1992. *Status Report and Protocol for the Mexican Long-nosed Bat* (Leptonycteris nivalis). National Park Service, Big Bend National Park, Texas. 10 pp.

Schmidly, David J. 1991. *The Bats of Texas*. Texas A&M University Press. College Station, TX. 188 pp.

Wilson, D.E. 1985. *Status Report:* Leptonycteris nivalis (Saussure) *Mexican Long-nosed Bat*. U.S. Fish and Wildlife Service, Denver Wildlife Research Center, National Museum of Natural History, Washington, D.C. 33 pp.

Funds for the production of this leaflet were provided by the U.S. Fish and Wildlife Service, under Section 6 of the Endangered Species Act.

Black-footed Ferret

Scientific Name: *Mustela nigripes*

Federal Status: Endangered, 3/11/67 • State Status: Endangered

Description

Black-footed Ferrets are buckskin-tan in color with distinctive body markings, including a black face-mask, dark "saddle" on the back, black feet and legs, and a black-tipped tail. The breast and stomach are light tan to cream in color. Adult ferrets range in total length from 18 to 24 inches. Their tail is approximately one-quarter the length of the body. The ferret is a member of the weasel family.

Black-footed Ferret
© USFWS Dean Biggins

Black-footed Ferrets can be confused with the smaller Long-tailed Weasel. Adult Long-tailed Weasels are about 12 to 20 inches in total length, and have a proportionately longer tail, nearly half or more of body length. The south-western color phase of the Long-tailed Weasel is brown in color with yellowish-white underparts and white patches on the forehead and below the ears. These weasels have a black tip on the tail but do not have black feet. Southwestern Long-tailed Weasels are sometimes referred to as "bridled weasels."

Black-footed Ferrets can also be confused with domestic European Ferrets, which are sold as pets. These animals have long, coarse guard hairs and a completely dark tail. They may have a faint face mask. European Ferrets are yellow to black in body color and often have black legs. Their muzzle is more pointed than that of the Black-footed ferret.

Habitat

The Black-footed Ferret once inhabited extensive areas of the western plains. Ferrets rely on prairie dogs for food and shelter. Because of this, active prairie dog colonies provide potential habitat for Black-footed Ferrets. It is estimated that over 100 million acres of western rangelands were occupied by prairie dogs in the early 1900's. Early accounts of huge prairie dog towns are common. For example, Bailey in 1905 recorded an almost continuous prairie dog town extending in a strip about 100 miles wide and 250 miles long on the high plains of Texas. Until about 60 years ago, prairie dog colonies provided a nearly continuous patchwork of ferret habitat, interrupted only by areas of undisturbed rangeland, mountain ranges, and large rivers.

Historically, the range of the Black-footed Ferret coincided closely with the range of prairie dogs throughout the Great Plains, semi-arid grasslands, and mountain basins of North America. Based on written accounts and specimens collected since its identification, the historical range of the ferret in the U.S. included Arizona, Colorado, Kansas, Montana, Nebraska, New Mexico, North Dakota, Oklahoma, South Dakota, Texas, Utah, and Wyoming, in addition to the Canadian Province of Saskatchewan and the Mexican State of Chihuahua. Black-footed Ferrets may have occupied nearly all adequate prairie dog habitat available to them regardless of prairie dog species, vegetation, soils, or climate.

Three of the five species of prairie dogs are known to have supported Black-footed Ferrets: Black-tailed Prairie Dogs on the shortgrass prairies of the Great Plains and Southwest; White-tailed Prairie Dogs in Wyoming, and northern Utah and Colorado; and Gunnison's Prairie Dogs in Arizona, New Mexico, and southern Utah and Colorado. The other two species of prairie dogs, Utah and Mexican, may have also supported ferrets.

In Texas, the Black-tailed Prairie Dog historically occurred throughout the High Plains, Rolling Plains, and Trans-Pecos regions. Today, the largest active prairie dog colonies in Texas occur in the Panhandle, although some areas in the Trans-Pecos also support large prairie dog towns. Colonies also exist on public lands such as the Rita Blanca National Grasslands in Dallam county, Muleshoe National Wildlife Refuge (NWR) in Bailey county, and Buffalo Lake NWR in Randall County. It is estimated that about 53,700 acres of prairie

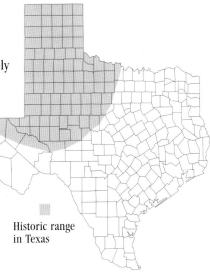

Historic range
in Texas

dog towns exist in the Texas Panhandle.

There have been no confirmed reports of Black-footed Ferrets in Texas since 1963. It is believed that existing prairie dog colonies are either too small or isolated from one another to support Black-footed Ferrets. However, the larger prairie dog colonies in the northern

Panhandle may still provide habitat for these endangered animals.

Life History

Black-footed Ferrets hunt primarily at night, so they are rarely seen. They live in burrows made by prairie dogs. Prairie dogs comprise about 90 percent of the ferret's diet, although they also eat rabbits, mice, voles, ground squirrels, pocket gophers, birds, and insects.

Little is known regarding the life history of Black-footed Ferrets in the wild. Only two populations have been studied; one in South Dakota and one in Wyoming. From the study in South Dakota, we know that a ferret family consisting of one female and young require a minimum of about 100 acres of prairie dog colony. The area required to support a sustainable breeding population of 40 to 60 adult ferrets is estimated to be about 6000 acres of prairie dog towns, either contiguous or located within about 4 miles of one another.

Ferrets have not been observed mating in the wild, but captive ferrets have been observed breeding in March and early April. Captive ferrets have a gestation period of 41 to 45 days, and litter sizes range from 3 to 5. The female alone cares for the young, even though the male may stay in the same prairie dog town. By early July, the young ferrets make their first appearance above ground, usually in the early morning. They begin to occupy separate burrows by late August or early September. By September, young ferrets are nearly full grown and begin to disperse from their birthplace to unoccupied territories within the colony or to nearby prairie dog towns. It is during this dispersal period that the young are exposed to the greatest danger. Ferrets do not hibernate and are usually solitary during the late fall and winter.

Many things can kill Black-footed Ferrets. Predators such as owls, eagles, hawks, coyotes, badgers, foxes, and bobcats are the main cause of death for wild ferrets. Some ferrets are killed crossing roads, particularly during the fall dispersal period. Canine distemper, to which ferrets have no natural immunity, has caused serious losses, especially in Wyoming. Ferrets are probably also susceptible to rabies, tularemia, leptospirosis, mange, and various other infections.

Threats and Reasons for Decline

In Texas, reasons for decline in the prairie dog population, and thus the Black-footed Ferret, include conversion of rangeland to cropland, elimination of prairie dog towns, urban development, and introduced diseases such as sylvatic plague. Sylvatic plague, a disease affecting prairie dogs and other rodents, is a fairly common occurrence in the Panhandle, and is a significant mortality factor in some years. For example, the prairie dog population on the Muleshoe National Wildlife Refuge was nearly eliminated by plague during a 2 week period in 1974. Although there have been no documented cases of sylvatic plague affecting Black-footed Ferrets directly, the indirect effects of a reduced food supply would certainly have serious consequences.

It is estimated that less than one percent of historical prairie dog habitat remains in Texas. The presence of large, healthy prairie dog towns may not always seem compatible with agricultural grazing interests. Prairie dogs feed on many of the same grasses and forbs that livestock do. They therefore reduce the amount of forage available for livestock, although studies show this reduction may be partially offset by improved nutritional content of forage. The competition between prairie dogs and livestock is a major factor in the human-caused decline of prairie dogs and Black-footed Ferrets. Also, many prairie dog towns adjacent to cropland have been eliminated to prevent crop depradation, which can be significant, particularly on winter wheat.

Isolation of habitat may have also contributed to the decline of prairie dogs and Black-footed Ferrets in Texas. The inability of young ferrets to find suitable habitat after leaving their birthplace is a major cause of mortality. Habitat fragmentation affects the exchange of individuals and thus genetic material, which is necessary to maintain viable breeding populations.

Maintaining prairie dog colonies is vital to recovery of the Black-footed Ferret in Texas. Prairie dog towns are the basis for a unique ecosystem which supports many other species. One study identified more that 140 species of wildlife associated with prairie dog towns. Vacant prairie dog burrows provide homes for Burrowing Owls, Cottontail Rabbits, and various small rodents and reptiles. Birds of prey, such as the Ferruginous Hawk are attracted by the abundance of small mammals. Mountain Plovers feed on insects and nest in areas of shortgrass and bare ground. Songbirds frequently appear in greater numbers on prairie dog towns than in surrounding prairie,

Shortgrass prairie
© TPWD

since seeds and insects are often more abundant and visible. These unique patches of habitat provide for a wide variety of plants and animals, adding valuable biological diversity to the landscape.

Recovery Efforts

State and federal agencies, in cooperation with private landowners and conservation groups, are beginning to reintroduce Black-footed Ferrets to the wild. Reintroduction efforts have begun in Wyoming, and other states plan to follow. The first releases are planned on public land and will be experimental, as researchers learn the best ways to return Black-footed Ferrets to their native habitat. Research with captive ferrets is attempting to answer the many questions regarding reproduction and behavior. Black-footed Ferrets are also being maintained and bred at several zoos and other facilites around the country. In Texas, efforts are being made to inform landowners and the general public regarding the importance of conserving and managing prairie dog colonies.

Prairie dogs
© TPWD Glen Mills

How You Can Help

You can be involved with the conservation of Texas' wildlife resources by supporting the Special Nongame and Endangered Species Conservation Fund. Special nongame stamps and decals are available at Texas Parks and Wildlife Department (TPWD) field offices, most state parks, and the License Branch of TPWD headquarters in Austin. If you see a Black-footed Ferret in the wild, report it to the Texas Parks and Wildlife Department or the U.S. Fish and Wildlife Service.

If you own or manage land with prairie dog colonies, you can contact the Texas Parks and Wildlife Department or U.S. Natural Resources Conservation Service for range and wildlife management recommendations that will benefit your ranching operation and maintain the diversity of native wildlife found on your property.

For More Information Contact

Texas Parks and Wildlife Department
Endangered Resources Branch
4200 Smith School Road
Austin, Texas 78744
(512) 912-7011 or (800) 792-1112
or
U.S. Fish and Wildlife Service
Ecological Services Field Office
10711 Burnet Road, Suite 200
Austin, Texas 78758
(512) 490-0057

Management guidelines are available from the Texas Parks and Wildlife Department or U.S. Fish and Wildlife Service for landowners and managers wishing to conserve and manage prairie dog communities.

References

Bonham, C.D., and A. Lerwick. 1976. *Vegetation changes induced by prairie dogs on shortgrass range.* J. Range Manage. 29(3):221-225.

Davis, W.B. 1974. *Mammals of Texas.* Texas Parks and Wildlife Bull. 41. p. 101-102.

Forrest, S.C., T.W. Clark, L. Richardson, and T.M. Campbell III. 1985. *Black-footed ferret habitat: some management and reintroduction considerations.* Wyoming BLM Wildlife Technical Bull. No. 2. 48pp.

Foster, N.S., and S.E. Hygnstrom. 1990. *Prairie dogs and their ecosystem.* Univ. of Nebraska-Lincoln, Dept. of Forestry, Fisheries, and Wildlife.

O'Meilia, M.E., F.L. Knopf, and J.C. Lewis. 1982. *Some consequences of competition between prairie dogs and beef cattle.* J. Range Manage. 35(5):580-585.

Texas Parks and Wildlife Department. 1991. *Black-footed ferret reintroduction evaluation status survey.* Final Section 6 Report. Project No. E-1-3.

U.S. Fish and Wildlife Service. 1988. *Black-footed ferret recovery plan.* Denver, CO. 154 pp.

Whicker, A.D., and J.K. Detling. *Ecological consequences of prairie dog disturbances.* BioScience 38(11):778-785.

Funds for the production of this leaflet were provided by the U.S. Fish and Wildlife Service, under Section 6 of the Endangered Species Act.

Management Guidelines for the Black-footed Ferret

The following guidelines address management practices that can be used to conserve prairie dog colonies and the wildlife they support. They are intended primarily to serve as general guidance for landowners and managers of livestock and wildlife operations in Texas.

Prairie dog
© TPWD Glen Mills

Conservation and Management of Prairie Dog Colonies

Conservation of prairie dog colonies is vital, since the Black-footed Ferret is totally dependent on prairie dogs for survival. Prairie dogs play an important role in their ecosystem by creating islands of unique habitat. Their daily activities change the physical characteristics of the community, which leads to increased plant and animal diversity. More that 100 other wildlife species can live in or use prairie dog towns. Prairie dogs are a source of food for predators, and their burrows provide homes for a variety of animals, including a number of increasingly rare species such as the Texas Horned Lizard. They also provide recreational opportunities for natural history study, photography, and hunters.

Where prairie dog population management is needed, directed and managed hunting is a preferred method. Hunting, as opposed to poisons, gas, or rodenticides, kills only prairie dogs. It also ensures that not all of the prairie dogs in a colony are killed, thus leaving a smaller, yet viable population. Hunting also has the advantage of providing recreational opportunity and income to the landowner.

If chemical control methods must be used for prairie dog management, read and carefully follow all label directions. Before chemical control measures are undertaken, the colony should be surveyed for signs of Black-footed Ferrets by a biologist familiar with the species. As with any chemical control method used on rangeland, whether for mesquite or prairie dogs, the economics must be evaluated very carefully to be certain that the costs do not exceed the expected benefits.

It is important to prevent damage to non-target wildlife whenever chemicals are used. Effects on Burrowing Owls, foxes, badgers, rabbits, reptiles, and songbirds can be minimized by discriminating between burrows occupied by prairie dogs and those occupied by other species. A burrow hole diameter of 3 to 5 inches with single or multiple entrances, dirt mounded up around the entrance, and scat which is 3/4 to 1 1/4 inches long, are signs that prairie dogs occupy the burrow. Prairie dog scat is light brown in color and composed of plant material. Burrows which are 8 to 12 inches in diameter, with dirt loosely piled or spread away from the entrance, are likely occupied by foxes or badgers. Owl burrows often have white droppings, owl pellets, feathers, or shredded cow manure around the opening. Toxic bait is especially hazardous to birds. If used, it should be scattered at the edge of mounds only. Bait should not be applied in a pile. Land managers with questions concerning

prairie dog population management are advised to contact the nearest office of the Texas Parks and Wildlife Department or the Texas Animal Damage Control.

Landowners interested in conserving prairie dog ecosystems should maintain a minimum of 100 to 150 acres per colony. Colonies should be located within about 4 miles of one another. Cooperative agreements between adjacent landowners can be used to manage larger areas for prairie dogs and the species they support.

Compatibility With Domestic Livestock

Prairie dogs are frequently described as competitors with livestock for range forage. The degree of competition, however, depends on both the density of prairie dogs and the stocking rate of livestock. As most ranchers know, a necessary part of good range management is adjusting stocking rates and allocating forage for all grazing animals, both wild and domestic. Controlling grazing pressure is basic to maintaining rangeland in good condition with high productivity and economic returns. By allocating some forage to the prairie dogs and the community of plants and animals they support, ranchers can help conserve an important part of the natural heritage of Texas.

Numerous studies have been done to understand the relationship between prairie dogs and other grazers. Prairie dogs influence the plant composition in areas where they occur. Shortgrasses, such as buffalograss and other plants that can withstand continuous grazing pressure, tend to increase while midgrasses decrease. Research results indicate that although prairie dogs reduce the total amount of forage available for livestock, this reduction is partially compensated by the improved nutritional content of forage that is available. When evaluating livestock performance, one should consider the tradeoff between reduction in forage quantity and increased forage quality. Increases in forage quality have been attributed to a higher percentage of young, rapidly growing plants, and higher plant diversity, allowing for greater selection by livestock.

Efforts by the Texas Parks and Wildlife Department, U.S. Fish and Wildlife Service, and various conservation groups are currently underway to develop incentives for management of endangered species on private lands in Texas. Hopefully, we can work together to conserve the prairie dog ecosystem and perhaps return the Black-footed Ferret to Texas.

For More Information

Technical assistance in range and wildlife management, including management for endangered species, is available to landowners and managers by contacting the Texas Parks and Wildlife Department (TPWD), U.S. Natural Resources Conservation Service (formerly Soil Conservation Service), or Texas Agricultural Extension Service. Further guidance and specific questions concerning Black-footed Ferret recovery efforts, should be directed to the U.S. Fish and Wildlife Service.

Funds for the production of this leaflet were provided by the U.S. Fish and Wildlife Service, under Section 6 of the Endangered Species Act.

Jaguarundi

Scientific Name: *Felis yagouaroundi cacomitli*

Federal Status: Endangered, 6/14/76 • State Status: Endangered

Description

The Jaguarundi is a small, slender-bodied, unspotted cat, slightly larger than a domestic cat (8-16 pounds). Other characteristics include a long tail; short legs; a small flattened head; and short, rounded, widely spaced ears. There are two color phases: a rusty-brown and a charcoal gray. The Jaguarundi tends to move in a quick, weasel-like manner. Because of similarity in appearance, the Jaguarundi can easily be confused with a large feral cat, especially when seen in low light or dense cover.

Jaguarundi
© USFWS Gary Halvorsen

Habitat

Little is known about the habitat of Jaguarundis in Texas. It is thought that they occur in the dense thorny shrublands of the Rio Grande Valley and Rio Grande Plains. Their habitat may be very similar to that of the Ocelot, although sightings and information from Mexico indicate that the Jaguarundi may be more tolerant of open areas than the Ocelot.

Typical habitat consists of mixed thornshrub species such as spiny hackberry, brasil, desert yaupon, wolfberry, lotebush, amargosa, whitebrush, catclaw, blackbrush, lantana, guayacan, cenizo, elbowbush, and Texas persimmon. Interspersed trees such as mesquite, live oak, ebony, and hackberry may also occur. Riparian habitats along rivers or creeks are sometimes used by Jaguarundis. Deep, fertile clay or loamy soils are generally needed to produce suitable habitat.

Canopy cover and density of shrubs are important considerations in identifying suitable habitat. Little information exists concerning optimal habitat for the Jaguarundi in Texas. Scientists speculate that these elusive cats are similar to the Ocelot in their requirement for dense brush cover.

Tracts of at least 100 acres of isolated dense brush, or 75 acres of brush interconnected with other habitat tracts by brush corridors, are considered important habitat. Even tracts as small as 5 acres, when adjacent to larger areas of habitat, may be used by Jaguarundis. Roads, narrow water bodies, and rights-of-way are not considered breaks in habitat. Brushy fencelines, water courses, and other brush strips connecting areas of habitat are very important in providing escape and protective cover. These strip corridors are considered important habitat.

Texas counties where Jaguarundis are thought to occur include Cameron and Willacy.

Life History

Little information is available concerning the biology of the Jaguarundi in Texas. Most of what is known comes from anecdotal or historical writings and information gained through the study of Ocelots in south Texas.

Jaguarundis hunt primarily in the morning and evening. They are less nocturnal than the Ocelot and have been observed more often during the day. Jaguarundis forage mainly on the ground, but they are agile climbers. Prey includes birds, rabbits, and small rodents. Historical accounts from Mexico suggest that Jaguarundis are good swimmers and enter the water freely.

Little is known regarding Jaguarundi reproduction in Texas. In Mexico, Jaguarundis are said to be solitary, except during the mating season of November and December. Kittens have been reported in March and also in August. It is not known whether females produce one or two litters each season. The gestation period is 9 to 10 weeks, and litters contain two to four young.

Threats and Reasons for Decline

Historically, the South Texas Plains supported grassland or savanna-type climax vegetation with dense mixed brush along dry washes and flood plains of the Rio Grande. The extensive shrublands of the Lower Rio Grande Valley have been converted to agriculture and urban development over the past 60 years. Much of this land, particularly the more fertile soils, has been cleared for production of vegetables, citrus, sugarcane, cotton, and other crops. Unfortunately for the Jaguarundi and Ocelot (another endangered South Texas cat), the best soil types also grow the thickest brush and thus produce the best habitat. Less than 5 percent of the original vegetation remains.

The Jaguarundi is one of the rarest cats in Texas, with only the Jaguar and Margay, which have not been reported in recent years, being more rare. Information about this species is urgently needed. Unless vigorous conservation measures are taken soon, this elusive cat may join the list of species extirpated from the United States.

Recovery Efforts

Very little is known concerning Jaguarundi biology in south Texas. Research regarding capture techniques, reproduction, rearing of young, dispersal, home range, and movements is urgently needed. Recently initiated Jaguarundi research in northeast Mexico, where they are more common, will enable biologists to better understand the requirements for a viable population. This information can then be used to assist conservation efforts for the Jaguarundi in Texas. Efforts to inform landowners and the public about the habitat needs, land management options, and biology of the Jaguarundi are also critical to recovery.

Conservation of remaining habitat, and maintenance or creation of brush corridors connecting these habitats are necessary for survival of the Jaguarundi population in Texas. The U.S. Fish and Wildlife Service, Texas Parks and Wildlife Department, and The Nature Conservancy of Texas have been working for several years to link the few remaining blocks of riparian forest along the Rio Grande. Without these corridors of riparian woodland or chaparral, the isolated populations of endangered or rare tropical species such as the Jaguarundi, Ocelot, Coatimundi, Red-billed pigeon, Rose-throated Becard, and Northern Gray Hawk will remain extremely vulnerable.

Recently, Texas Parks and Wildlife Department, The Nature Conservancy of Texas, and local landowners have joined in a cooperative effort to restore habitat for the Jaguarundi, Ocelot, neotropical migratory birds and other rare species in the Lower Rio Grande Valley. The objective of the project is to plant trees, shrubs and other native plants creating approximately 300 acres of new habitat. The project will focus on restoration of quality habitat in strategic locations, expanding and connecting significant parcels of public and private land in the lower Rio Grande Valley. The project will involve native plant nursery efforts and cost-sharing for landowners interested in restoring native brush vegetation corridors on their land.

Where To Learn More About Jaguarundis
The best places to visit to learn more about the Jaguarundi are the Laguna Atascosa National Wildlife Refuge near Rio Hondo (210) 748-3607, Santa Ana National Wildlife Refuge near Alamo (210) 787-3079, Bentsen-Rio Grande Valley State Park near Mission (210) 585-1107, Las Palomas Wildlife Management Area near Edinburg (210) 383-8982, and Audubon's Sabal Palm Grove Sanctuary near Brownsville (210)541-8034.

How You Can Help
You can be involved with the conservation of Texas' nongame wildlife resources by supporting the Special Nongame and Endangered Species Conservation Fund. Special nongame stamps and decals are available at Texas Parks and Wildlife Department (TPWD) field offices, most state parks, and the License Branch of TPWD headquarters in Austin. The Feline Research Program at the Caesar Kleberg Wildlife Research Institute (Texas A&M University-Kingsville) also accepts contributions to its Cat Conservation Fund. These funds are dedicated to the research and recovery of free-ranging wild cats of

Rio Grande resaca
© TPWD

Texas. For more information, contact the Feline Research Program at (512) 595-3922. Report sightings of Jaguarundis to the Feline Research Program, Texas Parks and Wildlife Department, or U.S. Fish and Wildlife Service. Be sure to note size, color, habitat, behavior, location, date, and time of day seen.

For More Information Contact
Texas Parks and Wildlife Department
Endangered Resources Branch
4200 Smith School Road
Austin, Texas 78744
(512) 912-7011 or (800) 792-1112
      or
U.S. Fish and Wildlife Service
Ecological Services Field Office
10711 Burnet Road, Suite 200
Austin, Texas 78758
(512) 490-0057

Management guidelines are available from the Texas Parks and Wildlife Department or U.S. Fish and Wildlife Service for landowners and managers wishing to conserve and improve habitat for the Jaguarundi.

References
Burt, W.H. and R.P. Grossenheider. 1964. *A field guide to the mammals.* Houghton Mifflin Company, Boston, Mass. 284pp.

Davis, W.B. and D.J. Schmidly. 1994. *The Mammals of Texas.* Texas Parks and Wildlife Press. Austin, Texas. 338pp.

Tewes, M.E. and D.J. Schmidly. 1987. "The Neotropical Felids: Jaguar, Ocelot, Margay, and Jaguarundi." In M. Novak, J. Baker, M.E. Obbard and B. Malloch (eds.) *Wild Furbearer Management and Conservation in North America.* Ministry of Natural Resources, Ontario. 703-705.

U.S. Fish and Wildlife Service. 1990. *Listed cats of Texas and Arizona recovery plan (with emphasis on the ocelot).* Endangered Species Office, Albuquerque, N.M.

Walker, E.P., F. Warnick, K.I. Lange, H.E. Uible, and P.F. Wright. 1975. *Mammals of the world.* Vol. 2. John Hopkins Univ. Press, Baltimore. 1500pp.

Funds for the production of this leaflet were provided by the U.S. Fish and Wildlife Service, under Section 6 of the Endangered Species Act.

Ocelot

Scientific Name: *Felis pardalis*

Federal Status: Endangered, 3/30/72 • State Status: Endangered

Description

The Ocelot is a beautiful medium-sized spotted cat with body dimensions similar to the bobcat (30-41 inches long and 15-30 lbs). Its body coloration is variable; with the upper parts gray or buff with dark brown or black spots, small rings, blotches, and short bars. The underparts are white spotted with black. The Ocelot's long tail is ringed or marked with dark bars on the upper surface. The backs of the rounded ears are black with a white central spot.

Ocelot
© USFWS Tom Smylie

Ocelot kittens
© USFWS Linda Laack

Habitat

In Texas, Ocelots occur in the dense thorny shrublands of the Lower Rio Grande Valley and Rio Grande Plains. Deep, fertile clay or loamy soils are generally needed to produce suitable habitat. Typical habitat consists of mixed brush species such as spiny hackberry, brasil, desert yaupon, wolfberry, lotebush, amargosa, whitebrush, catclaw, blackbrush, lantana, guayacan, cenizo, elbowbush, and Texas persimmon. Interspersed trees such as mesquite, live oak, ebony, and hackberry also occur.

Canopy cover and density of shrubs are important considerations in identifying suitable habitat. Optimal habitat has at least 95 percent canopy cover of shrubs, whereas marginal habitat has 75 to 95 percent canopy cover. Shrub density below the four foot level is the most important component of Ocelot habitat. Shrub density should be such that the depth of vision from outside the brush line is restricted to about five feet. Because of the density of brush below the four foot level, human movement within the brush stand would be restricted to crawling.

Tracts of at least 100 acres of isolated dense brush, or 75 acres of brush interconnected with other habitat tracts by brush corridors, are considered very important. Even tracts as small as 5 acres, when adjacent to larger areas of habitat, may be used by Ocelots. Roads, narrow water bodies, and rights-of-way are not considered breaks in habitat. Brushy fencelines, water courses, and other brush strips connecting areas of habitat are very important. These strip corridors are also considered important habitat.

Historical records indicate that the Ocelot once occurred throughout south Texas, the southern Edwards Plateau Region, and along the Coastal Plain. Over the years, the Ocelot population declined primarily due to loss of habitat and predator control activities. Today, Texas counties that contain areas identified as occupied habitat are: Cameron, Duval, Hidalgo, Jim Wells, Kenedy, Kleberg, Live Oak, McMullen, Nueces, San Patricio, Starr, Willacy, and Zapata.

Life History

Ocelots normally begin their activities at dusk, when they set out on nightly hunts for rabbits, small rodents, and birds. They move around during the night, usually within a well-established home range (area of activity) of one to two square miles for females and three to four square miles for males. Each morning they bed down in a different spot within the territory. Male Ocelots tend to travel more than females. Males generally cover an extensive area in a short time, whereas females cover less area but use the home range more intensively.

Female Ocelots prepare a den for their kittens in thick brush or dense bunchgrass areas surrounded

by brush. The den is often a slight depression with the dead leaves and mulch scraped away. The usual litter size is one or two kittens. The mother goes off to hunt at night, but spends each day at the den site. The kittens begin to accompany their mother on hunts at about 3 months of age. They stay with her until they are about a year old. Studies have shown that kittens are born from late spring through December.

Threats and Reasons for Decline

Historically, the South Texas Plains supported grassland or savanna-type climax vegetation with dense mixed brush along dry washes and flood plains of the Rio Grande. The extensive shrublands of the Lower Rio Grande Valley have been converted to agriculture and urban development over the past 60 years. Much of this land, particularly the more fertile soils, has been cleared for production of vegetables, citrus, sugarcane, cotton, and other crops. Unfortunately for the Ocelot, the best soil types also grow the thickest brush and thus produce the best habitat. Less than 5 percent of the original vegetation remains.

Only about 1 percent of the South Texas area supports what is currently defined as optimal habitat. Most of this habitat occurs in scattered patches probably too small to support Ocelots for extended periods. As a result, young cats dispersing from areas of suitable habitat have no place to go and most are probably hit by cars or die of starvation.

The Ocelot population in Texas is very small, probably no more than 80 to 120 individuals (1993 estimate). Approximately 30 to 35 live in the chaparral remaining at or near the Laguna Atascosa National Wildlife Refuge. Unless vigorous conservation measures are taken soon, this beautiful cat may join the list of species extirpated from the United States.

Recovery Efforts

Much information has been obtained recently concerning Ocelot biology in south Texas. However, there is still much to be learned regarding reproduction, rearing of young, dispersal, home range, and movements. Efforts to inform landowners and the public about the habitat needs, land management options, and biology of the Ocelot are critical to recovery.

Conservation of remaining habitat, and maintenance or creation of brush corridors connecting these habitats, are necessary for survival of the Ocelot population in Texas. The U.S. Fish and Wildlife Service, Texas Parks and Wildlife Department, and The Nature Conservancy of Texas have been working for several years to link the few remaining blocks of riparian forest along the Rio Grande. Without a corridor of riparian forest and

chaparral, the isolated populations of endangered or rare tropical species such as the Ocelot, Jaguarundi, Coatimundi, Red-billed Pigeon, Rose-throated Becard, and Northern Gray Hawk will remain extremely vulnerable.

Recently, Texas Parks and Wildlife Department, The Nature Conservancy of Texas, and local landowners have joined in a cooperative effort to restore habitat for the Jaguarundi, Ocelot, neotropical migratory birds and other rare species in the Lower Rio Grande Valley. The objective of the project is to plant trees, shrubs and other native plants creating approximately 300 acres of new habitat. The project will focus on restoration of quality habitat in strategic locations, expanding and connecting significant parcels of public and private land in the Lower Rio Grande Valley. The project will involve native plant nursery efforts and cost-sharing for landowners interested in restoring native brush vegetation corridors on their land.

Where To Learn More About Ocelots

The best places to visit to learn more about the Ocelot are the Laguna Atascosa National Wildlife Refuge near Rio Hondo (210) 748-3607, Santa Ana National Wildlife Refuge near Alamo (210) 787-3079, Bentsen-Rio Grande Valley State Park near Mission (210) 585-1107, Las Palomas Wildlife Management Area near Edinburg (210) 383-8982, and Audubon's Sabal Palm Grove Sanctuary near Brownsville (210) 541-8034.

How You Can Help

You can be involved with the conservation of Texas' nongame wildlife resources by supporting the Special Nongame and Endangered Species Conservation Fund. Special nongame stamps and decals are available at Texas Parks and Wildlife Department (TPWD) field offices, most state parks, and the License Branch of TPWD headquarters in Austin. The Feline Research Program at the Caesar Kleberg Wildlife Research Institute (Texas A&M University-Kingsville) also accepts contributions to its Cat Conservation Fund. These funds are dedicated to the research and

Sub-tropical forest habitat
© TPWD

Habitat loss in the Lower Rio Grande Valley
© TPWD Bill Reaves

recovery of free-ranging wild cats of Texas. For more information, contact the Feline Research Program at (512) 595-3922.

Report sightings of Ocelots to the Feline Research Program, Texas Parks and Wildlife Department, or U.S. Fish and Wildlife Service. Be sure to note size, color, habitat, behavior, location, date, and time of day seen.

For More Information Contact

Texas Parks and Wildlife Department
Endangered Resources Branch
4200 Smith School Road
Austin, Texas 78744
(512) 912-7011 or (800) 792-1112
     or
U.S. Fish and Wildlife Service
Ecological Services Field Office
10711 Burnet Road, Suite 200
Austin, Texas 78758
(512) 490-0057

Management guidelines are available from the Texas Parks and Wildlife Department or U.S. Fish and Wildlife Service for landowners and managers wishing to conserve and improve habitat for the Ocelot.

References

Burt, W.H. and R.P. Grossenheider. 1964. *A Field Guide to the Mammals.* Houghton Mifflin Company, Boston, Mass. 284pp.

Davis, W.B. and D.J. Schmidly. 1994. *The Mammals of Texas.* Texas Parks and Wildlife Press. Austin, Texas. 338pp.

Tewes, M.E. and D.J. Schmidly. 1987. "The Neotropical Felids: Jaguar, Ocelot, Margay, and Jaguarundi." In M. Novak, J. Baker, M.E. Obbard and B. Malloch (eds.) *Wild Furbearer Management and Conservation in North America.* Ministry of Natural Resources, Ontario. 697-711.

U.S. Fish and Wildlife Service. 1990. *Listed Cats of Texas and Arizona Recovery Plan (with emphasis on the Ocelot).* Endangered Species Office, Albuquerque, N.M.

Walker, E.P., F. Warnick, K.I. Lange, H.E. Uible, and P.F. Wright. 1975. *Mammals of the World. Vol. 2.* John Hopkins Univ. Press, Baltimore. 1500pp.

Funds for the production of this leaflet were provided by the U.S. Fish and Wildlife Service, under Section 6 of the Endangered Species Act.

Management Guidelines for the Jaguarundi and Ocelot

The following guidelines address land management practices that can be used to maintain, enhance, or create habitat for the Jaguarundi and Ocelot. They are intended primarily to serve as general guidance for landowners or managers of livestock/wildlife operations in South Texas. The guidelines are based on our current understanding of the biology of these species.

Habitat restoration – planting native brush species
© David Diamond

Dense mixed brush habitat
© David Diamond

Habitat Preservation

Conservation of dense stands of mixed thornshrub, which serve as habitat for the Ocelot and Jaguarundi, is vital to the survival of these cats in Texas. Habitat preservation around the Laguna Atascosa National Wildlife Refuge, in the Lower Rio Grande Valley, and in counties directly north of this area is particularly important.

Mechanical or chemical brush control, including prescribed burning, should not be conducted in habitat areas or in brushy corridors connecting larger areas of habitat. In everyday agricultural operations (i.e. livestock water facilities, fence construction), it is important to minimize disturbances that would destroy the integrity of a habitat tract or corridor. Tracts of at least 100 acres of isolated brush (of the required density and structure), or 75 acres of brush interconnected with other habitat tracts by brush corridors, are considered important habitat. Useful habitat can be provided by smaller tracts especially if these tracts are adjacent to larger areas of habitat.

On rangeland that does not provide the required brush cover and density (non-habitat areas), normal brush management practices, including prescribed burning, are not considered detrimental.

Habitat Restoration

Where dense mixed brush has developed into a tree form, or shrub density below four feet is inadequate, mechanical brush treatment methods such as chaining or roller chopping may be used to restore or create suitable habitat. These mechanical methods encourage basal sprouting by breaking off limbs or trunks of established plants, and can be used to increase cover and density of brush below the four foot level.

Adapted native shrubs, such as ebony, brasil, and granjeno, can be planted to increase habitat or to provide interconnecting corridors to existing habitat. Methods are currently being developed to allow for more successful establishment of these species.

Technical assistance in habitat management is available to landowners and managers by contacting the Texas Parks and Wildlife Department, U.S. Natural Resources Conservation Service (formerly Soil Conservation Service), U.S. Fish and Wildlife Service, Texas Agricultural Extension Service, or the Caesar Kleberg Wildlife Research Institute.

Funds for the production of this leaflet were provided by the U.S. Fish and Wildlife Service, under Section 6 of the Endangered Species Act.

Golden-cheeked Warbler

Scientific Name: *Dendroica chrysoparia*

Federal Status: Endangered, 5/4/90 • State Status: Endangered

Description

The Golden-cheeked Warbler is a small, migratory songbird, 4.5 to 5 inches long, with a wingspan of about 8 inches. The male has a black back, throat, and cap; and yellow cheeks with a black stripe through the eye. Females are similar, but less colorful. The lower breast and belly of both sexes are white with black streaks on the flanks.

Male Golden-cheeked Warbler
© Greg W. Lasley

Female Golden-cheeked Warbler
© Greg W. Lasley

Habitat

Typical nesting habitat is found in tall, dense, mature stands of Ashe juniper (blueberry cedar) mixed with trees such as Texas (Spanish) oak, Lacey oak, shin (scalybark) oak, live oak, post oak, Texas ash, cedar elm, hackberry, bigtooth maple, sycamore, Arizona walnut, escarpment cherry, and pecan. This type of woodland generally grows in relatively moist areas such as steep-sided canyons and slopes. A mix of juniper and deciduous trees on the slopes, along drainage bottoms, and in creeks and draws provide an ideal mix of vegetation for these birds. Warblers are also occasionally found in drier, upland juniper-oak (i.e. live oak, post oak, blackjack oak) woodlands over flat topography.

It is important to note that not all woodlands, such as those described above, are used by Golden-cheeked Warblers. Only habitat actually used by endangered or threatened animals is subject to protection by the Endangered Species Act (ESA).

Warblers need a combination of mature Ashe juniper and hardwood trees in their nesting habitat. Mature juniper trees vary in age and growth form, depending on site factors. Generally, trees required for nesting habitat are at least 20 years old and 15 feet tall. The essential element is that juniper trees have shredding bark, at least near the base of the tree.

Although the composition of woody vegetation varies within suitable warbler habitat, Ashe juniper is often, but not always, the dominant species. Studies have shown that juniper comprises anywhere from 10 to 90 percent of total trees in occupied habitat at 27 sites scattered throughout the breeding range.

In general, Golden-cheeked Warblers prefer areas with a moderate to high density of older trees, and dense foliage in the upper canopy. Higher warbler densities are associated with greater average tree height, greater variability in tree heights, and greater density of deciduous trees.

Golden-cheeked Warblers have been found in patches of habitat smaller than 12 acres, although they are believed to do better in larger tracts. With increasingly fragmented habitat, smaller patches may become more important to warblers, particularly those located near areas of occupied habitat.

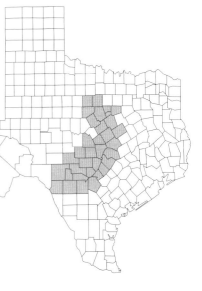

Life History

The Golden-cheeked Warbler's entire nesting range is currently confined to about 33 counties in central Texas. The birds are dependent on Ashe juniper (blueberry juniper or cedar) for fine bark strips used in nest construction. Although nests may be placed in various species of trees, such as juniper, Texas oak, live oak, and cedar elm, all nests contain strips of Ashe juniper bark woven together with spider webs.

Warblers feed almost entirely on caterpillars, spiders, beetles, and other insects found in foliage. The birds are thought to take advantage of insect blooms associated with different plants as the growing season progresses. For example, broad-leaved trees and shrubs, especially oaks, are particularly important in providing habitat for insects during the first part of the nesting season. Later in the season, warblers are frequently seen foraging in Ashe juniper. Mesic (relatively moist) conditions, such as those found on wooded slopes, canyon bottoms, and along creeks and draws, are especially favorable for the production of insect foods.

Depending on the location and quality of habitat, Golden-cheeked Warblers forage and nest in areas of habitat ranging in size from five to 20 acres per pair. Within suitable nesting habitat, male Golden-cheeked Warblers occupy an area, called a territory, which is vigorously defended against all other male Golden-cheeked Warblers. Nesting territories range in size from three to six acres. Banding studies show that males often occupy the same territory in subsequent breeding seasons. Male warblers can often be located through their territorial song, described as a rather hurried, buzzy "tweah-tweah-twee-sy." Single, sharp "chipping" calls can frequently be heard as Golden-cheeks forage among the trees.

The female does most of the work of nest building and incubating the eggs. The cup-like nest is often neatly tucked into the fork of a vertical limb and camouflaged to blend with the bark of the tree. Nests are constructed at an average height of 15 feet above ground, although they have been found as low as five feet and as high as 32 feet. The male stays nearby, singing his distinctive song and defending his territory during incubation.

During April, a single clutch of three to four eggs is laid. Warblers usually nest only once per season, unless a nest is lost to accident or predation. The eggs hatch in 12 days, and both parents care for the young. After the young hatch, male singing declines, although they can still be heard into June. Nestlings fledge eight or nine days after hatching, but remain in the vicinity of the territory for at least

four weeks while being cared for by both parents.

Golden-cheeked Warblers migrate to their wintering grounds in the pine-oak woodlands of southern Mexico (Chiapas), Guatemala, Honduras, and Nicaragua from late June to mid August. They return to Texas in early to mid-March.

Threats and Reasons for Decline

The most serious problem facing the Golden-cheeked Warbler today, as in the recent past, is habitat loss and fragmentation. Since warblers have limited and specific habitat requirements, direct habitat loss has resulted in population reduction, although precise comparisons of historic and current populations are not available.

Recently, serious losses in nesting habitat have occurred in counties such as Travis, Williamson, and Bexar, where rapid urban development has spread into oak-juniper woodlands associated with canyonlands. Flood control and other impoundments have also reduced habitat for the warbler by inundating the juniper-oak woodlands existing on canyon slopes and bottoms along springs, streams, and rivers. Construction of large reservoirs has also led to loss of warbler habitat due to development of lake-side communities.

Historically, some warbler habitat was lost as a result of clearing juniper/oak woodlands for increased livestock production or improved livestock handling. Stands of large juniper trees were also cut for sale as fenceposts and other timber products, especially before 1940. Overbrowsing by white-tailed deer, goats, and exotic ungulates is believed to contribute to habitat degradation by reducing the survival of seedling oaks and other deciduous trees, which are a vital component of warbler habitat. Also, the deeper and more fertile soils in much of the Hill Country are found in small floodplains along creeks or intermittent streams associated with hillside drainage. Many of these areas, some of them supporting a variety of deciduous trees, were cleared and converted to forage crops and pasture, often resulting in a decrease in the amount of warbler habitat.

Female warbler with insect
© TPWD Dean Keddy-Hector

Warbler at a nest
© TPWD Dean Keddy-Hector

Golden-cheeked Warbler habitat
© TPWD David Riskind

Juniper with peeling bark
© TPWD D. Keddy-Hector

Closed canopy habitat
© Carol Beardmore

Creek bottom habitat
© TPWD Glen Mills

Habitat loss may be obscured by the increase in juniper on rangeland throughout central Texas. The invasion of juniper on upland sites is often the result of fire suppression, overgrazing, or a combination of both. These young juniper stands invading open rangelands generally lack the kinds and numbers of hardwood trees required by warblers. Warblers are usually not found in monocultures (pure stands) where juniper comprises over 90 percent of the composition throughout a large area.

Poor grazing management practices and fire suppression result in a decline in the diversity and productivity of rangeland. The decline in range condition associated with improper management has led to increases in juniper throughout the Hill Country.

Nest parasitism by Brown-headed Cowbirds may threaten successful reproduction of Golden-cheeked Warblers, although the degree of impact of cowbird parasitism on warbler productivity is not fully understood. Cowbirds lay their eggs in other birds' nests, leaving the host bird to raise the cowbird young. Golden-cheeked Warblers apparently will either abandon parasitized nests, or raise young cowbirds in addition to or in place of their own young. Warblers that abandon parasitized nests may renest later in the season. However, abandonment of first clutches, or raising cowbird young in addition to their own, decreases the total number and survivability of Golden-cheeked warbler young produced.

Finally, habitat fragmentation reduces the quality and quantity of warbler habitat. In small woodland patches, the increased proportion of habitat edge to interior area may increase rates of nest parasitism and predation, so that the surviving populations cannot maintain themselves. Also, increased distance between patches may make recolonization of vacated habitat more difficult.

Habitat management and protection, in Texas and in Mexico and Central America, responsible land stewardship, and incentives for landowners to maintain and develop habitat, are keys to the survival and recovery of the Golden-cheeked Warbler. The diverse mix of hardwoods and junipers in canyons, and on slopes and adjacent hilltops, provide ideal habitat for the warbler. Numerous beautiful and interesting native plants and animals are also found in these canyons.

Recovery Efforts

Research is underway to better understand the life history, habitat requirements, limiting factors, and land management practices affecting the Golden-cheeked Warbler. Population surveys during the breeding season are being conducted in known and potential habitat areas. Efforts to provide information and educational opportunities to landowners and the public regarding life history and habitat requirements of the warbler are also a vital part of the recovery effort.

Additional research in Mexico is planned to gather information concerning life history and habitat requirements on the wintering range. Studies are needed to assess the potential for income generating activities, such as selective harvest of juniper, which may be compatible with habitat protection.

Where To See the Golden-cheeked Warbler

A number of state lands, including Colorado Bend State Park (SP), Dinosaur Valley SP, Garner SP, Guadalupe River SP, Honey Creek State Natural Area (SNA), Hill Country SNA, Kerr Wildlife Management Area, Longhorn Cavern SP, Lost Maples SNA, Meridian SP, Pedernales Falls SP, and Possum Kingdom SP offer opportunities for people to see Golden-cheeked Warblers and their habitat. Other locations include the Travis Audubon Sanctuary, Wild Basin Preserve, and Emma Long City Park in the Austin area; and Friedrich Wilderness Park near San Antonio. Once they are opened to the public, the Balcones Canyonlands National Wildlife Refuge, located northwest of Austin, and Government Canyon State Park, located northwest of San Antonio, will offer additional opportunities to see Golden-cheeked Warblers.

Because the Golden-cheeked Warbler is an endangered species, birders and other observers should carefully follow certain viewing ethics. Recorded calls of the Golden-cheeked Warbler or Screech Owl should not be used to attract birds and observers should be careful not to disturb or stress birds.

How You Can Help

You can help by providing encouragement and support for private landowners who are managing their land to protect natural diversity and endangered species habitat. Landowners are encouraged to learn the facts about the Golden-cheeked Warbler and its habitat needs, and to protect areas of habitat found on their property.

The Golden-cheeked Warbler is a beautiful songbird, and is much sought after among people who enjoy birdwatching and nature study. Possibilities exist for landowners to take advantage of the growing demand for natural history tours and vacations. Landowners interested in more information concerning ecotourism opportunities should contact the Nongame and Urban Fish and Wildlife Program, Texas Parks and Wildlife Department, Austin (800-792-1112).

Finally, you can be involved in the conservation of Texas' nongame wildlife resources by supporting the Special Nongame and Endangered

Species Conservation Fund. Special nongame stamps and decals are available at Texas Parks and Wildlife Department (TPWD) field offices, most state parks, and the License Branch of TPWD headquarters in Austin. Each dollar contributed to this fund helps TPWD conduct research and management and acquire habitat for nongame and endangered wildlife. Conservation Passports, available from Texas Parks and Wildlife, are valid for one year and allow unlimited access to most State Parks, State Natural Areas, and Wildlife Management Areas. Conservation organizations in Texas also welcome your participation and support.

For More Information Contact

Texas Parks and Wildlife Department
Endangered Resources Branch
4200 Smith School Road
Austin, Texas 78744
(512) 912-7011 or (800) 792-1112
or
U.S. Fish and Wildlife Service
Ecological Services Field Office
10711 Burnet Road, Suite 200
Austin, Texas 78758
(512) 490-0057

Management guidelines are available from the Texas Parks and Wildlife Department and U.S. Fish and Wildlife Service for landowners and managers wishing to maintain and improve habitat for the Golden-cheeked Warbler.

Golden-cheeked Warbler habitat
© TPWD Bill Reaves

Urban expansion
© USFWS Wyman Meinzer

References

Huss, D.L. 1954. *Factors Influencing Plant Succession Following Fire in Ashe Juniper Woodland Types in Real County, Texas.* MS Thesis, Texas A&M University, College Station, Texas. 77pp.

Oberholser, H.C. 1974. *The Bird Life of Texas.* University of Texas Press, Austin, Texas.

Pulich, W. 1976. *The Golden-cheeked Warbler, A Bioecological Study.* Texas Parks and Wildlife Department, Austin, Texas. 172pp.

U.S. Fish and Wildlife Service (USFWS). 1992. *Golden-cheeked Warbler Recovery Plan.* USFWS, Endangered Species Office, Albuquerque, NM. 88pp.

Wahl, R., D.D. Diamond, and D. Shaw. 1990. *The Golden-Cheeked Warbler: A Status Review.* U.S. Fish and Wildlife Service, Ecological Services Office, Austin, Texas.

Funds for the production of this leaflet were provided by the U.S. Fish and Wildlife Service, under Section 6 of the Endangered Species Act.

Warbler with identification band
© TPWD

Management Guidelines for the Golden-cheeked Warbler

The descriptions presented in this document are intended to help landowners determine if they have Golden-cheeked Warbler habitat on their property. Not all sites within the habitat types described will be used by Golden-cheeked Warblers. It is only where individuals of this species occupy the identified habitat types during the breeding season that special management considerations such as those provided in these guidelines need to be considered.

Private landowners have a tremendous opportunity to conserve and manage the fish and wildlife resources of Texas. The objective of these guidelines is to provide landowners with recommendations about how typically-used land management practices could be conducted so that it would be unlikely that golden-cheeked warblers would be adversely impacted. The guidelines will be updated periodically to make them more practical and useful to rural landowners. The guidelines are based on the best available information and current understanding about the biology of the warbler, but may be refined as more complete biological data are collected. TPWD biologists have prepared these guidelines in consultation with USFWS biologists to assure landowners who carry out land management practices within the guidelines that they would know, with the greatest certainty possible, that they would not be in violation of the E.S.A.

This document also provides information on land management practices that are appropriate for protection and/or enhancement of habitat. The categories were chosen to represent commonly encountered vegetation types and to address common questions regarding the effect of management practices on Golden-cheeked Warblers. In addition, suggestions are offered that promote conservation of soil, water, plant, and wildlife resources.

Habitat Descriptions

Habitat Types Where Warblers Are Expected To Occur

Woodlands with mature Ashe juniper (cedar) in a natural mix with oaks, elms, and other hardwoods, in relatively moist (mesic) areas such as steep canyons and slopes, are considered habitat types that are highly likely to be used by warblers. These areas generally will have a nearly continuous canopy cover of trees with 50 to 100 percent canopy closure. This habitat type is also important for deer, turkey, songbirds, and a variety of other wildlife due to the diversity of vegetation and topography and, in many cases, proximity to water. Woodlands of this description should be retained wherever they occur, especially along creeks and draws, and on steep slopes and generally rough terrain. Landowners with woodlands that fit the above description should assume that warblers may be using the area and are advised to follow the management guidelines presented here. Additional information regarding habitat types and their potential to support Golden-cheeked Warblers is presented in Table 1.

Habitat Types That May Be Used By Warblers

It is relatively easy to recognize the above described high quality habitat types where Golden-cheeked Warblers are likely to occur. However, there are a number of other vegetation types that may also be used by warblers, depending on the location, size of tract, land use, adjacent landscape features, and vegetation structure. These habitat types are most often used by warblers when they are located adjacent to or near areas of high quality habitat.

The four habitat types discussed below are associated with a variety of tree canopy cover, ranging from 35 to 100 percent. Although not representative of what is typically thought of as the "best" warbler habitat, these areas may support Golden-cheeked Warblers, especially fledglings (young birds that have left the nest). These habitats may be relatively more important to warblers nesting in the western and northern portions of the species' breeding range, or in areas where optimal habitat no longer exists. Although these habitat types may occupy a large geographic area within the Hill Country, little is known about warbler occupancy when the sites are not close to the optimal habitat types. Landowners are advised, however, to treat the following vegetation types as occupied habitat until technical assistance is obtained or a survey done to determine whether or not specific areas support warblers:

1. Stands of mature Ashe juniper (trees with shredding bark), over 10 feet in height, with scattered live oaks (at least 10% total canopy cover), where the total canopy cover of trees exceeds 35 percent.
2. Bottomlands along creeks and drainages which support at least a 35 percent canopy of deciduous trees, with mature Ashe juniper growing either in the bottom or on nearby slopes.
3. Mixed stands of post oak and/or blackjack oak with scattered mature Ashe juniper (10-30% canopy cover), where the total canopy cover of trees exceeds 35 percent.
4. Mixed stands of shin (scaly-bark) oak with scattered mature Ashe juniper (10-30% canopy cover), where the total canopy cover of trees exceeds 35 percent (See Table 1).

Table 1. Ecological site types and Range Sites with plant communities that may provide habitat for Golden-cheeked Warblers. On flat or rolling uplands, warblers are most likely to occupy larger patches of woodlands adjacent to canyon systems. Most of the flat and rolling uplands within these Range Sites have other plant communities, like open savannahs, that do not support warblers. Sites that are not used by warblers are described in the Habitat Descriptions section of this leaflet.

Site Description	Range Site	Typical Plant Communities that may support Golden-cheeked Warblers	Potential for Golden-cheeked Warblers
Slopes and canyons, and associated creek bottoms[1]	Adobe Clay Loam[2] Loamy Bottomland[2] Steep Adobe Steep Rocky	Continuous canopy woodland* of Ashe Juniper, Texas Oak, Live Oak, Lacey Oak, Cedar Elm, Escarpment Blackcherry, Texas Ash, Pecan, and other deciduous trees	Highly likely to be used
Flat or rolling uplands with shallow, rocky soils of variable depth[3]	Adobe Low Stony Hill Shallow Very Shallow	Continuous canopy woodland* of Live Oak, Shin Oak, Vasey Oak, Cedar Elm, Hackberry, Redbud, Ashe Juniper, and other hardwood trees	Highly likely to be used
		Patchy woodlands+ or interspersed mottes of mature Live Oak, Shin Oak, Ashe Juniper, and other shrubs	May be used
Flat or rolling uplands with reddish soils[4]	Deep Redland[5] Gravelly Redland[5] Redland[5]	Continuous canopy woodland* of Live Oak, Blackjack Oak, Post Oak, and Ashe Juniper	Highly likely to be used
		Patchy woodlands+ or interspersed mottes of mature Live Oak, Blackjack Oak, Post Oak, and Ashe Juniper	May be used
Flat or rolling uplands with shallow but more continuous rocky soils over limestone[6]	Low Stony Hill	Continuous canopy woodland* of Ashe Juniper, Live Oak, and Shin Oak	May be used
		Patchy woodlands+ or interspersed mottes of mature Live Oak, Ashe Juniper, Hackberry, Cedar Elm, and Mesquite	May be used

*Defined as 50-100% canopy cover of trees at least 15 feet in height or greater.
+Defined as 35-50% canopy cover of trees at least 15 feet in height or greater.

[1]Common woody plants include Ashe Juniper, Texas Oak, Live Oak, Lacey Oak, Chinkapin Oak, Cedar Elm, Escarpment Blackcherry, Texas Ash, Bigtooth Maple, Redbud, Hackberry, Texas Persimmon, Deciduous Holly, Arizona Walnut, Carolina Buckthorn, Carolina Basswood, Roughleaf Dogwood, Pecan, Sycamore, and Bald Cypress.

[2]Stream bottoms in and near canyon systems.

[3]Common woody plants include Live Oak, Shin Oak, Vasey Oak (West), Cedar Elm, Hackberry, Redbud, Ashe Juniper, Texas Persimmon, Texas Ash, Texas Oak, and Lacey Oak.

[4]Common woody plants include Live Oak, Blackjack Oak, Post Oak, Shin Oak, Lacey Oak, Texas Oak, Ashe Juniper, Cedar Elm, Hackberry, and Texas Madrone.

[5]Golden-cheeked Warblers may occur on Redland Range Sites adjacent to slope and canyon habitat. It is not known whether or not warblers occur on Redland Sites isolated from canyon systems.

[6]Common woody plants include Hackberry, Texas Persimmon, Texas Ash, Live Oak, Texas Oak, Ashe Juniper, Evergreen Sumac, Cedar Elm, and Mesquite.

Areas Where Warblers Are Not Expected To Occur

Although junipers occur abundantly over much of the Hill Country, a relatively small portion of them are actually a part of good warbler habitat. The following types of areas are not warbler habitat and are unlikely to be used by warblers. As long as these areas are not in close (within 300 ft.) proximity to warbler habitat, neither surveys nor permits are required for activities within these areas.

1. Stands of small Ashe juniper, averaging less than 10 feet in height, are not habitat. This includes "regrowth cedar" that invades open rangelands, previously cleared areas, or old fields. These areas are often dry and relatively flat, and lack oaks and other broad-leaved trees and shrubs. Generally, areas such as those described above that have been cleared within the last 20 years are not considered habitat.
2. Pure stands of larger (greater than 10 feet in height) Ashe juniper, with few or no oaks or other hardwoods.
3. Open park-like woodlands or savannahs (even with old junipers) where canopy cover of trees is less than 35 percent. These areas often have scattered live oaks and other trees.
4. Small junipers and other trees coming up along existing fencelines.
5. Small junipers coming up under larger hardwoods where junipers have been removed in the past 20 years, unless the junipers have shredding bark.

Controlling juniper on these areas by prescribed burning, hand-cutting, or well-planned mechanical methods is often desirable to improve range condition and plant diversity, and is compatible with protection of Golden-cheeked Warbler habitat. Maintaining a 300 feet wide buffer of woodland (or woody) vegetation adjacent to and around Golden-cheeked Warbler habitat is beneficial. However, when necessary brush management and maintenance activities near habitat should not occur during the March-August nesting season to avoid disturbance of possible nesting and feeding activities. Since brush management activities can affect habitat for the Black-capped Vireo as well as the Golden-cheeked Warbler, landowners are encouraged to learn about the habitat requirements of both endangered songbirds.

It is important in wildlife management in general, and in endangered species management in particular, to consider the "big picture" with regard to how land types relate to one another. For example, when brush management practices are planned in non-habitat areas, one should consider the proximity of the area to habitat used by warblers.

Management Practices in Golden-cheeked Warbler Habitat

Disruption of the tree canopy should be avoided when planning ranch improvements or maintenance work in Golden-cheeked Warbler habitat. It is recommended that new fencelines and livestock watering facilities (pipelines, storage tanks, ponds) be planned to avoid areas of habitat whenever possible. However, narrow linear openings, such as those needed for traditional agricultural management (fencelines, ranch roads, livestock water pipelines) will not harm Golden-cheeked Warblers. Typically, fencelines and other linear openings of about 16 feet in width are large enough to allow for maintenance, while permitting the hardwood tree canopy to grow over the gap. New developments in permanent electric fencing may enable landowners to crossfence areas of rough terrain with little or no disturbance to the tree canopy. Often, these power fences are the most cost effective way to crossfence areas of steep topography and shallow soils. Fencing and other ranch improvement work in Golden-cheeked Warbler habitat should be done during the non-nesting period (September-February).

Dozing or handcutting in habitat with closed tree canopy and steep slopes not only destroys warbler habitat, but mechanical disturbance also can create serious soil erosion problems. In addition, clearing these areas is generally not cost effective due to higher clearing costs, lower forage production potential, and grazing distribution problems associated with steep slopes. Selective removal of young "bushy" juniper less than 10 feet in height within habitat is not a problem as long as the tree canopy is not disturbed. Any selective removal of juniper within or adjacent to habitat should be done during the non-nesting period (September-February).

When mature juniper trees are abundant in the habitat, incidental removal of juniper for use as fenceposts on the ranch will have little impact on warbler habitat. The number of trees cut depends on the density of Ashe juniper in the habitat. For example, more trees could be removed from an area with a high density of juniper compared with the density of hardwoods. The idea should always be to provide a mix of juniper and hardwoods. When posting is done, trees should be selected to avoid disturbance to the tree canopy. One way to do this is to select trees with a relatively small individual canopy and scatter your tree selections over the area. Posting should

Open savannah – not habitat
© Matt Wagner

Regrowth cedar – not habitat
© Matt Wagner

not occur in habitat during the nesting period (March-August).

In habitat areas and on rangelands immediately adjacent to habitat, it is important to manage grazing pressure by deer and livestock to prevent overbrowsing of broad-leaved shrubs and trees, and to maintain plant diversity and productivity. Controlling the number of browsing animals (deer, exotic animals, and livestock) is important to maintain hardwood seedlings and ensure eventual replacement of deciduous trees in the canopy. Range condition improvement in and adjacent to habitat areas, through proper grazing management and planned deferment, will likely prove beneficial to livestock and wildlife, including the Golden-cheeked Warbler.

Landowners with questions regarding how ranch improvements and management practices will affect habitat are advised to seek technical assistance from the Texas Parks and Wildlife Department, U.S. Natural Resources Conservation Service (formerly Soil Conservation Service), or U.S. Fish and Wildlife Service. For activities other than those described above, land managers should seek assistance from the U.S. Fish and Wildlife Service, since permits may be required.

Other Management Suggestions

Reducing Impacts From Predation and Cowbird Parasitism

Reducing the impacts of predation and nest parasitism by Brown-headed Cowbirds may be important for successful reproduction in some populations of Golden-cheeked Warblers. This may be particularly true where warblers nest near grazed land or grain crops. Research is currently underway to better understand the impacts of cowbirds on Golden-cheeked Warblers.

Planned grazing systems designed to rotate livestock away from known nesting areas during the breeding season (March-August) may be desirable to reduce cowbird impacts. Periodic rest also has important benefits for improving

range condition and productivity. Since cowbirds are attracted to easily available food sources, spilling or scattering grain should be avoided. Supplemental feeding areas should be moved frequently, located away from nesting habitat, and kept free from accumulations of waste grain.

Leaving woodland vegetation adjacent to Golden-cheeked Warbler habitat is often desirable to reduce predation and nest parasitism by Brown-headed Cowbirds. Woodland strips of 300 feet or more are preferable.

Finally, controlling cowbirds through trapping may be effective in reducing warbler nest parasitism. Mounted mobile traps, placed near watering sites as livestock are rotated through pastures, have been used successfully to reduce cowbird numbers. Contact Texas Parks and Wildlife Department or the U.S. Fish and Wildlife Service for information and assistance in implementing a cowbird control program.

Habitat Restoration

The following suggestions are offered for landowners wishing to restore or create habitat for the Golden-cheeked Warbler in areas that currently do not support warblers. One type of restorable habitat is the relatively mesic (moist) area, with a diversity of deciduous trees, where junipers have been previously removed. Allowing the reestablishment of juniper on these sites would eventually result in the mature oak-juniper woodland preferred by Golden-cheeked Warblers.

Other situations where restoring habitat may be a possibility include relatively mesic areas dominated by juniper, where heavy browsing pressure by deer or livestock has prevented the establishment of hardwood seedlings. In these areas, control of deer numbers and planned deferment from livestock grazing would promote reestablishment of broad-leaved shrubs and trees, eventually resulting in a mature juniper-oak woodland.

In mesic areas where small junipers (10 ft. or less) are dominant, small junipers could be thinned to favor faster growth of remaining trees. Thinning would encourage hardwood regeneration,

especially if some slash is left in place to provide protection for hardwood seedlings. If large junipers are dominant, several small openings per acre would encourage hardwood regeneration. These openings should be protected from browsing and left to regenerate naturally, or planted to native hardwoods. In each of these examples, the idea is to restore areas that may once have provided habitat to the natural oak-juniper woodland capable of growing on the site.

Further Guidance Concerning the ESA

Good range management practices such as proper stocking, rotational grazing, prescribed burning, periodic deferments, carefully planned brush control, and attention to plant and animal resource needs will help prevent loss of Golden-cheeked Warbler habitat. Habitat where Golden-cheeked Warblers are likely to occur should be protected from activities that alter the composition or structure of trees and shrubs, except as provided for in these guidelines. Likewise, management activities in areas that may be used by warblers should be carefully planned to avoid altering vegetation composition and structure and timed to avoid the breeding season until a survey is done to determine if warblers are using the area.

Landowners who are not sure whether or not they have suitable Golden-cheeked Warbler habitat, or whether a planned activity will affect these birds, may want to consult a biologist familiar with the species. An on-site visit by a biologist familiar with the warbler can determine if warbler habitat is present and whether the planned activity falls under the guidelines presented here. Also, a biologist who has a scientific permit from the U.S. Fish and Wildlife Service and Texas Parks and Wildlife Department to do Golden-cheeked Warbler survey work will know how to conduct a breeding season survey (approximately March 20 to May 15) to determine if warblers are present in the area for which a management activity is planned. Finally, important habitat components such as the ratio of mature juniper to deciduous trees, and canopy structure and height, should be retained whenever possible to enable population recovery.

Technical Assistance

Technical assistance in range and wildlife management, including management for endangered species, is available to landowners and managers by contacting the Texas Parks and Wildlife Department, U.S. Natural Resources Conservation Service, or U.S. Fish and Wildlife Service. Additional information is available from the Texas Agricultural Extension Service. Further guidance and specific questions concerning Golden-cheeked Warbler research, endangered species management and recovery, and landowner responsibilities under the Endangered Species Act, should be directed to the Texas Parks and Wildlife Department or U.S. Fish and Wildlife Service.

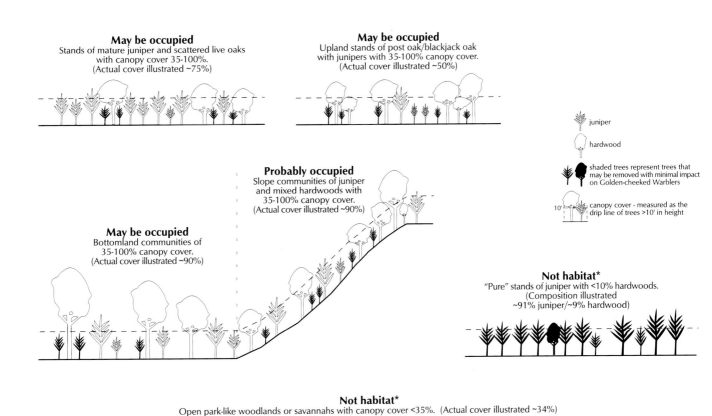

May be occupied
Stands of mature juniper and scattered live oaks with canopy cover 35-100%.
(Actual cover illustrated ~75%)

May be occupied
Upland stands of post oak/blackjack oak with junipers with 35-100% canopy cover.
(Actual cover illustrated ~50%)

juniper

hardwood

shaded trees represent trees that may be removed with minimal impact on Golden-cheeked Warblers

canopy cover - measured as the drip line of trees >10' in height

Probably occupied
Slope communities of juniper and mixed hardwoods with 35-100% canopy cover.
(Actual cover illustrated ~90%)

May be occupied
Bottomland communities of 35-100% canopy cover.
(Actual cover illustrated ~90%)

Not habitat*
"Pure" stands of juniper with <10% hardwoods.
(Composition illustrated ~91% juniper/~9% hardwood)

Not habitat*
Open park-like woodlands or savannahs with canopy cover <35%. (Actual cover illustrated ~34%)

*As long as these areas are not in close (within 300 feet) proximity to "probably occupied" or "may be occupied" habitat, neither surveys nor permits are required for activities within these areas.

Funds for the production of this leaflet were provided by the U.S. Fish and Wildlife Service, under Section 6 of the Endangered Species Act.

Black-capped Vireo

Scientific Name: *Vireo atricapillus*

Federal Status: Endangered, 10/6/87 • State Status: Endangered

Description

The Black-capped Vireo is a 4.5 inch insect-eating songbird. Mature males are olive green above and white below with faint greenish-yellow flanks. The crown and upper half of the head is black with a partial white eye-ring. The iris is brownish-red and the bill black. The plumage of the female is duller than the male. Females have a dark slate gray head.

Male Black-capped Vireo
© TPWD

Female Black-capped Vireo
© USFWS A. Shull

Distribution and Habitat

Historical records from 1852-1956 show that the Black-capped Vireo once occurred from central Kansas, Oklahoma, Texas and into Mexico. These records show that vireos bred in Kansas, Oklahoma, Texas, and central Coahuila, Mexico. Today, Black-capped Vireos breed locally in central Texas, a few counties in central Oklahoma, and central Coahuila, Mexico, although little is known of their status in Mexico. Black-capped Vireos winter along the western coast of Mexico.

In Texas, vireo habitat is found on rocky limestone soils of the Edwards Plateau, Cross Timbers and Prairies, eastern Trans-Pecos and, to a limited extent, on igneous soils in the Chisos Mountains. Although Black-capped Vireo habitat throughout Texas is highly variable with regard to plant species, soils, temperature, and rainfall, all habitat types are similar in vegetation structure; i.e. the "overall look" is somewhat similar although the plant species vary. Vireos require shrub vegetation reaching to ground level for nesting cover. They typically nest in shrublands and open woodlands with a distinctive patchy structure. Typical habitat is characterized by shrub vegetation extending from the ground to about 6 feet and covering about 30 to 60 percent or greater of the total area. In the eastern portion of the vireo's range, the shrub layer is often combined with an open, sparse to moderate tree canopy. Open grassland separates the clumps of shrubs and trees.

In the Edwards Plateau and Cross Timbers Regions, vireo habitat occurs where soils, topography, and land use produce scattered hardwoods with abundant low cover. Common broad-leaved plants in vireo habitat include: Texas (Spanish) oak, Lacey oak, shin oak, Durand (scaleybark) oak, live oak, mountain laurel, evergreen sumac, skunkbush sumac, flameleaf sumac, redbud, Texas persimmon, mesquite, and agarita. Although Ashe juniper is often part of the plant composition in vireo habitat, preferred areas usually have a low density and cover of juniper.

In the western Edwards Plateau and Trans-Pecos Regions, on the western edge of the vireo's range, the birds are often found in canyon bottoms and slopes where sufficient moisture is available to support diverse shrub vegetation. Dominant woody plants in this habitat type include sandpaper oak, vasey shin oak, Texas kidneywood, Mexican walnut, and fragrant ash, mountain laurel, and guajillo.

For all habitat types, the plant composition appears to be less important than the presence of adequate broad-leaved shrubs, foliage to ground level, and mixture of open grassland and woody cover. Deciduous and broad-leaved shrubs and trees throughout the vireo's range are also important in providing habitat for insects on which the vireo feeds.

Life History

Black-capped Vireos arrive in Texas from mid-March to mid-April. Adult males often arrive before females and first-year males to select their territories. Vireos' territories are

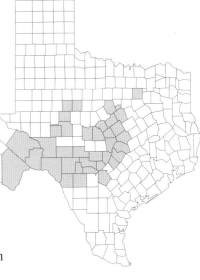

often clustered in patches of suitable habitat. Although territories range in size from 1 to 16 acres, most territories are 2 to 4 acres. Males sing to attract mates and defend territories. Many males can be heard singing throughout the breeding season, but singing begins to decline by July. The vireo's song is described as hurried and harsh, composed of various phrases and syllables with a restless quality.

Nesting begins after the females arrive in late March to early April. Both the male and female select the nest site, and the female completes the nest. Nest building usually requires 2 to 3 days. The cup-shaped nest is suspended from its rim in a fork of a branch about 1 to 6 feet above the ground. However, most Black-capped Vireos nest at about "doorknob" height. Nests have been found in shin oak, scalybark oak, Texas oak, sumac, Texas persimmon, juniper, and Texas mountain laurel.

The vireo may nest more than once in the same year. A new nest is constructed each time. Three to four eggs are usually laid in the first nesting attempt, but later clutches may contain only 2 to 3 eggs. The first egg is usually laid one day after completion of the nest, with one egg being laid each subsequent day. Incubation takes 14 to 17 days, and is shared by the male and female.

Vireo chicks are fed by both adults. The young fledge (leave the nest) 10 to 12 days after hatching. Fledglings are cared for by the female alone, the male alone, or by both adults. Sometimes the parents split the brood and each care for several young. Occasionally, males or females will leave the care of the young to their mate, and attempt another nesting effort.

Vireos may live for more than five years, and usually return year after year to the same territory, or one nearby. The birds migrate to their wintering grounds on Mexico's western coast beginning in July, and are gone from Texas by mid-September.

Threats and Reasons for Decline

The Black-capped Vireo is vulnerable to changes in the relative abundance of its habitat. For any given site, good vireo habitat may become unsuitable because of natural plant succession or because of human activities. Active, well-planned land management is often required to maintain good vireo habitat, especially in the eastern portion of its range. Factors that can adversely affect vireo habitat include broad-scale or improper brush clearing, fire suppression, overbrowsing by deer and livestock, and urbanization. Loss of tropical wintering habitat is also a concern.

Poorly planned brush management practices on rangeland may remove too much low growing woody cover, especially when large acreages are treated at one time. This eliminates or reduces habitat value for vireos and for other wildlife, such as White-tailed deer, quail, small mammals, and various songbirds. Overbrowsing of broad-leaved shrubs by goats, deer, and exotic animals reduces the vegetation in the 2 to 4 foot zone, making it unsuitable for vireo nesting. Continued overuse of these preferred browse plants over many years may eventually eliminate them from the plant community, thus permanently altering the habitat.

The role of fire in maintaining, improving, or creating vireo habitat is also an important consideration. The rangelands of central Texas, and the various plant communities these lands support, evolved under the influence of periodic fires. Historically, these natural and man-made fires maintained an open grassland with scattered clumps of trees and shrubs. Fire stimulated shrubs to sprout at the base, thus providing areas of dense foliage at the 2 to 4 foot level, required by vireos. In the past, fire was responsible for maintaining or periodically returning some areas to vireo habitat. Today, prescribed burning, a valuable range and wildlife management tool, occurs on many ranches throughout Texas. However, the combination of overgrazing and lack of fire in the recent past has reduced vireo habitat in many other areas.

Human activities have provided favorable habitat for the Brown-headed Cowbird, which parasitizes vireo nests. The cowbird is usually associated with livestock, farms,

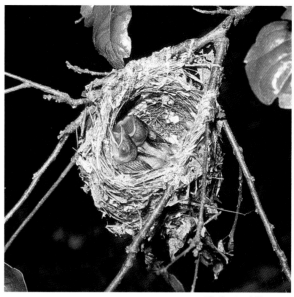

Black-capped Vireo nest
© TPWD Glen Mills

Nesting vireo
© Greg W. Lasley

and grain fields, where it benefits from waste grain and insects. They may also be attracted to backyard bird feeders, trash dumps, or other urban areas where food and water are available. Cowbirds lay their eggs in other birds' nests, leaving the host bird to raise their young. A cowbird chick can expel or outcompete the host birds' eggs and young, leaving only the cowbird chick to be fed by the host. While some birds remove cowbird eggs from their nest, the vireo does not. When nest parasitism occurs, vireos tend to abandon their nest, and thus parasitized nests usually fail to produce vireos. When their nest is parasitized, vireos often attempt to renest. The amount of nest parasitism varies greatly from one population to another throughout the

Habitat at Kickapoo Caverns State Park
© Matt Wagner

Habitat with low-growing shrubs
© Matt Wagner

Habitat in Big Bend National Park
© USFWS A. Shull

state, ranging from 10 to 90 percent of the nests.

Direct habitat loss and fragmentation due to urban and suburban development is a major threat in expanding urban areas of Travis, McLennan, Dallas, Bexar, and Kerr counties. Problems associated with suburban expansion, such as increases in predation by dogs, cats, raccoons, skunks, and jays, have also impacted the vireo.

In summary, protection and proper management of known vireo nesting areas, management for large patches of quality habitat, and reduction of the problem of parasitism are essential to the protection of this species and other plant and animal species associated with the Black-capped Vireo in Texas.

Recovery Efforts

Research is underway to better understand the life history, habitat requirements, and land management practices affecting the Black-capped Vireo. Research is also in progress regarding the impact of cowbirds on vireo populations in Texas. Research efforts in Mexico are planned to gather information concerning life history and habitat requirements on the wintering range.

Habitat conservation planning is underway in counties such as Travis and Bexar to direct urban expansion and development away from endangered species habitat. Finally, efforts to provide information, technical assistance, and incentives for private landowners to incorporate management for Black-capped Vireos into their livestock and wildlife operations are an essential part of the recovery process.

Where To See the Black-capped Vireo

A number of state lands offer opportunities to see and learn more about the Black-capped Vireo. These include Black Gap Wildlife Management Area (WMA), Colorado Bend State Park (SP), Devils River State Natural Area (SNA), Dinosaur Valley SP, Kerr WMA, Kickapoo Caverns SP, Lost Maples SNA, South Llano River SP, and Buck WMA. Also, once open to the public, the Balcones Canyonlands National Wildlife Refuge near Austin and Government Canyon State Park near San Antonio will offer additional opportunities to see Black-capped Vireos.

Because the Black-capped Vireo is an endangered species, birders and other observers should carefully follow certain viewing ethics. Observers should be careful not to flush birds from the nest or disturb nests or young. Black-capped Vireos should be viewed only from a distance with binoculars. Do not use recorded calls of the Black-capped Vireo or the Screech Owl to attract birds, and be careful that your presence does not unduly disturb or stress the birds.

How You Can Help

Landowners can help by learning more about the habitat requirements of the Black-capped Vireo and incorporating management practices which create or maintain habitat for these birds. You can also encourage and support private landowners who are managing their land to protect and provide habitat for endangered species.

You can be involved with the conservation of Texas' nongame wildlife resources by supporting the Special Nongame and Endangered Species Conservation Fund. Special nongame stamps and decals are available at Texas Parks and Wildlife Department (TPWD) field offices, most state parks, and the License Branch of TPWD headquarters in Austin. Part of the proceeds from the sale of these items are used to conserve habitat and provide information to the public concerning endangered species. Conservation Passports, available from TPWD, are valid for one year and allow unlimited access to most State Parks, State Natural Areas, and Wildlife Management Areas throughout Texas. Conservation organizations in Texas also welcome your participation and support.

For More Information Contact

Texas Parks and Wildlife Department
Endangered Resources Branch
4200 Smith School Road
Austin, Texas 78744
(512) 912-7011 or (800) 792-1112
    or
U.S. Fish and Wildlife Service
Ecological Services Field Office
10711 Burnet Road, Suite 200
Austin, Texas 78758
(512) 490-0057

Management guidelines are available from the Texas Parks and Wildlife Department and U.S. Fish and Wildlife Service for landowners and managers wishing to know more about rangeland management practices which improve habitat for the Black-capped Vireo.

Cowbird egg (spotted) in Black-Capped Vireo nest
© Glen Mills

References

Armstrong, W.E., M.W. Lockwood, and D.K. Stuart. 1992. *Performance Report: Black-capped Vireo Management on Texas Parks and Wildlife Department Lands.* Federal Aid Project No. E-1-4, Job No. 3.2.

Armstrong, W.E., C. Travis, and B.G. Alexander. 1989. *Final Report: Black-capped Vireo Management.* Federal Aid Project No. W-103-R-19, Job No. 60.

Graber, J.W. 1961. *Distribution, Habitat Requirements, and Life History of the Black-capped Vireo.* Ecol. Mon. 31:313-336.

Oberholser, H.C. 1974. *The Bird Life of Texas.* Edgar Kincaid, Ed., University of Texas Press, Austin, Texas. Vol. 2, 1069 pp.

U.S. Fish and Wildlife Service. 1991. *Black-capped Vireo Recovery Plan.* Endangered Species Office, Albuquerque, N.M.

Funds for the production of this leaflet were provided by the U.S. Fish and Wildlife Service, under Section 6 of the Endangered Species Act.

Management Guidelines for Black-capped Vireo

The following guidelines address land management practices that can be used to maintain, enhance, or create Black-capped Vireo habitat. They are intended primarily to serve as general guidance for rural landowners and others managing land for livestock and/or wildlife in Texas. The guidelines are based on our current understanding of the biology of this species.

Prescribed Burning

Prescribed burning is an excellent tool used to maintain the desired vegetation structure for vireo nesting; i.e. a mosaic of shrubs and open grassland with abundant

Prescribed burning
© Matt Wagner

Selective handcutting of juniper
© TPWD Glen Mills

woody foliage below 6 feet. Cool season burns, conducted prior to March 15, are often recommended to control small juniper, thus maintaining the relatively open shrublands preferred by vireos. Prescribed burns conducted during late spring and early fall, under hotter conditions, can be used to set back plant succession in order to create vireo habitat; however, warm season burns should be done only in areas that do not currently support Black-capped Vireos. On grazed rangeland, prescribed burns should be coordinated with livestock rotation to allow for needed deferments. It is best to avoid burning relatively small areas within large pastures to prevent heavy grazing pressure by livestock and/or deer on burned areas.

Desirable burn intervals for cool season burns vary throughout the state, depending on rainfall and vegetation type. Field experience shows that, for much of the Hill Country, a burning interval of 4 to 7 years is considered desirable to keep Ashe juniper (cedar) invasion in check and to allow regrowth of broad-leaved shrubs. Maintaining open grassland areas between clumps of shrubs is important for good vireo habitat. Research is needed to better understand the use of prescribed burning to maintain and create vireo habitat, and to develop guidelines on desirable burn intervals throughout the vireo's range in Texas.

Assistance from people experienced with the use of prescribed burning is highly recommended. Landowners are encouraged to have a complete written prescribed burn plan addressing the objectives of the burn, required weather conditions, grazing deferments, fireguard preparations, personnel and equipment needed, a detailed map showing how the burn will be conducted, and notification and safety procedures.

Fire is a natural component of Texas rangelands, and prescribed burning has many range and wildlife management benefits. These include improved forage quality and availability for livestock and deer, and maintenance of desirable plant composition and structure. Landowners are advised to contact local representatives of the Texas Parks and Wildlife Department, U.S. Natural Resources Conservation Service (formerly Soil Conservation Service), or Texas Agricultural Extension Service for help in developing and implementing a prescribed burning program designed specifically for your property and management objectives.

Selective Brush Management

Increases in juniper (cedar) and other woody species can easily cause the vegetation to grow (succeed) out of the patchy, low shrub cover that provides suitable habitat. In the eastern portion of the vireo's range, good nesting habitat generally has between 30 and 60 percent shrub canopy. Selective brush removal with herbicides or mechanical means can be used to keep the habitat favorable for vireo nesting. For example, the selective removal of juniper, mesquite, or pricklypear (less desirable to the vireo and to the rancher) serves to maintain a relatively open shrub canopy and encourages growth of associated broad-leaved shrubs. Selective brush removal should strive to maintain the low shrubby structure. Also, radical changes in shrub canopy from one year to the next over large areas should be avoided. Western Edwards Plateau rangelands comprised primarily of mesquite, often referred to as mesquite flats, are not considered Black-capped Vireo habitat; therefore, mesquite control in these areas will not affect vireos.

When using herbicides, careful attention to the kinds, amounts, timing, and application technique will achieve the best control of target species at minimum cost. Precise application also reduces the risk of environmental contamination and off-site effects. It is best to choose highly selective individual plant treatment methods, whenever practical, to avoid damage to desirable shrubs such as live oak, shin oak, Texas oak, hackberry, Texas persimmon, sumac, redbud, and elm. Herbicides should always be used in strict accordance with label directions, including those for proper storage and disposal of containers and rinse water. Herbicide applications should not occur during the breeding season, except for basal applications or individual plant treatment of prickly pear pads.

Handcutting or carefully planned mechanical methods of brush management such as chaining, roller chopping, or shredding can be used to stimulate basal sprouting of key woody species in order to maintain, enhance, or create vireo habitat. Mechanical methods should only be used during the non-breeding season (October-February). Remember that good grazing management and moderate stocking rates can reduce woody plant invasion and therefore the need for expensive brush control practices.

Finally, although brush management practices can be used to change the structure and composition of vegetation so that vireos may occupy the habitat, landowners should seek technical assistance when planning brush management practices in habitat that is known to be occupied by Black-capped Vireos. Since brush management activities can affect habitat for the Golden-cheeked Warbler as well as the Black-capped Vireo, landowners are encouraged to learn about the habitat requirements of both endangered songbirds (see leaflet on the Golden-cheeked Warbler).

Grazing and Browsing Management

Excessive browsing by goats, exotic animals, and White-tailed deer destroys the thick woody growth needed for nest concealment. Livestock and deer management, which allows woody plants such as live oak, shin oak, sumac, Texas persimmon, elbowbush, redbud, and hackberry to make dense growth from 0 to 6 feet, is needed. On ranches throughout Texas, moderate stocking, rotation of livestock, controlling deer numbers, and proper use of desirable browse plants will benefit deer and livestock as well as Black-capped Vireos.

To provide adequate nesting cover for vireos, woody plants should receive only limited browsing during the spring and summer. If animals (livestock, deer, and exotics) are well-managed and kept within recommended stocking rates, this can be achieved. Experience has shown that, in general, ranges stocked with cattle and deer tend to maintain better vireo nesting cover than ranges stocked with goats and exotic animals. Browsing surveys should pay more attention to stem growth than leaf growth, since leaf production in many shrubs varies widely, depending on season and weather conditions. Also, the amount of leaf production depends in part on the amount of stem and bud growth available on the plant. Research is lacking concerning how various levels of browsing pressure affect habitat structure and nesting use. However, based on field experience, a conservative approach would be to limit browsing pressure, especially during the growing season, to no more than 50% of the total annual growth (young, tender twigs) within reach of animals on any given plant. This will maintain plants that are already vigorous and allow for improvement of those with less than ideal structure. As a rule of thumb, if you can "see through" a browse plant, then too much stem and leaf growth has been removed.

Careful management of woody plants will not only provide for the habitat needs of Black-capped Vireos, but will also create high quality habitat for deer and other wildlife as well as livestock. Technical assistance in determining proper use of browse plants is available from the Texas Parks and Wildlife

Cattle rotation
© TPWD

Overgrazed range with low-growing cover removed
© TPWD

Department and U.S. Natural Resources Conservation Service.

Reducing Impacts From Cowbirds

Brood parasitism by Brown-headed Cowbirds poses a serious threat to successful reproduction in some populations of Black-capped Vireos. Research is currently underway to better understand the impacts of cowbirds on vireos. Because cattle attract cowbirds, management to reduce cowbird impacts is important on grazed land.

Because cowbirds are attracted to easily available sources of food, avoid spilling or scattering grain. Supplemental feeding areas should be moved frequently and kept free from accumulations of waste grain. This would help to prevent sparsely vegetated areas of compacted soils, which also tend to attract cowbirds.

Grazing management can be used to remove cattle from areas where vireos nest. For example, cattle can be rotated away from prime nesting habitat during the breeding season. Another option is to graze stocker cattle during the fall and winter, resting pastures during the spring/summer nesting season. Resting pastures periodi-

Cowbird trap
© TPWD

cally improves range condition and may also help reduce nest parasitism.

Finally, trapping and/or shooting cowbirds can be effective in reducing vireo brood parasitism. Mounted mobile traps, placed near watering sites as livestock are rotated through pastures, have been used successfully to reduce cowbird numbers. Shooting cowbirds at places where they congregate is another option, although this method is often not selective for the cowbirds responsible for the parasitism. Contact Texas Parks and Wildlife Department or the U.S. Fish and Wildlife Service for assistance with implementing a cowbird control program for your property.

Habitat Restoration

For landowners wishing to restore or create habitat for the Black-capped Vireo in areas currently unoccupied by vireos, the following suggestions are offered.

One type of restorable habitat is an open shrubland capable of growing a diversity of woody plants, where much of the low-growing cover has been removed through overbrowsing by livestock or deer. Controlling browsing pressure by reducing animal numbers and providing pasture rest will allow the natural reestablishment of low-growing shrub cover needed by vireos.

Habitat restoration may also be possible in areas where the shrub layer has become too tall or dense to provide good vireo habitat. In these areas, well-planned use of controlled fire can reduce overall shrub height, stimulate basal sprouting of shrubs, and reduce shrub density to produce more favorable habitat for vireos.

Also, in areas where the brush has become too dense, selective thinning could be done to produce a more open habitat. Carefully planned brush management could be used to encourage regeneration and lateral branching of desirable shrubs by allowing sunlight to reach the ground. In each of these examples, the idea is to restore areas that may once have provided habitat to the relatively open, low-growing shrub/grassland vegetation preferred by vireos.

Summary

Periodic prescribed burning, selective brush management, control of deer and exotic wildlife numbers, and good grazing manage-

ment practices, including proper stocking and rotational grazing, are management options that can be used to create and maintain Black-capped Vireo habitat. These same management tools will also maintain diverse and productive rangelands. In addition to providing food, fiber, and support for rural landowners, well-managed rangelands provide habitat for a wide variety of wildlife, and benefits such as clean water, natural diversity, and recreational opportunities for all Texans.

Technical assistance in range and wildlife management, including grazing management, determination of proper stocking rates, prescribed burning, brush management, and management for endangered species, is available to landowners and managers by contacting the Texas Parks and Wildlife Department or U.S. Natural Resources Conservation Service. Information is also available from the Texas Agricultural Extension Service. Further guidance and specific questions concerning Black-capped Vireo research, endangered species management and recovery, and landowner responsibilities under the Endangered Species Act, should be directed to the U.S. Fish and Wildlife Service or Texas Parks and Wildlife Department. If, after reading this leaflet, you are still unsure whether or not your management plans will adversely affect the Vireo or its habitat, please contact the U.S. Fish and Wildlife Service for assistance.

Funds for the production of this leaflet were provided by the U.S. Fish and Wildlife Service, under Section 6 of the Endangered Species Act.

Red-cockaded Woodpecker

Scientific Name: *Picoides borealis*

Federal Status: Endangered, 10/13/70 • State Status: Endangered

Description

An eight inch long woodpecker with a solid black cap and nape, and prominent white cheek patches. The male has a tiny red streak behind the eye and near the ear (the cockade). The cockade is seldom visible in the field, making it difficult to distinguish males from females. The Red-cockaded Woodpecker is similar to the Downy and Hairy Woodpeckers in general appearance, except that it has a barred back, spotted breast, and the male has red on either side of the head rather than on the nape.

Male (left) and female Red-cockaded Woodpeckers
© TPWD Frank Aquilar

Habitat

The Red-cockaded Woodpecker is found in mature pine forests of east Texas and the southeastern United States. It is the only species of woodpecker that excavates its cavity exclusively in living pines. In Texas, cavities have been found in longleaf, loblolly, shortleaf, and slash pines. Most cavities are found in trees 60 to 70 years old or older. The tree must have enough heartwood (older, non-living, inner portion of wood) to contain the roosting chamber, since a chamber in sapwood (younger, living portion of wood) would fill with resin. Since heartwood is very hard, a large percentage of cavities is found in pines infected with a heart rot fungus called red heart. This fungus weakens the heartwood and makes cavity excavation easier.

A cluster site is a stand of trees containing and surrounding the cavity trees in which a group of woodpeckers nest and roost. In most clusters, all the cavity trees are located within a circle about 1500 feet in diameter. Preferred cluster sites are mature, park-like pine stands with 50 to 80 square feet of basal area per acre (about 90 to 145 trees averging 10 inches in diameter). Ideally, cluster sites should have a grassy understory with few or no hardwood or pine trees above 6 feet in height. Controlling midstory growth is especially critical within 50 feet of all cavity trees. Once the midstory grows to the level of the cavities (20 to 50 feet above the ground), a high rate of cavity abandonment occurs. A few widely scattered hardwood trees and shrubs do not harm the woodpeckers and are beneficial to other wildlife. However, control of dense midstory vegetation is essential to maintain the cluster site.

An important function of the cluster site is to provide a source of new cavity trees. Cavity trees are generally used for several years, but an average of 5 percent of loblolly and shortleaf, and 1 percent of longleaf pines die each year. Causes of mortality include bark beetles, wind snap, and fire. Also, cavity enlargement by Pileated Woodpeckers often makes cavities unusable by the Red-cockaded Woodpecker. The cluster site should be at least 10 acres in size, with 10 to 30 mature pines, to ensure cavity trees for the future.

The best cluster site will not be used if the foraging or food gathering habitat is not suitable. Red-cockaded Woodpeckers exhibit a distinct preference for large living pines as foraging sites. Good foraging habitat consists of pine stands with trees 10 inches and larger in diameter measured at 4.5 feet above the ground. These birds also forage in pole stands, consisting of pines 4 to 10 inches in diameter. However, little use is made of sapling stands, which contain pines less than 4 inches in diameter. Also, Red-cockaded Woodpeckers are known to actively seek and forage extensively on pines infested by southern pine beetles (bark beetles).

The quality of the foraging habitat determines the amount needed to support a group of woodpeckers. While 125 acres of well-stocked (100-140, 10-inch diameter trees per acre), mature pine is sufficient for some groups; where habitat conditions are less ideal, groups may require several hundred acres to meet their foraging needs.

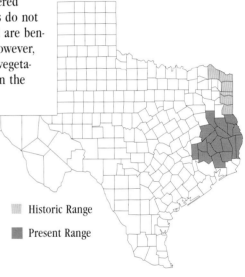

Historic Range

Present Range

Life History

The Red-cockaded Woodpecker has a complex social system. These birds live in groups, which usually have two to six birds, although as many as nine birds have been observed. The group may consist of only a mated pair; a mated pair with their current year's offspring; or a mated pair, their current year's offspring and helpers. These helpers are one to three year old adult birds, typically sons of one or both of the breeders. Helpers assist in incubating the eggs, feeding young, constructing new cavities, and defending the group's territory.

Although Red-cockaded Woodpecker groups may consist of a number of adult birds during the nesting season, there is only one mated pair. A breeding male may live for several years; and when he dies, one of his helper sons generally becomes the breeding male.

A woodpecker group roosts and nests in a cluster of cavity trees. The cluster may include one to 30 cavity trees. Most clusters have some cavities under construction, some completed and in use, and some abandoned, often occupied by competitors.

Generally, each member of a woodpecker group has its own cavity for roosting. Red-cockaded Woodpeckers defend their cavities from members of other groups and from other animals. Major competitors for nest cavities include other woodpeckers (Red-headed, Red-bellied, and Pileated) and Flying Squirrels.

Red-cockaded Woodpeckers nest from April through July. Group members assist with incubating the eggs during the day, and the breeding male stays with the eggs at night. The eggs hatch in 10 to 12 days. Young birds leave the nest in about 26 days, but remain with the group. Studies have shown higher nestling survival at nests attended by helpers.

The diet of the Red-cockaded Woodpecker consists mainly of insects (85%), but also includes small fruits and seeds (15%). The birds concentrate their search for food on the trunks and limbs of live pine trees. They scale the bark and dig into dead limbs for insects and larvae.

Compared to decayed wood, the sapwood and heartwood of a living pine is very hard and difficult to excavate. The average time required to excavate a cavity is 1 to 3 years for loblolly and shortleaf pine, and 4 to 7 years for longleaf. Once the sapwood is penetrated, the abundant resin flow that occurs creates another barrier. Most of the work on cavities occurs in summer after the young leave the nest. Cavity excavation occurs primarily in the morning, but can occur any

time during the day. Once completed, a cavity is used for several years. Cavities in longleaf pine are sometimes used for 20 and even 30 years.

Cavities are constructed by tunneling at an upward slope through the sapwood so that the resin or pitch will drain from the hole. Once the birds have tunneled into the heartwood a sufficient distance, they excavate downward, forming a gourd-shaped chamber about 6 to 10 inches deep and 3 to 5 inches wide. Near the cavity entrance, numerous small holes called resin wells are chipped through the bark. The birds regularly peck at resin wells to keep resin flowing.

Red-cockaded Woodpeckers maintain open cavity holes by removing the growing tissue from around the holes. Eventually, the birds expose the sapwood for several inches around the entrance. This exposed area is called the plate. Pitch from the plate and resin wells coats the trunk of the cavity tree. The continuous flow of resin deters predators, especially snakes. Actively used trees have clear, sticky pitch, and freshly chipped, reddish bark around the resin wells and plate.

Threats and Reasons for Decline

The main threat to the survival of the Red-cockaded Woodpecker is the decrease in the quality and quantity of old growth forest nesting habitat, primarily due to short rotation timber management. Fire suppression has also been detrimental due to the importance of controlling the midstory in Red-cockaded habitat. Because of this bird's requirement for old age pines, habitat loss takes a long time to rectify. It may take 60 to 70 years to begin to provide suitable nesting habitat. Ideally, rotation ages of 100 years for loblolly, and 120 years or more for shortleaf and longleaf pine are needed to produce trees with the required amount of heartwood and frequency of red heart fungus.

Some of the potential adverse effects of modern forestry on Red-cockaded Woodpecker habitat are: (1) short timber rotations (30 to

Red-cockaded Woodpecker at cavity
© TPWD Glen Mills

Active cavity with resin flow
© R. N. Conner

Habitat with tall, large widely-spaced pines
© TPWD Glen Mills

Old growth logging
© TPWD

Midstory encroachment leads to cavity abandonment
© Brent Ortego

45 years) which result in loss of suitable nesting and roosting habitat, (2) leaving only cavity trees and cutting all others within a cluster reduces foraging habitat and does not allow for cavity tree replacement, (3) leaving isolated clusters surrounded by harvested areas reduces foraging habitat and may increase predation by forcing birds to cross large open areas, (4) removing all dead and dying trees results in loss of habitat for other cavity-nesters, thereby increasing competition for Red-cockaded nest cavities, (5) preserving cavity trees and removing other dominant trees in a colony makes the cavity tree the tallest in the area and subject to lightning strikes and wind damage, (6) careless use of pesticides may poison the birds directly or decrease their food supply below the minimum level needed for reproduction, and (7) noise and activity of forestry operations in the vicinity of a colony during the breeding season can disrupt nesting success.

Finally, southern pine beetle infestations have been found to be a major cause of cavity tree loss in Texas. This is particularly true during southern pine beetle epidemics, such as the one that occurred on the Sam Houston National Forest in 1983 following hurricane Alicia. Active management is needed to reduce the loss of cavity trees to southern pine beetles.

The 1994 post-breeding population estimate for the Red-cockaded Woodpecker in Texas was 925 birds. An estimated 685 birds (74%) were found on federal lands (National Forests and National Park), 181 birds (20%) on private lands (timber companies and other private landowners), and 59 birds (6%) on state lands (State Forests and other state lands).

Recovery Efforts

Despite the problems facing the Red-cockaded Woodpecker, recovery efforts are proceeding on private, state, and federal lands. State and Federal agencies are working with private landowners interested in developing Red-cockaded woodpecker conservation and habitat management plans for their property. Efforts are also underway to create corridors of continuous habitat or chains of high quality habitat islands between populations to facilitate exchange of birds and enhance opportunities for reproduction. Conservation and habitat management, providing information to landowners and the public, and monitoring woodpecker populations are all important parts of the recovery process.

Red-cockaded Woodpecker populations on all four National Forests are increasing as a result of habitat improvements (removal of midstory vegetation), insertion of artificial cavities (nest boxes placed on the inside of the tree), and augmentation (moving young females and males to single bird clusters in an effort to start new clusters). Recent techniques such as artificial cavities and augmentation are helping to prolong the useful life of some cavities, to create man-made cavities where suitable natural cavities are limited, and to address short-term problems of isolation and fragmentation.

Where To See Red-cockaded Woodpeckers

A number of state and federal properties offer opportunities to see and learn more about Red-cockaded Woodpeckers. These include the Alabama Creek, Bannister, and Moore Plantation Wildlife Management Areas; the Jones and Fairchild State Forests; the Sam Houston, Davy Crockett, Angelina, and Sabine National Forests; the Alabama-Coushatta Indian Reservation; and the Big Thicket National Preserve.

How You Can Help

You can be involved with the conservation of Texas' nongame wildlife resources by supporting the Special Nongame and Endangered Species Conservation Fund. Special nongame stamps and decals are available at Texas Parks and Wildlife Department (TPWD) field offices, most state parks, and the License Branch of TPWD headquarters in Austin. Conservation Passports, available from TPWD, are valid for one year and allow unlimited access to most State Parks, State Natural Areas, and Wildlife Management Areas throughout Texas. Conservation organizations in Texas also welcome your participation and support. Finally, you can encourage and support private landowners who are managing their land to protect endangered species and their habitat.

For More Information Contact

Texas Parks and Wildlife Department
Endangered Resources Branch
4200 Smith School Road
Austin, Texas 78744
(512) 912-7011 or (800) 792-1112
    or
U.S. Fish and Wildlife Service
Ecological Services Field Office
10711 Burnet Road, Suite 200
Austin, Texas 78758
(512) 490-0057

Management guidelines are available from the Texas Parks and Wildlife Department and U.S. Fish and Wildlife Service for landowners and managers wishing to manage timberlands to benefit the Red-cockaded Woodpecker.

Red-cockaded Woodpecker cavity enlarged by a raven
© Brent Ortego

Cavity hole restrictor plate
© Brent Ortego

Artificial cavity nest box
© R. N. Conner

Artificial cavity nest box with restrictor plate installed
© R. N. Conner

References

Carpenter, J., and T. Hayes. 1991. *Managing forests for Red-cockaded woodpeckers-guidelines for private landowners in southeast Texas.* Texas Nature Conservancy.

Conner, R.N., D.C. Rudolph, D.L. Kulhavy, and A.E. Snow. 1991. *Causes of mortality of Red-cockaded woodpecker cavity trees.* J. Wildl. Manage. 55(3):531-537.

Conner, R.N., and D.C. Rudolph. 1991. *Effects of midstory reduction and thinning in Red-cockaded woodpecker cavity tree clusters.* Wild. Soc. Bull. 19:63-66.

Costa, R. 1992. *Draft Red-cockaded woodpecker procedures manual for private lands.* U.S. Fish and Wildlife Service. Atlanta, GA. 35 pp.

Hooper, R.G, A.F. Robinson, Jr., and J.A. Jackson. 1980. *The Red-cockaded woodpecker: notes on life history and management.* USDA Forest Service, General Report SA-GR 9.

Ortego, B., M. Krueger, and E. Barron. 1995. *Status and management needs of Red-cockaded woodpeckers on state and private land in Texas.* Pp. 477-481, *in Red-cockaded woodpecker: recovery, ecology and management* (D.L. Kulhavy, R.G. Hooper, and R. Costa, eds.). Center for Applied Studies in Forestry, Stephen F. Austin University, Nacogdoches, 551 pp.

Rudolph, D.C., and R.N. Conner. 1991. *Cavity tree selection by Red-cockaded woodpeckers in relation to tree age.* Wilson Bull. 103(3):458-467.

Rudolph, D.C., R.N. Conner, and J. Turner. 1990. *Competition for Red-cockaded woodpecker roost and nest cavities: effects of resin age and entrance diameter.* Wilson Bull. 102(1):23-36.

Swepston, D. 1980. *Results of Red-cockaded woodpecker research in Texas between 1969 and 1973.* Species Report. Texas Parks and Wildlife Department, P-R Project W-103-R-9.

U.S. Fish and Wildlife Service (USFWS). 1985. *Red-cockaded woodpecker recovery plan.* USFWS, Endangered Species Office, Atlanta, GA.

Funds for the production of this leaflet were provided by the U.S. Fish and Wildlife Service, under Section 6 of the Endangered Species Act.

Management Guidelines for the Red-cockaded Woodpecker

Landowners with Red-cockaded Woodpeckers can implement management practices that enhance survival, regardless of the size of their property. However, because these birds forage over large areas, forest conditions on adjacent land may ultimately determine the fate of the birds. On larger tracts, particularly those 200 acres or larger, these birds can be maintained with

Prescribed burning
© Craig Rudolph

Longleaf pine habitat
© Brent Ortego

greater assurance. Successful management for Red-cockaded Woodpeckers must do five things: (1) retain existing cavity trees, (2) provide trees for new cavities, (3) provide adequate foraging habitat, (4) control hardwood and pine midstory in the cluster site, and (5) provide for future cluster sites.

Cluster Site
Do not remove or damage active cavity trees. Selective cutting within cluster sites can be used to maintain the desired basal area.

However, thinning within a cluster site should not be done if stocking is below 50 square feet of basal area per acre of stems 10 inches DBH or larger. Also, all potential cavity trees (older, relict pines) within the cluster should be retained for replacement cavities. Do not isolate cluster sites from foraging areas of pines 4 inches or greater in diameter.

Burning or otherwise treating cluster areas to control midstory vegetation is vital. Do not allow midstory to exceed 6 feet in height, especially within 50 feet of the cavity trees. In cluster sites lacking past hardwood control, the fuel load may be too great to burn without destroying the cavity trees. In these cases, it may be necessary to remove them by cutting or use of herbicide. Raking to remove mulch at the base of cavity trees is also helpful in preventing fire damage. Regular, periodic prescribed burning should be implemented to control midstory growth and maintain the open forest preferred by the birds.

Pine stands surrounding cluster sites should be thinned to 50 to 80 square feet of basal area per acre. Maintain groups of larger pines (10 to 12 inches or larger DBH) within the surrounding forest for future cluster sites. Leave some dead and abandoned cavity trees of both pine and hardwood for other cavity nesters, to reduce competition for the Red-cockaded cavities. Maintain a spacing of 20 to 25 feet between trees to maintain stand vigor and minimize the probability of southern pine beetle infestation and spread.

Foraging Area
Provide adequate foraging habitat to support existing clusters and to facilitate establishment of new territories. A minimum of 3,000 square feet of pine basal area (10-inch DBH or larger) should be provided on at least 60 acres and up to 300 acres for each active cluster. Avoid isolat-

ing cluster sites from foraging areas. Most of the foraging acreage should be adjacent to (within 300 ft.) or within 1/4 mile of the cluster site. Thin sapling and pole stands to improve diameter growth and open the pine stand to a condition more favorable for the woodpecker. Prescribe burn for hardwood control. When regenerating stands, plant pines at 10x10 or 12x12 foot spacing to encourage rapid stand development. Use natural regeneration, such as seed tree, shelterwood, and group selection to develop an open park-like stand of pines. Favor longleaf pine over loblolly and shortleaf whenever possible.

Rotation Age
Generally, the longer the rotation age, the greater the opportunity the Red-cockaded Woodpecker has to maintain existing clusters and to create new ones. Rotation cycles of 80 to 120 years are encouraged. When it is not feasible to have long rotations over the entire ownership, setting aside smaller acreages of older pines will benefit the bird. Also, leaving old-growth remnant groups of trees well distributed throughout younger stands, and maintaining small remnant stands or patches of old-growth pines throughout the forest are helpful.

For More Information Contact
For detailed timber management guidelines, private landowners are referred to the U.S. Fish and Wildlife Service, Draft Red-cockaded Woodpecker Procedures Manual for Private Lands, by Ralph Costa. A number of management options are available for landowners with Red-cockaded Woodpeckers on their land. Contact the Texas Parks and Wildlife Department at (800) 792-1112 (Austin), (512) 912-7011 (Austin), or (409) 564-7145 (Nacogdoches); or the U.S. Fish and Wildlife Service at (409) 639-8546 (Lufkin) for more information.

Funds for the production of this leaflet were provided by the U.S. Fish and Wildlife Service, under Section 6 of the Endangered Species Act.

Attwater's Prairie Chicken

Scientific Name: *Tympanuchus cupido*

Federal Status: Endangered, 3/11/67 • State Status: Endangered

Description

The Attwater's Prairie Chicken is a brownish, strongly black-barred, medium-sized grouse with a short, rounded, blackish tail. Males have long tufts on the sides of the neck, called pinnae, which point forward during courtship. Males also have a yellow-orange comb above the eyes, and, on each side of the neck, an area of yellow-orange skin that inflates during courtship display.

Male Attwater's Prairie Chicken
© Ben Brown

Female Attwater's Prairie Chicken
© Gary Halvorsen

Habitat

Attwater's Prairie Chickens are found only in the coastal prairie of Texas. They use different areas of coastal prairie grassland for various activities; so a mixture of native grasses at different heights is optimum. For example, the birds use shortgrass cover (less than 10 inches in height) for courtship, feeding, and to avoid moisture during heavy dew or after rains. Midgrass areas (10 to 16 inches in height) are used for roosting and feeding. Tall grasses (16 to 24 inches in height) are needed for nesting, loafing, feeding, and escape cover. Very dense stands of grass are generally avoided, but are occasionally used for shade during summer, and as protection against inclement weather and predators. Studies have shown that prime habitat consists of tallgrass prairie dominated by bunchgrasses such as little bluestem, indiangrass, switchgrass and big bluestem; along with flowering plants such as Ruellia, yellow falsegarlic, and ragweed. The birds prefer open prairies without any woody cover, and avoid areas with more than 25 percent cover of shrubs. Preferred habitat is also characterized by knolls and ridges, with the minor variations in topography and soils on these sites resulting in a variety of vegetation types.

Life History

Prairie chicken breeding activity occurs on or near leks. A lek or booming ground is a specific area typically used year after year. They are usually located on bare ground or shortgrass areas which allow the males to be seen by the females. Booming grounds vary in size from one-eighth acre to several acres. They may be naturally occurring short grass flats or artificially maintained areas such as roads, runways, oil well pads, and drainage ditches. Areas around windmills, ponds, and other cattle concentration areas are often heavily grazed, and therefore provide the shortgrass cover used for booming sites. Active booming grounds are usually in close proximity to mid and tallgrass cover.

Males begin to set up territories on the booming grounds in late January to February. Fighting ensues when one male enters the territory of another. This fighting early in the booming season determines the social structure of the males on the lek. Usually one or two males will be dominant. Booming is usually heard from about daylight to 9 a.m. and in the late evening.

The hens start coming to the booming grounds in late February and early March. They appear quietly, often staying on the edge of the booming ground. When a hen is on the booming ground, the males become much more vocal and active. This increased activity often causes males not on the ground to fly in and start booming. Most mating occurs in early March, with one or two dominant males doing the majority of the breeding. Booming activity gradually ceases during the last week of April and the first two weeks of May. By mid May, the males have abandoned the booming grounds.

Nesting is usually initiated in early March. Most nests are located within one-half mile of the booming ground. The nest is a well-concealed, shallow depression about eight inches in diameter lined with dry grass and feathers from the hen. Hens prefer to nest in mid to tall grass cover with the grass canopy concealing the nest. Also preferred are areas with openings that facilitate walking, including cow trails used for access to their nests.

Clutch size ranges from 4 to 15 eggs, with the average being 12 eggs. During the 26 to 28 day incubation period, the hen leaves the nest only for short periods (45 to 90 minutes) during the morning and again in the afternoon to feed nearby (usually within 1/4 mile). The peak of the hatch is in late April to early May.

If a nest is destroyed, a hen will renest; although renesting attempts are limited because males leave the booming grounds by mid-May. Nesting losses are often the result of predators such as snakes, raccoons, oppossums, skunks, and coyotes, and flooding of nests. Because of the flat nature of coastal prairie rangeland, nests and small young are unable to survive heavy rains and flooding. The most detrimental rainfall pattern for nests is heavy rains in late April and early May. The April rains destroy initial nests, and May rains ruin renesting attempts. Hailstorms and human activities such as shredding during the nesting season can also destroy nests.

When the eggs hatch, the hen leaves the nest site. She takes her brood into more open areas, since it is difficult for young chicks to travel in dense vegetation, although some heavy cover is important for escape areas. The chicks are quite mobile at hatching, and can fly short distances by two weeks of age. Heavy or frequent rainfall during May are especially detrimental to young chicks. Death loss of birds over four weeks drastically declines, since by this age they are large enough to escape predators and can fly fairly well.

Prairie chickens feed on a wide variety of plant parts and insects. Potential food sources, both vegetation and insects, vary by season, location, and availability. Studies have shown that green foliage and seeds make up most of the diet, whereas insects are important seasonally. The foliage and seeds of native forbs (flowering plants) are particularly important in the diet. Most commonly consumed plants include Ruellia, yellow falsegarlic, upright prairie-coneflower, leavenworth vetch, stargrass, bedstraw, doveweed, and ragweed. Predators that feed on prairie chickens include hawks and coyotes.

Insects make up the majority of the diet of chicks. The chicks generally hatch when insect populations are high. Hens take their broods to weedy areas where insect density is greatest.

Threats and Reasons for Decline

Habitat loss and alteration are the primary reasons for the population decline of Attwater's Prairie Chicken. Loss of habitat due to land use changes since 1930 are particularly significant. It is estimated that 6 million acres of coastal Texas were once covered with suitable tallgrass prairie habitat. Only a few patches of this immense expanse of prairie chicken habitat now remain. Currently, it is estimated that less than 200,000 acres of suitable habitat remain. This represents a 97% loss of habitat within the historic range, and a 57% loss since 1937.

This loss of habitat has been the result of several factors. The biggest single change was brought about by the the start of rice production along the Gulf Coast. From about 1892 to present, about two million acres of grassland were converted to rice production.

Other factors, such as overgrazing by cattle in some locations and conversion of rangeland to introduced grass pastures have also reduced habitat. High stocking rates and continuous grazing over a period of many years have caused declines in range condition on parts of the Coastal Prairie. The climax tallgrass plant community with its associated native wildlife, which existed before the influence of European man, was ideal habitat for the prairie chicken. Unfortunately, tallgrasses such as big bluestem, little bluestem, and indiangrass required by prairie chickens for nesting are also preferred cattle forage. Without proper grazing management, continuous selective grazing by livestock will reduce desirable grasses and forbs and replace them with a plant community unable to support the nesting and food requirements of prairie chickens.

Also, much coastal prairie rangeland has been converted to introduced grasses such as coastal bermudagrass. Over a million acres have been planted to introduced grass pastures in an effort to boost livestock production. The conversion was especially rapid from 1940 to 1970, when fertilizer on which introduced grass

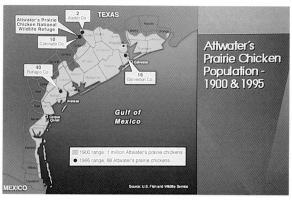

© TPWD

Coastal tallgrass prairie habitat
© David Diamond

Attwater's Prairie Chicken chick
© Gary Montoya

Attwater's Prairie Chicken nest
© Mike Morrow

Coastal rice production
© Gary Montoya

Industrialization on the Gulf Coast
© R. W. Jurries

Introduced grass pasture
© R. W. Jurries

production depends was relatively inexpensive. This was another setback for the prairie chicken, since introduced grass pastures do not provide habitat.

The invasion of woody species such as Chinese tallow and Macartney rose (introduced exotics), wax myrtle, Baccharis, running liveoak, huisache, and mesquite have also contributed to loss of over a million acres of coastal prairie habitat. The invasion of brush is the result of overgrazing combined with lack of fire. Historically, the coastal prairie burned periodically. These natural and man-made fires helped to maintain a healthy and diverse grassland.

Finally, urbanization and industrial expansion have taken their toll on prairie chicken habitat. Losses have been most evident along the upper Texas coast. The considerable urban sprawl of Houston, Galveston, and other coastal cities have led to irreplaceable habitat losses. The loss of diverse tallgrass prairie has not only affected the prairie chicken, but also plants such as Texas windmillgrass (*Chloris texensis*), Texas prairie dawn (*Hymenoxys texana*), and Houston machaeranthera (*Machaeranthera aurea*), which have become rare components of the ecosystem.

In 1995, fewer than 100 birds remain in fragmented pieces of habitat scattered across four Texas counties. We must find a way to reverse the factors contributing to the loss of tallgrass coastal prairie and the life it supports. The Attwater's prairie chicken now literally stands on the brink of extinction. Time is running out for this spectacular inhabitant of our coastal grasslands.

Recovery Efforts

Research is continuing regarding the interaction of limiting factors on prairie chicken populations. Efforts to provide information and incentives for private landowners to manage rangeland for the benefit of prairie chickens as well as livestock are an essential part of the recovery process. Recent successes with captive breeding are also encouraging. Cooperative habitat management projects involving private landowners, Texas Parks and Wildlife Department, and the U.S. Fish and Wildlife Service have made a start at reversing the devastating habitat losses.

Where To Learn More About the Attwater's Prairie Chicken

The best place to visit to learn more about prairie chickens is the Attwater's Prairie Chicken National Wildlife Refuge. The refuge is located off FM 3013 about 6 miles northeast of Eagle Lake, Texas.

How You Can Help

You can be involved with the conservation of Texas' nongame wildlife resources by supporting the Special Nongame and Endangered Species Conservation Fund. Special nongame stamps and decals are available at Texas Parks and Wildlife Department (TPWD) field offices, most state parks, and the License Branch of TPWD headquarters in Austin. The Gulf Coastal Prairies Foundation, a nonprofit organization, also accepts gifts. For more information, contact the Attwater Prairie Chicken National Wildlife Refuge at (409) 234-3021.

For More Information Contact

Texas Parks and Wildlife Department
Endangered Resources Branch
4200 Smith School Road
Austin, Texas 78744
(512) 912-7011 or (800) 792-1112
 or
U.S. Fish and Wildlife Service
Ecological Services Field Office
10711 Burnet Road, Suite 200
Austin, Texas 78758
(512) 490-0057

Management guidelines are available from Texas Parks and Wildlife Department for landowners and managers wishing to improve habitat for Attwater's Prairie Chicken.

References

Jurries, R. 1979. *Attwater's Prairie Chicken*. Texas Parks and Wildlife Department. Series F.S., no. 18, Project W-100-R. 36 pp.

Lehmann, V.M. 1941. *Attwater's prairie chicken, its life history and management*. U.S. Fish and Wildlife Service, North American Fauna No. 57. 65 pp.

U.S. Fish and Wildlife Service. 1993. *Attwater's Prairie Chicken Recovery Plan*. Endangered Species Office, Albuquerque, N.M.

Funds for the production of this leaflet were provided by the U.S. Fish and Wildlife Service, under Section 6 of the Endangered Species Act.

Management Guidelines for Attwater's Prairie Chicken

Habitat for the Attwater's Prairie Chicken consists of open tallgrass coastal prairie dominated by bunchgrasses such as little bluestem, indiangrass, switchgrass, and big bluestem, along with various flowering plants. Preferred habitat is characterized by high plant diversity and variations in grass height.

Control of Chinese tallow and baccharis with hydroax
© Matt Wagner

Prescribed burn
© TPWD

Management for Attwater's Prairie Chicken involves good grazing management and carefully planned prescribed burning and brush management. Range management practices aimed at achieving and maintaining Good and Excellent Range Condition (i.e. greater than 50% climax vegetation present) will benefit the prairie chicken, as well as other plants and animals that share its habitat, including livestock.

Grazing Management

The tallgrass prairie evolved under grazing by bison and other herbivores. Carefully managed livestock grazing is a beneficial tool for maintaining healthy and diverse tallgrass prairie habitat for prairie chickens. Cattle recycle nutrients, break up homogeneous grass stands, and provide trails. Prairie chickens are known to nest in proximity of these trails and other openings. Grazing also produces a patchy, open cover, and a diversity of forbs; which provide the bulk of the adult prairie chicken's diet.

Prairie chickens need rangeland in Good to Excellent Condition, with a high percentage of decreaser plants (plants which decrease with continued heavy grazing pressure) such as little bluestem and indiangrass in the plant composition. Proper stocking and periodic deferment are the keys to preventing overuse of the range and a decline in range condition. Animal numbers should be managed to maintain the proper degree of use (i.e. no more than 50% use of annual forage production). Grazing pressure should also be balanced with soil types and rainfall. Flexible stocking and timely responses to changing environmental conditions are necessary. Implementation of rotational grazing is necessary to prevent decline of highly desirable plants through selective grazing. These desirable tallgrasses and forbs provide nesting habitat and food for prairie chickens. In summary, good range management which achieves maintenance and restoration of tallgrass prairie (i.e. rangeland in Good to Excellent Condition) will benefit sustained livestock production and prairie chickens.

Prescribed Burning

The coastal tallgrass prairie evolved under the influence of natural and man-caused fires. Prescribed burning, therefore, is an excellent management tool for maintaining healthy grassland and improving prairie chicken habitat. Periodic burning keeps woody plant invasion under control. It also reduces rank growth of vegetation, which is unpalatable for cattle and too dense for prairie chickens. Burned areas are often used for booming grounds, especially if shortgrass areas are in short supply. Prescribed burning also improves plant diversity and, in the case of winter burns, provides succulent food for prairie chickens during the winter and early spring. Prescribed burning should be completed by late February.

Pastures generally need to be rested following a prescribed burn to allow vegetation to recover without selective grazing pressure. It may also be necessary to rest a pasture prior to the planned burn to accumulate enough grass fuel to accomplish the burn objectives. Care must be taken to avoid burning only portions of large pastures, as this will concentrate grazing pressure on newly burned areas, leading to overuse of these areas and uneven grazing distribution. It is best to burn an entire pasture at one time, on about a 3 to 5 year rotation, depending on rainfall and other factors. The key to a successful prescribed burning program is to have a detailed written plan and help from experienced people. Technical assistance with prescribed burning is available by contacting the Texas Parks and Wildlife Department, U.S. Natural Resources Conservation Service (formerly Soil Conservation Service), or Texas Agricultural Extension Service.

In summary, prescribed burning can be used to improve grazing distribution and forage quality for livestock; reduce brush encroachment and maintain productive grassland; improve range condition and plant diversity; and improve availability of food, nesting sites, and booming grounds for prairie chickens.

Brush Management

Mechanical or chemical brush management techniques are often needed to provide initial control in areas of dense, large brush. Prescribed burning is not an option in many of these areas because there is not enough grass to carry the fire or brush is too large to be effectively controlled by fire. Each brush problem is unique, and technical assistance from knowledgeable people is helpful. Factors such as type, density and size of target species, range site and soils, past history of brush management, and surrounding land use must be considered.

The right kinds, amounts, and application techniques for herbicide treatments are important in achieving good control of target species. Many herbicides are very selective, so choosing the correct formulation of one or more herbicides is very important for successful treatment of a particular brush problem. Precise application also saves money and reduces the risk of environmental contamination. In some cases, timing of application can make the difference between good and poor results. As with any chemical, label directions should be strictly followed, including those concerning disposal of rinse water and used containers.

Combining methods of brush management, such as herbicide or mechanical control and prescribed burning, is often very effective. For example, on rangeland infested with Macartney rose, herbicide application followed by periodic prescribed burning can provide good results in reducing brush and restoring grassland. Mechanical methods such as dozing, roller chopping, or shredding can be followed by prescribed burning or herbicide application, depending on the target species. Prescriptions need to be carefully designed to achieve the best results at the lowest cost. As with any range management practice, good grazing management (i.e. proper stocking and rotational grazing) is vital to achieving cost effective treatment and improvement in range condition. Technical assistance in brush management is available from the Texas Parks and Wildlife Department, U.S. Natural Resources Conservation Service, and Texas Agricultural Extension Service.

Additional Management Practices

The following management practices are suggested as ways to further enhance habitat quality. However, the benefits they may provide are definitely secondary to the primary goal of providing large areas of high quality prairie habitat for nesting and brood rearing.

Food plots or weedy areas of three to five acres scattered throughout pastures provide an easily available food source, although food plots probably do not add much to habitat quality if good prairie habitat is available. When planning food plots, it is best to locate them in areas that have already been farmed or otherwise disturbed, rather than plowing additional grassland. Crops planted should be those normally recommended for the local area, and could possibly include native forbs and legumes, rice, grain sorghum, annual legumes, and cool season small grains. Narrow strip plantings are desirable to maximize prairie chicken use and minimize waterfowl depredation.

Mixtures of native mid and tall bunchgrasses, along with perennial forbs such as Illinois bundleflower, Maximilian sunflower, and Englemann daisy, should be used if needed for range seeding following mechanical brush removal or to revegetate former cropland fields. The goal is to use plants, preferably native species, that are commercially available and locally adapted, to approximate the species composition and structure of the tallgrass prairie.

Finally, mowing can be used to provide feeding areas and brood habitat, and to control undesirable plant growth. Shredding during the nesting and brooding season (March through June 15) should be avoided to prevent destruction of nests and young chicks unable to fly.

Funds for the production of this leaflet were provided by the U.S. Fish and Wildlife Service, under Section 6 of the Endangered Species Act.

Whooping Crane

Scientific Name: *Grus americana*

Federal Status: Endangered, 6/2/70 • State Status: Endangered

Description

The stately Whooping Crane is the tallest bird found in North America, with males approaching nearly five feet in height. Adult birds are white overall with some red and black on the head. Their inner wing feathers droop over the rump in a "bustle" that distinguishes cranes from herons. With a seven foot wingspan and a slow wingbeat, Whooping Cranes fly with their long necks and legs fully extended. When in flight, the birds' black wingtips or primary feathers

Whooping Crane
© USFWS Steve Van Riper

can be seen, and their long legs extend beyond their tail. Their dark olive-gray beaks are long and pointed. The area at the base of the beak is pink and the eyes are yellow. The Whooping Crane's call, from which it derives its name, has been described as a shrill, bugle-like trumpeting. Whooping Crane chicks are a reddish cinnamon color. At four months of age, white feathers begin

to appear on the neck and back. Juvenile feathers are replaced through the winter months. By the following spring, juvenile plumage is primarily white, with rusty colored feathers remaining only on the head, upper neck, and on the tips of wing feathers. Young birds generally have adult plumage by late in their second summer.

There are a number of birds which may appear similar to the Whooping Crane. The Sandhill Crane, the Whooping Crane's closest relative, is gray in color, not white. Also, Sandhill Cranes are somewhat smaller, with a wingspan of about five feet. Sandhill Cranes occur in flocks of two to hundreds, whereas Whooping Cranes are most often seen in flocks of two to as many as 10-15, although they sometimes migrate with Sandhill Cranes. Snow Geese and White Pelicans are white birds with black wingtips, however both of these birds have short legs that do not extend beyond the tail when in flight. In addition, Snow Geese generally occur in large flocks, are much smaller, and fly with a rapid wingbeat. White Pelicans fly with their neck folded and can be distinguished by their long yellow bill. Finally, swans are all white and have short legs, and herons and egrets fly with their long necks folded.

Status and Distribution

The historical range of the Whooping Crane extended from the Arctic coast south to central Mexico, and from Utah east to New Jersey, South Carolina, Georgia, and Florida. Distribution of fossil remains suggest a wider distribution during the cooler, wetter climate of the Pleistocene.

It has been estimated that between 500 and 1400 Whooping Cranes inhabited North America in 1870. Although the exact number is unknown, Whooping Cranes were uncommon, and their numbers rapidly declined by the late 19th century.

In the mid 1800's, the principal breeding range extended from central Illinois northwestward through northern Iowa, western Minnesota, northeastern North Dakota, southern Manitoba and

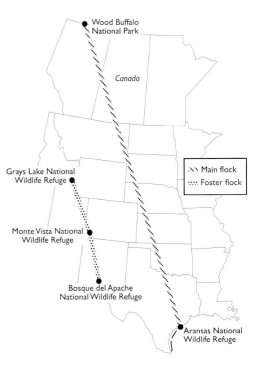

Saskatchewan, to the area near Edmonton, Alberta. The Whooping Crane disappeared from the heart of its breeding range in the north-central United States by the 1890's. The last documented nesting in southern Canada occurred in Saskatchewan in 1922. By 1937, only two small breeding populations remained; a nonmigratory population in southwestern Louisiana, and a migratory population which wintered on the Aransas National Wildlife Refuge (NWR) on the Texas coast and nested in a location which at that time was unknown. The remnant population in southwestern Louisiana was reduced from 13 to 6 birds following a hurricane in 1940, and the last individual was taken into captivity in 1950. In the winter of 1938-39, only 14 adult and 4 juvenile Whooping Cranes were found on the Aransas NWR. The nesting area of the Aransas Wildlife Refuge population was discovered in 1954 in Wood Buffalo National Park, Northwest Territories, Canada. This population is the only historical one that survives.

Whooping Cranes currently exist in three wild populations. The only self-sustaining wild population is the one that winters on the Texas coast and nests primarily within Wood Buffalo National Park. In 1995, this population consisted of 43 nesting pairs, with a total of 133 birds wintering in Texas.

Another wild flock includes eight individuals reared by wild sandhill cranes at Grays Lake National Wildlife Refuge in southeastern Idaho. In 1975, Whooping Crane eggs were transferred from Wood Buffalo to Grays Lake in an effort to establish a migratory population in the Rocky Mountains. The Rocky Mountain birds spend the summer in Idaho, western Wyoming, and southwestern Montana, and winter in the middle Rio Grande Valley of New Mexico.

The third wild population consists of 24 birds remaining from 51 captive-reared Whooping Cranes released in the Kissimmee Prairie of Florida from 1993-1995. These birds were released as the first step in an effort to establish a nonmigratory population in Florida.

Habitat
Within Wood Buffalo National Park, Whooping Cranes nest in poorly drained wetlands interspersed with numerous potholes (small areas of open water). These wetlands are separated by narrow ridges which support trees such as white and black spruce, tamarack, and willows, and shrubs such as dwarf birch, Labrador tea, and bearberry. Bulrush is the dominant plant in

areas used by nesting birds, although cattail, sedge, musk-grass and other aquatic plants are common. Nest sites are often located in the rushes or sedges of marshes and sloughs, or along lake margins. An abundance of invertebrates, such as mollusks, crustaceans, and aquatic insects have been found in the ponds near occupied nests.

Whooping Cranes use a variety of habitats during their long migrations between northern Canada and the Texas coast. Croplands are used for feeding, and large wetland areas are used for feeding and roosting. Whooping Cranes are known to roost in riverine habitat along the Platte, Middle Loup, and Niobrara Rivers in Nebraska, Cimarron River in Oklahoma, and the Red River in Texas. The birds often roost on submerged sandbars in wide unobstructed channels isolated from human disturbance. Whooping Cranes also use large wetland areas associated with lakes for roosting and feeding during migration.

The Whooping Crane's principal wintering habitat consists of about 22,500 acres of marshes and salt flats on Aransas National Wildlife Refuge and adjacent publicly and privately owned islands. Plants such as salt grass, saltwort, smooth cordgrass, glasswort, and sea ox-eye dominate the outer marshes. Further inland, Gulf cordgrass is more common. The interior portions of the refuge are characterized by oak mottes, grassland, swales, and ponds on gently rolling sandy soils. Live oak, redbay, and bluestems are typical plants found on upland sites. During the last 20 years, upland sites have been managed using grazing, mowing, and controlled burning. About 14,250 acres of grassland are managed for cranes, waterfowl, and other wildlife.

Life History
Whooping Cranes usually mate for life, although they will remate following the death of their mate. They mature at 3 to 4 years of age, and most females are capable of producing eggs by 4 years of age. It is estimated that Whooping Cranes can live up to 22 to 24 years in the wild. Captive individuals live 30 to 40 years.

Whooping Crane at Aransas National Wildlife Refuge
© TPWD Bill Reaves

Whooping Crane chick
© USFWS

Whooping Cranes begin leaving the Texas coast in late March and early April, returning to their nesting area in Wood Buffalo National Park by late April. Experienced pairs arrive first and normally nest in the same vicinity each year. Nesting territories vary considerably in size, ranging from 0.5 to 18 square miles. From the start of egg laying until the chicks are a few weeks old, the birds' activities are restricted to the breeding territory. Eggs are normally laid in late April to mid May, and hatching occurs one month later. Most nests contain 2 eggs. The eggs are light-brown or olive-buff in color with dark, purplish-brown blotches primarily at the blunt end. Whooping Cranes will renest if their first clutch is destroyed during the first half of the incubation period. They usually nest each year, but occasionally a

Aerial view of Aransas National Wildlife Refuge
© TPWD

*Whooping Crane
in flight*
© TPWD Bill Reaves

pair will skip a nesting season for no apparent reason. When nesting conditions are unsuitable, some pairs do not attempt to nest.

Whooping Crane parents share incubation and brood-rearing duties, and one member of the pair remains on the nest at all times. Females take the primary role in feeding and caring for the young. During the first 3 to 4 days after hatching, parents and young return to the nest each night. After that, the young are protected by their parents wherever they happen to be during inclement weather or at nightfall. During the first 20 days after hatching, families generally remain within 1 mile of the nest site.

Whooping cranes feed by probing the soil with their bills or taking food items from the soil surface or vegetation. Parents feed young chicks. Summer foods include large insect nymphs or larvae, frogs, rodents, small birds, minnows, and berries.

Fall migration begins in mid-September. Whooping Cranes normally migrate as a single, pair, family group, or in small flocks, sometimes accompanying Sandhill Cranes. Flocks of up to 10 subadults have been observed feeding at stopover areas. Whooping

Cranes migrate during the day, and make regular stops to feed and rest. Although they use a variety of habitats during migration, they prefer isolated areas away from human disturbance.

Whooping Cranes arrive on the Texas coast between late-October and mid-November. They spend almost 6 months on the wintering grounds at and near Aransas NWR. Pairs and family groups generally occupy and defend discrete territories, although close association with other Whooping Cranes is sometimes tolerated. Juveniles stay close to their parents throughout their first winter. Recent estimates of territory size average 292 acres. Studies indicate a declining territory size as the wintering population increases. Subadults and unpaired adults form small flocks and use areas outside occupied territories. Subadult birds often spend the winter near the territories where they spent their first year. Also, young adult pairs will often locate their first territory near the winter territory of one of their parents.

During the wintering period on the Texas coast, Whooping Cranes eat a variety of plant and animal foods. Blue crabs, clams, and the fruits of wolfberry are predominant in the winter diet. Clams are relatively more important in the diet when water depths are low and blue crabs are less abundant. Most clams and small blue crabs (2 inches or less in width) are swallowed whole. Larger crabs are pecked into pieces before being swallowed.

Whooping Cranes feed mostly in the brackish bays, marshes, and salt flats. Occasionally, they fly to upland sites for foods such as acorns, snails, crayfish, and insects, returning to the marshes in the evening to roost. Upland sites are more attractive when they are flooded by rainfall, burned to reduce plant cover, or when food is less available in the marshes and salt flats. Some Whooping Cranes use the upland parts of the refuge frequently in most years, but use of croplands adjacent to the refuge is rare.

As spring approaches, the courtship displays for which Whooping Cranes are famous begin. These displays include loud unison calling, wing flapping, head bow-

ing, and leaps into the air by one or both birds, increase in frequency. These rituals serve to forge and strengthen pair bonds, and indicate that the birds will soon leave for the breeding grounds. Family groups and pairs usually depart first, normally between March 25 and April 15. The last birds are usually gone by May 1, but occasional stragglers may stay into mid-May. During the 16-year period between 1938 and 1992, a total of 27 birds have remained at Aransas NWR throughout the summer. Many of these birds were ill or crippled or mates of birds which were crippled.

Parents separate from their young of the previous year at the beginning of spring migration, while in route to the breeding grounds, or soon after arrival on the breeding grounds. Most juveniles spend the summer near the area where they were born.

Threats and Reasons for Decline

Whooping Cranes gradually disappeared as agriculture claimed the northern Great Plains of the United States and Canada. Man's conversion of the native prairies and potholes to pasture and crop production made much of the original habitat unsuitable for Whooping Cranes. Rural electrification brought powerlines, resulting in an increase in death and serious injury due to collisions.

Human disturbance has also played a role in the decline of the Whooping Crane. The birds are wary on the breeding grounds. They will tolerate human intrusion for short intervals, but will not remain near constant human activity. The mere presence of humans during settlement of the midcontinental and coastal prairies may have interfered with the continued use of traditional breeding habitat by Whooping Cranes.

The Aransas population, the only population that is self-sustaining, remains vulnerable to accidental spills that could occur along the Gulf Intracoastal Waterway. The Intracoastal Waterway carries some of the heaviest barge traffic of any waterway in the world, and it runs right through the center of the Whooping Crane winter range. Much of the cargo is petrochemical products. Although spill response plans have been developed, an accident resulting in a spill could potentially destroy Whooping Cranes or their food resources.

Records of Whooping Cranes known to have died from gunshot or other causes from colonial times to 1948, show that about 66 percent of the losses occurred during migration. Shooting represented a substantial drain on the population, particularly from 1870 to 1920. Large and conspicuous, Whooping Cranes were shot for both meat and sport. Laws enacted to protect the birds have led to a decline in human caused mortality, but shootings still occur. The most recent known cases involved an adult female being mistaken for a snow goose near Aransas NWR in 1989, and an adult female shot by a vandal as she migrated northward through Texas in 1991.

Biological factors such as delayed sexual maturity and small clutch size prevent rapid population recovery. The major population of Whooping Cranes is now restricted to breeding grounds in northern Canada. This hampers productivity because the ice-free season is only 4 months, barely enough time to incubate their eggs for 29-31 days and rear their chicks to flight age in the remaining 3 months. Unless nest loss occurs early in the incubation period, there is rarely time to successfully rear a second clutch if the first clutch fails.

Drought during the breeding season presents a serious hazard because nest site availability and food supplies are reduced and newly hatched chicks are forced to travel long distances between wetlands. Drought also increases the exposure of eggs and chicks to predators such as ravens, bears, wolverines, foxes, and wolves.

Although little is known about the importance of disease and parasites as mortality factors, there have been documented cases of

Whooping Cranes dying of avian tuberculosis, avian cholera, and lead poisoning. Coccidia, a parasite which causes digestive tract disorder, has also been found in wild and captive birds.

Finally, Whooping Cranes are exposed to a variety of hazards and problems during their long migrations. Natural events such as snow, hail storms, low temperatures, and drought can make navigation hazardous or reduce food supplies. Collision with utility lines, predators, disease, and illegal shooting are other hazards that affect migrating cranes.

Recovery Efforts

The comeback story of the Whooping Crane has been heralded as one of the conservation victories of the 20th Century. The increase and stabilization of the Aransas/Wood Buffalo population has been a result of many factors, including legal protection, habitat protection, and biological research in both the United States and Canada.

In 1975, the U.S. Fish and Wildlife Service initiated a migration monitoring program to protect migrating Whooping Cranes from disease outbreaks and other potential hazards, and to compile information on the characteristics of stopover sites. This monitoring program is now coordinated with a network of people from the Canadian Wildlife Service, States, and Provinces along the migration corridor.

Flightless young Whooping Cranes were captured and marked with colored plastic legbands in Wood Buffalo National Park (NP) from 1977 through 1988. Of the 133 birds banded, 37 percent could still be identified in the spring of 1994. This marking program has provided a wealth of information on Whooping Crane biology. A radio tracking program, in which miniature radio transmitters were attached to the color legbands of young Whooping Cranes banded at Wood Buffalo NP, has also yielded valuable information concerning migration timing and routes, stopover locations, habitat use, social behavior, daily activity, and causes of death. Recently, tests of line marking devices have identi-

Oil spills are a potential threat
© TPWD

fied techniques effective in reducing collisions with utility lines.

The wintering territories of Whooping Cranes on the Texas coast place the birds in close proximity to human disturbance factors such as tour boats, boat and barge traffic along the Intracoastal Waterway, recreational and commercial fishing boats, and air traffic. A number of recent and ongoing studies have addressed the issue of how human disturbance factors might affect wintering birds. Additional research studies currently underway include evaluating human and wildlife competition for principal crane foods, and determining the nutritive composition of winter foods. Significant habitat research has also been conducted on the nesting grounds in Canada.

Prescribed burning is used on Aransas NWR to reduce height and density of grasses, topkill brush, and to modify plant composition on the uplands to make them more attractive to Whooping Cranes. Burned areas are immediately used by the birds. Currently, 10 prescribed burning units averaging 1,410 acres in size are burned on a 3 year rotation.

The most complete count of the Aransas/Wood Buffalo population is made during the winter. Aerial counts are made weekly throughout the winter period, although counts are made less frequently during mid-winter. These flights provide information on mortality, habitat use, pair formation, territory establishment, and age structure by identifying all color banded birds present. Additional protection of habitat outside Aransas NWR is provided by the National Audubon Society, which leases several offshore islands from the State of Texas. Monitoring of nesting pairs also takes place at Wood Buffalo NP.

Erosion control efforts along the Intracoastal Waterway at Aransas National Wildlife Refuge
© TPWD

Construction of the Gulf Intracoastal Waterway through the marshes of Aransas NWR in the early 1940's, and subsequent erosion by wind and boat wakes, has resulted in 11 percent loss of wintering habitat. Between 1989 and 1992, volunteers placed over 57,000 sacks of cement to protect 8,752 feet of shoreline. In 1992, the Corps of Engineers placed 2,013 feet of interlocking cement mats to stop erosion. They plan to armor an additional 14,000 feet of eroding shoreline in 1993 and 1994, and 2,000 feet each year thereafter until all areas are adequately protected.

Dredged material deposited from periodic maintenance of the Intracoastal Waterway has destroyed some marsh areas and unintentionally created others. In 1991, Mitchell Energy and Development Corporation built a dike around 10 acres of open shallow bay, filled the area with dredge spoil, and planted it to wetland vegetation. Whooping Cranes began using the area the following winter. In 1993, Mitchell Energy built 8 more acres of marsh adjacent to the first area. The Corps of Engineers is also currently evaluating beneficial uses of dredge spoil to create coastal marsh habitat for Whooping Cranes. In 1993, they created nearly 50 acres of marsh.

Several efforts have been initiated to establish new populations of Whooping Cranes as a means of safeguarding the species against a catastrophe in the Aransas/Wood Buffalo population. The effort in Idaho used sandhill cranes as foster parents to incubate Whooping Crane eggs, raise the chicks, and teach them migration paths to New Mexico. Foster-parenting has proved to be an unsuitable technique, however, as imprinting led to problems for the whoopers in establishing pair bonds. An effort in Florida is using techniques developed successfully with the endangered Mississippi Sandhill Crane to try to establish a non-migratory flock of Whooping Cranes. Meanwhile, new techniques for establishing a second migratory population continue to be explored. Several new techniques, such as finding appropriate migration routes through satellite telemetry of sandhill cranes, rearing young whoopers in captivity using humans costumed as Whooping Cranes, and teaching migration using ultralight aircraft hold significant promise.

These reintroduction efforts have been made possible by a successful captive breeding program for Whooping Cranes. Although whoopers at Wood Buffalo lay two eggs, usually only one hatches. Since 1967, biologists from the United States and Canada have collected eggs from wild nests in order to establish captive populations and support reintroduction efforts. Three captive breeding facilities exist, including Patuxent Wildlife Research Center in Maryland, the International Crane Foundation in Wisconsin, and Calgary Zoo in Alberta, Canada.

Finally, there is much evidence that people value Whooping Cranes. Numerous books, magazines articles, television programs, and nature documentary films have been produced about this magnificent bird. Each year 70,000 to 80,000 people visit Aransas NWR, most during the winter. These visitors spend a significant amount of money locally on lodging, gasoline, and supplies. In 1990, five tour boats offered trips to view Whooping Cranes along the Gulf Intracoastal Waterway. During 1990-91, approximately 17,000 people took these tours, paying an average of $20 per ticket, for a total seasonal amount of $340,000. The city of Rockport estimates that wildlife-related activities result in annual gross economic benefits of $6 million to the local economy. Some of these benefits result from the nearby presence of Whooping Cranes. The possibility of sighting Whooping Cranes, along with large numbers of migrating sandhill cranes, is an additional attraction to tourists in other areas of the United States. For example, approximately 80,000 people visit the Platte River area of Nebraska each year during the peak of spring crane migrations, spending approximately $15 million. The Chamber of Commerce of Grand Island, Nebraska has responded by sponsoring an annual festival, "Wings over the Platte," to further promote this interest in birds.

Where To See Whooping Cranes

Visit Aransas National Wildlife Refuge near Austwell, Texas during November through March to see Whooping Cranes as well as migratory waterfowl and other wildlife. As mentioned above, there are a number of commercially operated boat tours, departing from the Rockport/Fulton area, which offer visitors the chance for a close look at Whooping Cranes, waterfowl, shorebirds, herons, and hawks. Contact Aransas NWR at (512) 286-3559 or the Rockport Chamber of Commerce at (800) 242-0071 for more information. Also, the San Antonio Zoo exhibits captive Whooping Cranes as part of the recovery effort.

How You Can Help

Whooping Cranes migrate over north and east-central Texas on their way to and from Aransas NWR each fall and spring. The birds are particularly vulnerable to human disturbance and other hazards during this migration period. They sometimes stop in fields or wetlands near rivers or lakes to feed or rest. If you see migrating Whooping Cranes, view them from a distance and be careful not to disturb them. Report sightings to the Texas Parks and Wildlife Department or the U.S. Fish and Wildlife Service. Remember that harassing, shooting, or attempting to capture a Whooping Crane is a violation of Federal Law. If you find a dead or injured bird, report it immediately to one of the numbers listed below or to your local game warden. Since injured Whooping Cranes are delicate and require special care, you should quickly contact a representative of Texas Parks and Wildlife or U.S. Fish and Wildlife and carefully follow their instructions.

You can be involved in the conservation of Texas' nongame wildlife resources by supporting the Special Nongame and Endangered Species Conservation Fund. Special nongame stamps and decals are available at Texas Parks and Wildlife Department (TPWD) Field Offices, most State Parks, and the License Branch of TPWD headquarters in Austin. Part of the proceeds from the sale of these items are used to conserve habitat and provide information concerning rare and endangered species. Conservation organizations such as the Whooping Crane Conservation Association, National Audubon Society, International Crane Foundation, and The Nature Conservancy of Texas also welcome your participation and support.

For More Information Contact

Texas Parks and Wildlife Department
Endangered Resources Branch
4200 Smith School Road
Austin, Texas 78744
(512) 912-7011 or (800) 792-1112
        or
U.S. Fish and Wildlife Service
Ecological Services Field Office
10711 Burnet Road, Suite 200
Austin, Texas 78758
(512) 490-0057
        or
Aransas National Wildlife Refuge
P.O. Box 100
Austwell, Texas 77950
(512) 286-3559

References

Allen, R.P. 1952. *The Whooping Crane*. National Audubon Society Resource Report 3. 246 pp.

Bishop, M.A., and D.R. Blankinship. 1982. "Dynamics of Subadult Flocks of Whooping Cranes at Aransas National Wildlife Refuge, Texas, 1978-1981." Pages 180-189, in J.S. Lewis, eds. *Proceedings 1981 International Crane Workshop*. National Audubon Society, Tavernier, Florida.

Mabie, D.W., L.A. Johnson, B.C. Thompson, J.C. Barron, and R.B. Taylor. 1989. *Responses of Wintering Whooping Cranes to Airboat and Hunting Activities on the Texas Coast*. Wildlife Society Bulletin 17(3):249-253.

Mirande, C., R. Lacy, and U. Seal (Ed.). 1991. *Whooping Crane (*Grus americana*) - Conservation Viability Assessment Workshop Report*. Captive Breeding Specialist Group (CBSG/SSC/IUCN), Apple Valley, MN. 119 pp.

Slack, R.D., and H. Hunt. 1987. *Habitat Use By Whooping Cranes and Sandhill Cranes on the Aransas Wildlife Refuge*. U.S. Fish and Wildlife Service Contract No. 14-16-0002-82-220. 146 pp.

U.S. Fish and Wildlife Service. 1993. *Whooping Crane Recovery Plan*. Albuquerque, New Mexico. 76 pp.

Funds for the production of this leaflet were provided by the U.S. Fish and Wildlife Service, under Section 6 of the Endangered Species Act.

Eastern Brown Pelican

Scientific Name: *Pelecanus occidentalis occidentalis*

Federal Status: Endangered, 10/13/70 • State Status: Endangered

The Eastern Brown Pelican has recovered sufficiently in Florida, Alabama, and the United States Atlantic coast to be delisted. Although numbers are increasing in Louisiana and Texas, it is currently still listed as Endangered in Texas and Louisiana.

Description

With its 6 foot wingspread and 18-inch bill with pouch along the underside, no other bird could be easily mistaken for this unique seashore dweller. Possessing broad wings and a bulky body, a Brown Pelican weighs about 9 pounds. A graceful flier, the pelican's powerful wingbeat is one of the slowest among birds. Its feet are webbed to provide power while swimming in or under the water.

Brown Pelican
© TPWD Glen Mills

Nonbreeding adults have a white head and neck, often washed with yellow; a grayish-brown body; and a dark brown to black belly. In breeding birds, the back of the neck is a dark chestnut color with a yellow patch at the base of the foreneck. Some breeding birds develop red or plum colored pouches. Adults molting during incubation and chick-feeding have cream-colored heads and necks. Juveniles are grayish-brown above with whitish underparts. Young birds appear more brown in color as they age, acquiring adult plumage by their third year.

Distribution and Habitat

Historically, the Brown Pelican was found in large numbers along the Atlantic and Gulf coasts from South Carolina to Florida and west to Texas. Today, the birds occur throughout their historic range but their numbers have been greatly reduced.

The earliest population estimate of Brown Pelicans in Texas was that of Sennett in 1879, who estimated 5,000 adults nesting on two islands in Corpus Christi Bay. By 1918, the estimated number was 5,000 birds nesting on the entire Texas coast. The numbers continued to decline sharply from about 1,034 breeding birds on the central coast in 1939 to only 50 birds in 1964. During the period 1967-1974, the Texas population was estimated to be less than 100 birds, with fewer than 10 breeding pairs. Only 40 young were fledged on the entire Texas coast during this period.

Today, Brown Pelicans are found along the Texas coast from Chambers County on the upper coast to Cameron County on the lower coast. Most of the breeding birds nest on Pelican Island in Corpus Christi Bay and Sundown Island near Port O'Connor, both National Audubon Society Sanctuaries. Smaller groups or colonies occasionally nest on Bird Island in Matagorda Bay, a series of older spoil islands in West Matagorda Bay, Dressing Point Island in East Matagorda Bay, and islands in Aransas Bay. Pelican numbers have increased slowly from very low levels in the 1960's and 1970's to an estimated 2,400 breeding pairs in 1995.

Brown Pelicans nest on small, isolated coastal islands where they are safe from predators such as raccoons and coyotes. Nesting habitat ranges from mud banks and spoil islands to offshore islands covered with mangroves and other woody vegetation. Part of the Texas population spends the nonbreeding season along the Texas coast, while others migrate south to spend the winter along the eastern coast of Mexico.

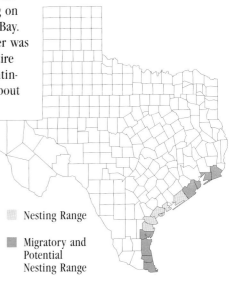

Nesting Range

Migratory and Potential Nesting Range

Life History

It is quite an experience to watch a Brown Pelican feeding. Soaring overhead, the bird spots a fish near the surface and keeps it in sight. Rotating into a dive, the pelican plunges 30 to 60 feet bill-first into the water. The impact of hitting the water with such force would stun an ordinary bird, but the Brown Pelican is equipped with air sacs just beneath the skin to cushion the blow. As it enters the water, the loose skin on the underside of the bill extends to form a scoop net with an amazing capacity of 2.5 gallons. If the dive is successful, the pelican quickly drains the water from its pouch and tosses its head back to swallow the fish.

Brown Pelicans can often be seen flying in formation with slow powerful wingbeats, searching the water for Menhaden and Mullet, which form the major portion of their diet. Several studies of food habits have shown that the diet of Brown Pelicans consists almost entirely of these fish. In one study, Menhaden was by far the most prevalent fish found regurgitated and left lying in pelican colonies. Since gamefish considered desirable by fisherman are not typically included in the pelican's diet, the birds do not compete with man for food.

Brown Pelicans breed in the spring, building their nests in mangrove trees or on the ground. Nests vary greatly in size and structure, consisting of piles of sticks, grass, reeds and other available vegetation. Pelicans usually lay two to four white eggs which are often stained brown by nest materials. The young hatch in about 30 days. Newly hatched pelicans appear helpless indeed, with their black, featherless, leathery skin. They are blind at first and completely dependent upon their parents for food and protection. Until the young birds develop a coat of down, about two weeks after hatching, it is often necessary for the adults to shade them from the direct rays of the sun, which can be fatal.

Young pelicans are fed by both parents. Using its pouch as a feeding trough, the adult regurgitates semidigested fish into it for the young to eat. As the young pelicans grow, they reach farther into the pouch, occasionally reaching down the parent's throat for food. The young are fed for about nine weeks. During this time, each nestling will devour about 150 pounds of fish. The parents spend most of every day catching fish to satisfy the ravenous appetites of their offspring.

Although mortality from predators, weather, and accidents is high for hatchlings, once on their own, Brown Pelicans have a fairly long life span. Adult survival approaches 80 percent per year, and some birds live 30 years or longer.

Threats and Reasons for Decline

Brown Pelican numbers in Texas began to decline sharply in the 1920' and 1930's, when adult birds were killed and nesting colonies destroyed by fisherman, in the mistaken belief that pelicans compete with man for food. It is estimated that pelican numbers declined by more than 80% in just 16 years, between 1918 and 1934.

Even more damaging, however, was the widespread use of DDT and similar insecticides beginning in the late 1940's. These insecticides were used on farmlands across the United States and in coastal areas to control mosquitoes. DDT does not usually kill adult birds, but it does interfere with calcium metabolism. The result is that the birds lay thin-shelled eggs that break during incubation or are too thin to protect the embryo. Pelicans are fish eaters, and fish are great accumulators of all toxic chemicals that get into coastal waters. The pelican's favorite food, Menhaden, a small filter-feeding fish, trap plankton for food. The plankton absorbed DDT residues from runoff. Thus, the concentration of DDT and Endrin in the environment had a devastating impact on the reproduction of Brown Pelicans, along with other top-of-the-food-chain birds such as Bald Eagles, Ospreys, and Peregrine Falcons. Recovery of these species has been steady since the early 1970's, when DDT and Endrin were banned in the United States.

In Texas today, the major threats to the continued recovery of the Brown Pelican appear to be human disturbance and loss of nesting habitat. Pelicans need safe places to nest, away from predators and man. Many former nesting sites have become accessible to both due to new construction and siltation. The hope is that as the pelican population expands, the birds will colonize the more remote islands still available as nesting sites.

Ongoing Recovery Efforts

The National Audubon Society, U.S. Fish and Wildlife Service, and Texas Parks and Wildlife Department have combined forces to count, band, and inspect the Brown Pelican nesting colonies. Brown Pelicans banded

Brown Pelican with young
© TPWD

Brown Pelican in non-breeding plumage
© TPWD Leory Williamson

on the central Texas coast have been reported from the Louisiana coast, Mobile Bay, Alabama, Naples, Florida, and the northeastern coast of Yucatan. Researchers are studying the migration patterns of Brown Pelicans, particularly movements between Texas and Mexico.

Biologists continue to monitor the nesting success of pelicans at existing colonies and surveying the bays for possible new nesting sites. One recently developed technique

Banding pelicans
© TPWD

involves placing pelican decoys near suitable islands in an effort to establish new nesting colonies.

Also, individuals from Texas Parks and Wildlife Department and the National Audubon Society regularly patrol the nesting islands to help minimize the effects of human disturbance. Many of the islands are owned or leased by the National Audubon Society as colonial waterbird nesting sanctuaries. These islands are regularly posted and patrolled.

Where To See Brown Pelicans

Matagorda Island and Mustang Island State Parks and Padre Island National Seashore offer visitors the opportunity to see and learn more about Brown Pelicans. Public piers and jetties, such as those in Port Aransas, are also good places to watch pelicans.

What You Can Do To Help

Brown Pelicans and other colonial nesting birds (herons, egrets, spoonbills, ibis, terns, gulls, and skimmers) nest on islands. Islands offer protection from predators, but the birds are still vulnerable to human disturbance. Since the hot sun can kill small chicks and embryos in unhatched eggs in a matter of minutes if the adults are flushed from the nests, you can help by staying off islands where birds are nesting. Islands maintained as bird sanctuaries are identified with posted

signs. Boaters wishing to observe the birds should bring binoculars and stay behind designated signs so as not to disturb the birds. And whatever you do, don't get off the boat. Pelicans (and other birds) will become agitated and leave their nests if approached. Remember that state and federal laws protect nongame and endangered species, and harassing the birds at any time is illegal. The Endangered Species Act provides protection for listed species against any action that significantly disrupts normal behavior patterns, including breeding, feeding, or sheltering.

Occasionally, a Brown Pelican will mistake a fishing lure or bait for a swimming fish and accidently gets hooked. If this happens to you, don't just cut the line and leave the bird with trailing line that can entangle and kill it. Gently reel the pelican in. Even though pelicans are big birds, they are not that strong, and this is easy to do. Grab the bill first and then fold the wings up to restrain the bird. Next, remove all fishing line and try to remove the hook. Cut the barb or push the hook through, just as you would for a person. If the hook is impossible to remove, leave it in and release the bird.

For years, pelicans reared in Texas have been banded. If you see a pelican with a colored plastic band or an aluminum U.S. Fish and Wildlife Service band on its leg, note which leg, the color of the band, the date, and the location. Send a post card to: Bird Banding Laboratory, U.S. Fish and Wildlife Service, Laurel, Maryland, 20811. This valuable information will help

biologists to better understand the life cycle and movements of Brown Pelicans in Texas.

You can be involved in the conservation of Texas' nongame wildlife resources by supporting the Special Nongame and Endangered Species Conservation Fund. Special nongame stamps and decals are available at Texas Parks and Wildlife Department (TPWD) Field Offices, most State Parks, and the License Branch of TPWD headquarters in Austin. Part of the proceeds from the sale of these items are used to conserve habitat and provide information concerning rare and endangered species. Conservation Passports, available from Texas Parks and Wildlife, are valid for one year and allow unlimited access to most State Parks, State Natural Areas, and Wildlife Management Areas. Conservation organizations in Texas also welcome your participation and support.

For More Information Contact

Texas Parks and Wildlife Department
Endangered Resources Branch
4200 Smith School Road
Austin, Texas 78744
(512) 912-7011 or (800) 792-1112
or
U.S. Fish and Wildlife Service
Ecological Services Field Office
10711 Burnet Road, Suite 200
Austin, Texas 78758
(512) 490-0057
or
National Audubon Society
P.O. Box 5052
Brownsville, Texas 78523
(210) 541-8034

References

King, K.A. and E.L. Flickinger. 1977. *The Decline of Brown Pelicans on the Louisiana and Texas Gulf Coast.* The Southwestern Naturalist 21(4):417-431.

Mabie, David. 1990. *Brown Pelican/Reddish Egret Colony Monitoring.* Texas Parks and Wildlife Department Section 6 Report. Project W-125-R-1, Job. No. 9.4. 4 pp.

Texas Parks and Wildlife Magazine:
Paul R.T. "Pelican Comeback." March 1977.
Middleton, R. "On the Way Back." November 1984.

U.S. Fish and Wildlife Service. 1979. *Eastern Brown Pelican Recovery Plan.* Endangered Species Office, Atlanta, Georgia.

Funds for the production of this leaflet were provided by the U.S. Fish and Wildlife Service, under Section 6 of the Endangered Species Act.

Eskimo Curlew

Scientific Name: *Numenius borealis*

Federal Status: Endangered, 3/11/67 • State Status: Endangered

Description

The Eskimo Curlew is a small shore-bird, about 12 inches in length, with a slightly decurved bill. It closely resembles its larger relative, the Whimbrel (*Numenius phaeopus*), which is about 17 inches in length. The Eskimo Curlew has a thin bill which is slightly decurved, whereas the Whimbrel has a bill which is thick at the base and strongly decurved. Other differences include a rich cinnamon color to the upperparts and underwing in Eskimo Curlew, as opposed to lighter grayish-brown upperparts and dark, heavily barred underwing in Whimbrels. Also, although both species have brown head stripes, the Eskimo Curlew's head is less strongly patterned, with an indistinct central crown stripe, whereas the Whimbrel has contrasting brown and buff stripes on the head. The call of the Eskimo Curlew has been described as soft, twittering whistles.

Eskimo Curlew
© TPWD

Distribution and Current Status

Thought to be very close to extinction, the Eskimo Curlew was once abundant. In the mid-1800's, huge flocks migrated north from South America to their nesting grounds in the Alaskan and Canadian Arctic, foraging on North American prairie grasslands as they made their way north. Historic reports tell of the skies being full of Eskimo Curlews as they migrated through the prairie states and provinces. A single flock alighting in Nebraska was said to have covered 40 to 50 acres of ground. In the fall, massive flocks of these birds gathered on the east coast of Canada to prepare for their trans-Atlantic flight to South American wintering grounds. Reminiscent of the immense flocks of Passenger Pigeons, Eskimo Curlews (commonly called prairie pigeons) may have been second in abundance only to the Lesser Golden-Plover among some 50 species of North American shorebirds.

During the last half of the 19th century, the Eskimo Curlew experienced a decline from great abundance to great scarcity. Unregulated hunting during the late 1800's, and loss of grassland habitat along the North American migration route and on South American wintering grounds, are thought to be the main reasons for the decline.

Only about 70 Eskimo Curlews have been seen anywhere in the last 50 years. They have not been reported with certainty in at least 30 of the last 86 years. Since 1916, sightings have most often been one or two birds at a time, and have always been of fewer than 25 birds at one time. The most recent sightings include one bird on the Platte River in Nebraska in mid-April 1987, at least two more along the Texas coast in late April and early May 1987, and a pair nesting in the Canadian Arctic in late May 1987. There may be no more than a few hundred Eskimo Curlews alive today.

Habitat

Like most birds with extensive migration routes, Eskimo Curlews use a variety of habitats. From breeding grounds on the grassy Arctic tundra, to fall concentration areas on the barren, low hills of Labrador, to wintering grounds on

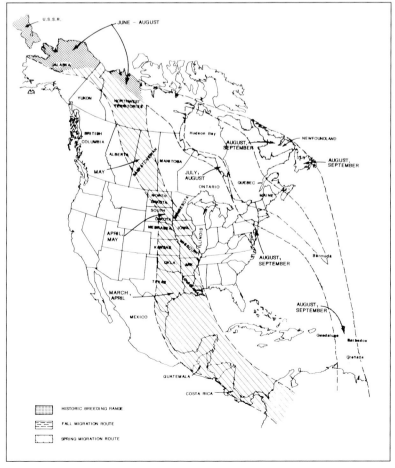

the Pampas grasslands of Argentina, Eskimo Curlews were found in open grasslands, fields, and wetlands. Recently burned prairies and marshes were particularly attractive to migrating curlews on midwestern grasslands.

Eskimo Curlews were once abundant on the Texas prairies during their spring migration from South America to breeding areas in the Arctic. Early observers describe the Eskimo Curlew as frequenting mainly the plains and prairies, both in the interior and coast region. Like many shorebirds, it was found near lakes, ponds, sloughs, and streams, but also ranged into dry prairies located away from water. Historical observations on Galveston Island suggest that Eskimo Curlews fed over wide areas of sand flats, shallow ponds, and grassy patches, as well as well-drained, gently rolling grazed pastures, with grass about 3 to 4 inches high.

Life History

Most of what we know today about the biology of the Eskimo Curlew comes from accounts written in the late 1800's. These birds formerly nested in the Arctic tundra of northwestern Canada between the MacKenzie and Coppermine Rivers. They probably also nested in the Alaskan tundra west to the Bering Sea. Early scientists described the Eskimo Curlew's nest as a shallow depression in the ground on open Arctic tundra. Nests were sparsely lined with decayed leaves and dried grasses. There were usually 4 eggs to a clutch. The eggs blended with the color of the grass, being dark green to brownish-green in color with brown blotches. Nests were found from late May through mid-June.

Fall migration began in July, and was in a southeasterly direction from the breeding grounds to feeding and staging areas on the coast of southern Labrador. After a brief stopover to fatten on crowberries and blueberries, the birds began their southward migration. They flew via Newfoundland and Nova Scotia, over the Atlantic Ocean, directly to eastern South America. The first curlew arrived on the wintering grounds of Uruguay and southern Argentina in September. Occasionally, Eskimo Curlews were forced by severe storms to land on the north Atlantic coast of the United States, Bermuda, and the eastern islands of the West Indies.

Spring migration began in late February, with the birds heading northwestward from the wintering area. Although not well documented, it is believed the migration took them across the Andes, Chile, the Pacific Ocean, Guatemala, and the Gulf of Mexico to the coasts of Texas and Louisiana. They arrived on the Texas Gulf coast in early March. From Texas and Louisiana, the the birds moved northward through the American tallgrass prairie, arriving at the Arctic breeding grounds before the end of May.

Regarding the Eskimo Curlew's Texas migration range, Oberholser noted that the species has been seen in Eliasville, Lampasas, Ft. Stockton, Boerne, and San Antonio. He also noted observations at Brownsville, North Padre Island, Corpus Christi, Galveston Island, Long Point, Rice, Gainesville, Clarksville, and Victoria, Calhoun, and Wise Counties.

The primary food of Eskimo Curlew in late summer on Arctic tundra, and at the migration staging area in Labrador, was crowberry and blueberry. Ants were also consumed on the tundra breeding grounds. A small species of snail, abundant on rocks in the intertidal areas of southern Labrador was also extensively eaten. During spring migration, grasshoppers and their eggs were an important food item. Egg pods and emerging young grasshoppers were obtained by probing grassland sod. On plowed land, the birds fed on white grubs and cutworms.

Threats and Reasons for Decline

There is overwhelming evidence that, between 1870 and 1890, unrestricted hunting and excessive killing by market hunters drastically and rapidly reduced populations of Eskimo Curlew. Considered a table delicacy, the Eskimo Curlew was killed by the thousands by market hunters, just as the Passenger Pigeon had been years earlier. The curlew's lack of fear and its habit of travelling in large flocks made it an easy target for market hunters. Eskimo Curlews were particularly vulnerable during northward spring migration through the midwestern prairies of the United States, and to a lesser degree during fall migration in southeastern Labrador. Occasionally, severe storms along the northeastern coast of the United States caused migrating curlews to land on the coast of Massachusetts, where they were rapidly killed. They were also hunted on the South American winter range.

In 1916, hunting in the United States was stopped by the Migratory Bird Treaty Act. Although other shorebirds with similar migration, breeding and wintering ranges recovered after hunting was prohibited, the Eskimo Curlew did not. Conversion of native grasslands to cropland in the main wintering area in South America, and along the migration route through the tall grass prairie of the United States, coincided with the population decline. This loss of grassland habitat has continued to the present and is thought to be the reason for failure of the species to recover. Although the Arctic tundra may still provide enough crowberries and blueberries for energy storage for fall migration, the South American and North American grasslands, now largely cultivated, may not provide enough suitable insect foods during winter and early spring to allow the curlews to travel their long traditional migration routes and then breed successfully.

Other factors that may have played a role in the population decline include unusually cold weather on the nesting grounds, severe storms over the Atlantic Ocean during fall migration, pesticide use on grasslands, and loss of habitat along the Gulf Coast due to urban and industrial development.

Recovery Efforts

Encouraged by recent sightings, biologists with the governments of the United States, Canada, and Argentina, along with several conservation organizations have begun efforts to save the Eskimo Curlew from extinction. In Texas, efforts are underway to characterize habitat for confirmed and possible sightings of Eskimo Curlews. The U.S. Fish and Wildlife Service and Texas Parks and Wildlife Department are cooperating in efforts to inform the public about the status of the Eskimo Curlew and enlisting their help in reporting sightings.

How You Can Help

Rare sightings of the Eskimo Curlew in Texas would most likely occur near the Texas coast in March and April. If you believe you have seen an Eskimo Curlew, please report your sighting to the U.S. Fish and Wildlife Service (USFWS) or Texas Parks and Wildlife Department (TPWD) in Austin at the telephone numbers listed below. You may also contact the USFWS in Arlington (817) 885-7830, Houston (713) 286-8282, or Corpus Christi (512) 888-3346; or the TPWD in Corpus Christi (512) 993-4492. Be sure to record notes concerning appearance, behavior, habitat being used, location, associated bird species, and local weather conditions. Take a photograph if possible, or record the bird's call. Observe the bird for as long as possible to be sure of your identification, but keep disturbance to a minimum.

You can be involved in the conservation of Texas' nongame wildlife resources by supporting the Special Nongame and Endangered Species Conservation Fund. Special nongame stamps and decals are available at Texas Parks and Wildlife Department (TPWD) Field Offices, most State Parks, and the License Branch of TPWD headquarters in Austin. Part of the proceeds from the sale of these items are used for endangered species habitat management and public information. Conservation organizations in Texas also welcome your participation and support. Finally, you can encourage and support efforts to conserve and properly manage coastal prairie grasslands in Texas.

For More Information Contact

Texas Parks and Wildlife Department
Endangered Resources Branch
4200 Smith School Road
Austin, Texas 78744
(512) 912-7011 or (800) 792-1112
    or
U.S. Fish and Wildlife Service
Ecological Services Field Office
10711 Burnet Road, Suite 200
Austin, Texas 78758
(512) 490-0057

References

Aldrich, J. 1978. *Eskimo Curlew*. Unpublished report of the U.S. Fish and Wildlife Service. 11 pp.

Atkinson, S.F., G.M. Church, and D.M. Shaw. 1991. *Characterization of Historical Eskimo Curlew Habitat in Texas*. Institute of Applied Sciences, Center for Remote Sensing and Landuse Analysis, University of North Texas, Denton, Texas. 39 pp.

Bent, A.C. 1962. *Life Histories of North American Shorebirds, Part 2*. Dover Publications, New York, N.Y.

Eubanks, T.L. and G.F. Collins. 1993. *The Status of the Eskimo Curlew Along the Upper Texas Coast*. Unpublished report of the U.S. Fish and Wildlife Service, Division of Technical Services, Order #2018110522.

Iversen, E.H. 1976. *On the Brink of Extinction*. Texas Parks and Wildlife 34(3):24-26.

Oberholser, H.C. 1974. *The Bird Life of Texas, Vol. 1*. University of Texas Press, Austin, Texas. 530 pp.

U.S. Fish and Wildlife Service. 1990. *Have You Seen an Eskimo Curlew?* Endangered Species Office, Grand Island, Nebraska.

Funds for the production of this leaflet were provided by the U.S. Fish and Wildlife Service, under Section 6 of the Endangered Species Act.

Piping Plover

Scientific Name: *Charadrius melodus*

Federal Status: Threatened in Northern Great Plains and Atlantic Coast, endangered in Great Lakes. The Piping Plover is being considered for endangered status in the Great Plains. • State Status: Threatened

Description

The Piping Plover is a small, stocky shorebird about 7 inches long with a wingspan of about 15 inches. Adults have a sand-colored upper body, white undersides, and orange legs throughout the year. A white rump, which is visible in flight, distinguishes this species from other small plovers. During the breeding season, adults acquire a dark narrow breast band, a dark strip across the forehead, and a black-tipped orange bill. The breast band is sometimes incomplete, especially in females. Juveniles are similar to nonbreeding adults in appearance.

Piping Plover
© Greg W. Lasley

Although post-breeding birds lose the dark bands and orange bills, they can be distinguished from Snowy Plovers (*Charadrius alexandrinus*) by their shorter bill and bright orange legs. Compared with the Semipalmated Plover (*Charadrius semipalmatus*), the Piping Plover's back is paler and more sand-colored.

Distribution and Habitat

The Piping Plover is a migratory North American shorebird. Historically, Piping Plovers were common in certain habitats along the Atlantic and Gulf coasts, along the river systems and lakes of the Northern Great Plains and Great Lakes region, and in the Bahamas and West Indies. Although populations have been drastically reduced, remnant populations occur through-

out the historic range. Currently, Piping Plovers breed on sandy beaches along the Atlantic Coast from Canada to North Carolina, along the sand and gravel shores of Lakes Michigan and Superior in Michigan, and on river sandbars and islands, barren shorelines of inland lakes, and alkali wetlands in the northern Great Plains of Canada and the United States. They winter primarily along Gulf Coast beaches from Florida to Mexico, and along the Atlantic Coast from North Carolina to Florida.

Sightings of color-banded Piping Plovers indicate that most of the birds from the Great Plains and Great Lakes breeding populations spend the winter along the Gulf Coast and adjacent barrier islands. Piping Plovers spend 60-70% of the year on the wintering grounds. Winter habitat includes beaches, sandflats, mudflats, algal mats, washover passes, and very small dunes where seaweed (*Sargassum*) or other debris has accumulated sand. Spoil islands along the Intracoastal Waterway are also used by wintering plovers. Texas is estimated to winter about 35 percent of the known population of Piping Plovers.

Wintering Piping Plovers in Texas seem to prefer sparsely-vegetated tidal mudflats, sandflats, or algal flats - areas which are periodically covered with water and then exposed either by tides or wind. The soft sand or mud covered by decaying material is rich with polychaetes. These invertebrates are a primary food of Piping Plovers. The extensive wind-tidal flats in the Laguna Madre of the lower coast are often covered with blue-green algae, which supports large numbers of insects and other invertebrates eaten by plovers. Tidal flats formed at the base of jetties and tidal passes are also important feeding areas, especially north of the Coastal Bend. Piping Plovers

also feed on beaches, especially when high tides cover the flats.

Piping Plovers often roost on beaches huddled down in the sand, or behind driftwood or clumps of seaweed and other debris. They also roost among debris in washover passes created by hurricanes and storms on barrier islands and peninsulas. Generally, roosting areas are close to feeding areas.

Life History

Piping Plovers spend about 3 to 4 months on their breeding grounds in the northern United States and southern Canada. They

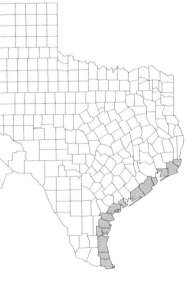

begin arriving from the wintering areas in mid-April. Courtship behavior includes aerial flights, digging of several nest scrapes, and ritualized stone tossing. Piping Plovers are monogamous, but mate-switching may occur both during the breeding season and between years.

Plover nests are shallow depressions in the sand, frequently lined with small pebbles or shell fragments. The nest cups are about an inch deep and 2.5 inches in diameter. Females lay four eggs, which are gray to pale sand-colored with a few dark spots. The eggs blend almost perfectly with the sand, making them very difficult to see. Both parents incubate the eggs for about 27 days. Most adults raise only one brood per year, and occasionally they will renest if their nest is destroyed.

Eggs begin to hatch from late May to mid-June. The chicks can feed themselves within hours after hatching. Both parents attend the young. Broods generally remain on the nesting territory, expanding their movements as they mature or are disturbed. The young are able to fly about 30 to 35 days after hatching. Females commonly leave broods when the young are 14 to 20 days of age, but males often remain with them until after they have reached flight age.

The Piping Plover's activity (home range) during the breeding season is limited to the section of lakeshore or beach on which the nest is located. Both adults defend an area (territory) surrounding the nest against intruders. This territory sometimes includes their foraging area. Plovers in some areas defend both nesting and feeding territories. Piping Plovers commonly nest in association with Least Terns, Arctic Terns, Common Terns, Killdeer and American Avocets. Adults begin migrating south from the breeding grounds by July or early August. Juveniles leave a few weeks later, and most are gone by late August.

Piping Plovers generally begin arriving on the Texas coast in mid-July. The number of plovers increases on the upper Texas coast through October, when the first cold front pushes them further down the coast. Plovers begin moving back up the Texas coast in March in preparation for their return to the breeding grounds. Most birds are gone from Texas by mid-April, although some may remain until mid-May.

On the wintering grounds, the diet of the Piping Plover consists of marine worms, flies, beetles, spiders, crustaceans, mollusks, and other small marine animals and

their eggs and larvae. Plovers are visual predators. They often run short distances, pausing to stare at the sand with a slightly tilted head, before picking a food item from the substrate. Plovers feed most aggressively during the falling tide, when the availability of exposed muddy flats is greatest.

When not feeding, plovers rest and preen. Although little is known about nocturnal behavior, Piping Plovers are thought to roost on beaches sheltered by driftwood or other debris, or on sand or algal flats. Plovers often roost together in small flocks.

During the wintering period on the Texas coast, Piping Plovers are often seen with other shorebirds. These associated species include the Snowy, Semipalmated, Wilson's, and Black-bellied Plovers; American Oystercatcher, American Avocet, Willet, Marbled Godwit, Ruddy Turnstone, Sanderling, Dowitchers, Dunlin, and Sandpipers.

Threats and Reasons for Decline

Habitat alteration and destruction are the primary causes for the decline of the Piping Plover. Loss of sandy beaches and lakeshores due to recreational, residential, and commercial development has reduced available habitat on the Great Lakes, Atlantic Coast, and the Gulf of Mexico. Reservoir construction, channelization of rivers, and modification of river flows have eliminated sandbar nesting habitat along hundreds of miles of the Missouri and Platte Rivers. Winter habitats along the Gulf coast are threatened by industrial and urban expansion and maintenance activities for commercial waterways. Pollution from spills of petrochemical products and other hazardous materials is also a concern.

On the breeding grounds, reproductive success can be curtailed by human disturbance. Vehicular and foot traffic destroys eggs and chicks. The presence of people on beaches and sandbar islands inhibits incubation and other breeding behavior. Changes in land use such as agricultural development, urbanization, and use of beaches has brought an increase in the number of unleashed pets

Wintering habitat along the Texas coast
© TPWD Leroy Williamson

Feeding
© TPWD Glen Mills

Resting
© Greg W. Lasley

and other predators such as gulls, skunks, and foxes.

Increased recreational use of Gulf beaches may also threaten the quality of wintering sites. Beach traffic, including vehicles and ATV's, disturb birds and degrade habitat. Beach raking, a practice associated with high recreational use, removes driftwood, seaweed, and other debris used by roosting plovers.

In 1991, the total population of Piping Plovers in North America was estimated to be 5,482 breeding adults. The Texas Gulf Coast had the highest wintering population, with about 1,900 individuals. It is up to Texans to insure that the wintering habitat so vital to the survival of this species is protected.

Recovery Efforts

State, federal, and private organizations are collaborating to monitor

Residential development along the Gulf coast
© Leroy Williamson

Recreational use of beach habitat
© Phil Glass

Piping Plover populations and assess current and potential habitat on breeding and wintering grounds. Research concerning reproductive success, food habits, habitat selection, and limiting factors is underway. The results of these studies will help biologists develop management plans designed to benefit Piping Plovers. Protective measures, such as signs or fences, are being implemented to reduce human disturbance to breeding birds. Vegetation management, predator control, pollution abatement, and habitat creation/restoration are management strategies being used to benefit Piping Plover populations. Biologists continue to assess habitat availability and quality throughout the plover's range in Texas, and identify essential habitat for management and protection. Finally, public information campaigns concerning Piping Plover conservation are a vital part of the recovery process.

Where To See Piping Plovers

Piping Plovers can be seen along the Texas coast from about mid-July through April. Padre Island National Seashore, along with Galveston Island, Bryan Beach, Matagorda Island, Mustang Island, and Goose Island State Parks, are good places to visit and observe

Piping Plovers and other shorebirds. Look for them on large mud, sand, or algal flats, or on Gulf beaches. Since these birds are sensitive to human disturbance, they should be observed from a safe distance with binoculars.

How You Can Help

Whether you enjoy fishing, boating, swimming, or viewing wildlife, please remember that your actions, especially when multiplied by thousands of other recreational users, can have an immense impact on the bays and estuaries of the Texas Coast. Responsible recreational use should include proper disposal of trash and other potential pollutants, respect for private property rights, preventing harm to plants and wildlife, and generally keeping human impacts to a minimum. Minimize driving on the beach and keep pets on a leash.

You can be involved in the conservation of Texas' nongame wildlife resources by supporting the Special Nongame and Endangered Species Conservation Fund. Special nongame stamps are available at

Texas Parks and Wildlife Department (TPWD) field offices, most state parks, and the License Branch of TPWD headquarters in Austin. Each dollar contributed to this fund can potentially provide TPWD with $4 to conduct research and manage habitat for nongame and endangered wildlife. Conservation Passports, available from Texas Parks and Wildlife, are valid for one year and allow unlimited access to most State Parks, State Natural Areas, and Wildlife Management Areas. Conservation organizations in Texas also welcome your participation and support.

For More Information Contact

Texas Parks and Wildlife Department
Endangered Resources Branch
4200 Smith School Road
Austin, Texas 78744
(512) 912-7011 or (800) 792-1112
or
U.S. Fish and Wildlife Service
Corpus Christi Field Office
CCSU, Campus Box 338
Corpus Christi, Texas 78412
(512) 994-9005

References

Eubanks, T. (in press). *The Status and Distribution of the Piping Plover in Texas*. Bulletin of the Texas Ornithological Society.

Haig, S.M. 1992. "The Piping Plover." In: *Birds of North America No. 2* (A. Poole, P. Stettenheim, F. Gill, eds.). American Ornithologists Union, Philadelphia, PA. pp. 1-18.

Haig, S.M. and J.H. Plissner. 1993. *Distribution and Abundance of Piping Plovers: Results and Implications of the 1991 International Census*. Condor 95:145-156.

Johnson, C.M. and G.A. Baldassarre. 1988. *Aspects of the Wintering Ecology of Piping Plovers in Coastal Alabama*. Wilson Bulletin 100(2):214-223.

Nicholls, J.L. and G.A. Baldassarre. 1990. *Winter Distribution of Piping Plovers Along the Atlantic and Gulf Coasts of the United States*. Wilson Bulletin 102(3):400-412.

U.S. Fish and Wildlife Service. 1994. *Great Lakes and Northern Great Plains Piping Plover Recovery Plan*. U.S. Fish and Wildlife Service, Twin Cities, MN. 116 pp.

Wilcox, L. 1959. *A Twenty Year Banding Study of the Piping Plover*. Auk 76(2):129-153.

Funds for the production of this leaflet were provided by the U.S. Fish and Wildlife Service, under Section 6 of the Endangered Species Act.

Interior Least Tern

Scientific Name: *Sterna antillarum athalassos*

Federal Status: Endangered, 6/27/85 • State Status: Endangered

Description

Least Terns are the smallest North American terns. Adults average 8 to 10 inches in length, with a 20 inch wingspan. Their narrow, pointed wings make them streamlined flyers. Males and females are similar in appearance. Breeding adults are gray above and white below, with a black cap, black nape and eye stripe, white forehead, yellow bill with a black or brown tip, and yellow to orange legs. Hatchlings are about the size of ping-pong balls and are yellow and buff with brown mottling. Fledglings (young birds that have left the nest) are grayish brown and buff colored, with white heads, dark bills and eye stripes, and stubby tails. Young terns acquire adult plumage after their first molt at about 1 year, but do not breed until they are 2 to 3 years old. The Least Tern's call has been described as a high pitched "kit," "zeep," or "zreep."

Distribution and Habitat

There are three subspecies of the Least Tern recognized in the United States. The subspecies are identical in appearance and are segregated on the basis of separate breeding ranges. The Eastern or Coastal Least Tern (*Sterna antillarum antillarum*), which is not federally listed as endangered or threatened, breeds along the Atlantic coast from Maine to Florida and west along the Gulf coast to south Texas. The California Least Tern (*Sterna antillarum browni*), federally listed as endangered since 1970, breeds along the Pacific coast from central California to southern Baja California. The endangered Interior Least Tern (*Sterna antillarum athalassos*) breeds inland along the Missouri, Mississippi, Colorado, Arkansas, Red, and Rio Grande River systems. Although these subspecies are generally recognized, recent evidence indicates that terns hatched on the Texas coast sometimes breed inland. Some biologists speculate that the interchange between coastal and river populations is greater than once thought.

The Interior Least Tern is migratory, breeding along inland river systems in the United States and wintering along the Central American coast and the northern coast of South America from Venezuela to northeastern Brazil. Historically, the birds bred on sandbars on the Canadian, Red, and Rio Grande River systems in Texas, and on the Arkansas, Missouri, Mississippi, Ohio and Platte River systems in other states. The breeding range extended from Texas to Montana and from eastern Colorado and New Mexico to southern Indiana. It included the braided rivers of

Breeding Range

Wintering Range

Oklahoma and southern Kansas, salt flats of northwest Oklahoma, and alkali flats near the Pecos River in southeast New Mexico.

Today, the Interior Least Tern continues to breed in most of the major river systems, but its distribution is generally restricted to the less altered and more natural or little disturbed river segments. In Texas, Interior Least Terns are found at three reservoirs along the Rio Grande River, on the Canadian River in the northern Panhandle, on the Prairie Dog Town Fork of the Red River in the eastern Panhandle, and along the Red River (Texas/Oklahoma boundary) into Arkansas.

Nesting habitat of the Interior Least Tern includes bare or sparsely

Interior Least Tern on nest
© Leroy Williamson

Least Tern and chick
© TPWD Glen Mills

vegetated sand, shell, and gravel beaches, sandbars, islands, and salt flats associated with rivers and reservoirs. The birds prefer open habitat, and tend to avoid thick vegetation and narrow beaches. Sand and gravel bars within a wide unobstructed river channel, or open flats along shorelines of lakes and reservoirs, provide favorable nesting habitat. Nesting locations are often at the higher elevations away from the water's edge, since nesting usually starts when river levels are high and relatively small amounts of sand are exposed. The size of nesting areas depends on water levels and the extent of associated sandbars and beaches. Highly adapted to nesting in disturbed sites, terns may move colony sites annually, depending on landscape disturbance and vegetation growth at established colonies.

For feeding, Interior Least Terns need shallow water with an abundance of small fish. Shallow water areas of lakes, ponds, and rivers located close to nesting areas are preferred.

As natural nesting sites have become scarce, the birds have used sand and gravel pits, ash disposal areas of power plants, reservoir shorelines, and other manmade sites.

Life History

Interior Least Terns arrive at breeding areas from early April to early June, and spend 3 to 5 months on the breeding grounds. Upon arrival, adult terns usually spend 2 to 3 weeks in noisy courtship. This includes finding a mate, selecting a nest site, and strengthening the pair bond. Courtship often includes the "fish flight," an aerial display involving aerobatics and pursuit, ending in a fish transfer on the ground between two displaying birds. Courtship behaviors also include nest preparation and a variety of postures and vocalizations.

Least Terns nest in colonies, where nests can be as close as 10 feet but are often 30 feet or more apart. The nest is a shallow depression in an open, sandy area,

gravelly patch, or exposed flat. Small twigs, pieces of wood, small stones or other debris usually lie near the nest.

Egg-laying begins in late May, with the female laying 2 to 3 eggs over a period of 3 to 5 days. The eggs are pale to olive buff and speckled or streaked with dark purplish-brown, chocolate, or blue-gray markings. Both parents incubate the eggs, with incubation lasting about 20 to 22 days. The chicks hatch within one day of each other and remain in the nest for about a week. As they mature, they begin to wander from the nest, seeking shade and shelter in clumped vegetation and debris. Chicks are capable of flight within 3 weeks, but the parents continue to feed them until migration. Least Terns will renest until late July if clutches or broods are lost.

The Interior Least Tern's activities during the breeding season are limited to the portion of river near the nesting site. Nesting adults defend an area surrounding the nest (territory) against intruders, and terns within a colony will defend any nest within that colony. When defending a territory, the incubating bird will fly up giving an alarm call, and then dive repeatedly at the intruder.

The breeding season is usually complete by late August. Prior to migration, the terns gather at staging areas with high fish concentrations. They gather to rest and eat prior to the long flight to southern wintering grounds. Low, wet sand or gravel bars at the mouths of tributary streams and floodplain wetlands are important staging areas. Interior Least Terns often return to the same breeding site, or one nearby, year after year.

Nesting success of terns at a particular location varies greatly from year to year. Because water levels fluctuate and nesting habitats such as sandbars and shorelines change over time, the terns are susceptible to habitat loss and frequent nest and chick loss.

The Interior Least Tern is primarily a fish-eater, feeding in shallow waters of rivers, streams, and lakes. The birds are opportunistic and tend to select any small fish within a certain size range. Feed-

Least Tern chicks
© TPWD Glen Mills

Nesting area and foraging site on the Canadian River
© Bruce C. Thompson

ing behavior involves hovering and diving for small fish and aquatic crustaceans, and occasionally skimming the water surface for insects.

In portions of the tern's range, shorebirds such as the Piping Plover and Snowy Plover often nest in close proximity. The Piping Plover is listed as Threatened by the U.S. Fish and Wildlife Service, and the interior nesting populations of Snowy Plovers are U.S. Fish and Wildlife Service candidates for listing.

Threats and Reasons for Decline

Channelization, irrigation, and the construction of reservoirs and pools have contributed to the elimination of much of the tern's natural nesting habitat in the major river systems of the midwest. Discharges from dams built along these river systems pose additional problems for the birds nesting in the remaining habitat. Before rivers were altered, summer flow patterns were more predictable. The nesting habits of the Least Tern evolved to coincide with natural declines in river flows. Today, flow regimes in many rivers differ greatly from his-

Dam on the Brazos River
© TPWD

toric regimes. High flow periods may now extend into the normal nesting period, thereby reducing the availability of quality nest sites and forcing terns to nest in poorer quality locations. Extreme fluctuations can inundate potential nesting areas, flood existing nests, and dry out feeding areas.

Historical flood regimes scoured areas of vegetation, providing additional nesting habitat. However, diversion of river flows into reservoirs has resulted in encroachment of vegetation and reduced channel width along many rivers, thereby reducing sandbar habitat. Reservoirs also trap much of the sediment load, limiting formation of suitable sandbar habitat.

In Texas and elsewhere, rivers are often the focus of recreational activities. For inland residents, sandbars are the recreational counterpart of coastal beaches. Activities such as fishing, camping, and ATV use on and near sandbar habitat are potential threats to nesting terns. Even sand and gravel pits, reservoirs, and other artificial nesting sites receive a high level of human use. Studies have shown that human presence reduces reproductive success, and human disturbance remains a threat throughout the bird's range.

Water pollution from pesticides and irrigation runoff is another potential threat. Pollutants entering rivers upstream and within breeding areas can adversely affect water quality and fish populations in tern feeding areas. Least Terns are known to accumulate contaminants that can affect reproduction and chick survival. Mercury, selenium, DDT derivatives, and PCB's have been found in Least Terns throughout their range at levels warranting concern, although reproductive difficulties have not been observed.

Finally, too little water in some river channels may be a common problem that reduces the birds' food supply and increases access to nesting areas by humans and predatory mammals. Potential predators include coyotes, gray foxes, raccoons, domestic dogs and cats, common crows, great egrets, and great blue herons.

Recovery Efforts

State, federal, and private organizations throughout the United States are collaborating to census the birds, conduct research, curtail human disturbance, and provide habitat. Continued monitoring of confirmed and potential colony sites is underway to assess population status and reproductive success. Protective measures, including signs and fences, are being implemented to restrict access to sites most threatened by human disturbance. Vegetation control at occupied sites, chick shelter enhancement, predator control, pollution abatement, and habitat creation/restoration at unoccupied sites are management strategies used to benefit Interior Least Tern populations.

Biologists continue to assess habitat availability and quality throughout the bird's range in Texas, and identify essential habitat for management and protection. Recently, in a cooperative effort between the Texas Parks and Wildlife Department, National Park Service, International Boundary and Water Commission, Comision Internacional de Limites y Aguas, Oficina de Ecologia Estado de Coahuila, and City of Del Rio, warning signs in both Spanish and English were erected to inform visitors about the effects of human disturbance on the terns. Also, the National Park Service recently initiated annual status surveys for Interior Least Terns at Amistad NRA. Finally, public information campaigns concerning Least Tern conservation are a vital part of the recovery process.

Where To See Interior Least Terns

Falcon State Park near Falcon Heights in Zapata County (512) 848-5327, Amistad National Recreation Area near Del Rio in Val Verde County (210) 775-7491, and Gene Howe Wildlife Management Area near Canadian in Hemphill County (806) 323-8642 offer visitors the opportunity to see and learn more about the Interior Least Tern. Often, the best opportunity to see the birds is by boat. Please remember that human disturbance during the nesting season reduces reproductive success and threatens survival. The terns should be viewed from a distance with binoculars or spotting scope.

How You Can Help

Interior Least Terns and other colonial nesting shore and water birds (plovers, herons, egrets, spoonbills, ibis, gulls, and skimmers) often nest on sandbars and islands. These areas offer protection from predators, but the birds are still vulnerable to human disturbance. Since the hot sun can quickly kill small chicks and embryos in unhatched eggs if the adults are flushed from the nest, you can help by staying off sandbars and islands and away from flats and shorelines where birds are nesting. Also, when

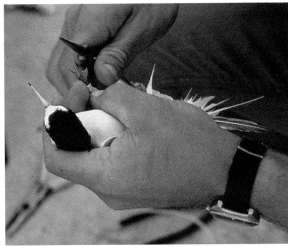

Banding Least Terns
© Bruce C. Thompson

adults are flushed from the nest, the eggs or young are more vulnerable to predation. Nesting areas maintained as bird sanctuaries are identified by official signs. If you want to observe the birds, bring binoculars and stay a safe distance away so you don't disturb the birds. Pets and livestock should also be kept off these areas while the terns are nesting. Remember that state and federal laws protect migratory and endangered birds, and harassing them at any time is illegal.

You can be involved in the conservation of Texas' nongame wildlife resources by supporting the Special Nongame and Endangered Species Conservation Fund. Special nongame stamps and decals are available at Texas Parks and Wildlife Department (TPWD) Field Offices, most State Parks, and the License Branch of TPWD headquarters in Austin. Conservation Passports, available from Texas Parks

and Wildlife, are valid for one year and allow unlimited access to most State Parks, State Natural Areas, and Wildlife Management Areas. Part of the proceeds from the sale of these items are used to protect habitat and to provide public information concerning endangered species conservation. Conservation organizations in Texas welcome your participation and support.

For More Information Contact

Texas Parks and Wildlife Department
Endangered Resources Branch
4200 Smith School Road
Austin, Texas 78744
(512) 912-7011 or (800) 792-1112
        or
U.S. Fish and Wildlife Service
Ecological Services Field Office
10711 Burnet Road, Suite 200
Austin, Texas 78758
(512) 490-0057

Bilingual "Do not Disturb" sign
© TPWD Sylvestre Sorola

References

Hill, L.A. 1992. *Status of the Least Tern and Snowy Plover on the Red River, 1991.* Interagency Agreement No. 14-16-0002-91-923 (FWS) and G040A10001 (BLM). U.S. Bureau of Land Management, Oklahoma Resource Area, Moore, OK. 29 pp.

Locknane, D.M. 1988. *Interior Least Tern Distribution and Taxonomy.* Texas Parks and Wildlife Dept., Federal Aid Project No. W-103-R-17, Job No. 54. 37 pp.

Thompson, B.C. 1985. *Interior Least Tern Distribution and Taxonomy.* Texas Parks and Wildlife Dept., Federal Aid Project No. W-103-R-14, Job No. 54. 11 pp.

U.S. Fish and Wildlife Service. 1990. *Recovery Plan for the Interior Population of the Least Tern* (Sterna antillarum). U.S. Fish and Wildlife Service, Twin Cities, Minnesota. 90 pp.

Whitman, P.L. 1988. *Biology and Conservation of the Endangered Interior Least Tern: A Literature Review.* U.S. Fish and Wildlife Service, Biological Report 88(3). 22 pp.

Funds for the production of this leaflet were provided by the U.S. Fish and Wildlife Service, under Section 6 of the Endangered Species Act.

Bald Eagle

Scientific Name: *Haliaeetus leucocephalus*

Federal Status: Threatened • State Status: Threatened

Description

The Bald Eagle is one of nature's most impressive birds of prey. Males generally measure 3 feet from head to tail, weigh 7 to 10 pounds, and have a wingspan of 6 to 7 feet. Females are larger, some reaching 14 pounds with a wingspan of up to 8 feet. Adults have a white head, neck, and tail and a large yellow bill.

Bald Eagle
© TPWD Martin Fulfer

First year birds are mostly dark and can be confused with immature Golden Eagles. Immature Bald Eagles have blotchy white on the underwing and tail, compared with the more sharply defined white pattern of Golden Eagles. While gliding or soaring, Bald Eagles keep their wings flat, and their wingbeats are slow and smooth. In contrast, Turkey Vultures soar with uplifted wings, and they fly with quick, choppy wingbeats. Bald Eagles require 4 or 5 years to reach full adult plumage, with distinctive white head and tail feathers.

Distribution and Habitat

The Bald Eagle, our National Symbol, occurs throughout the United States, Canada, and northern Mexico. Bald Eagles are present year-round throughout Texas as spring and fall migrants, breeders, or winter residents. The Bald Eagle population in Texas is divided into two populations; breeding birds and nonbreeding or wintering birds. Breeding populations occur primarily in the eastern half of the state and along coastal counties from Rockport to Houston. Nonbreeding or wintering populations are located primarily in the Panhandle, Central, and East Texas, and in other areas of suitable habitat throughout the state.

Nesting populations are gradually increasing in most areas of the country, including Texas. Between 1985 and 1990, a 47% increase in active nests and a 55% increase in numbers of fledglings were reported. Breeding territories are located mostly along rivers and near reservoirs in East Texas, the Post Oak region, and along the Gulf Coast. The colonization of inland reservoirs by nesting Bald Eagles is a rather recent event, since this habitat type was not used by eagles historically. As of 1994, Bald Eagle nests were known to occur in Angelina, Bastrop, Bowie, Brazoria, Calhoun, Chambers, Colorado, Cooke, Fannin, Fayette, Fort Bend, Goliad, Grimes, Harris, Houston, Jackson, Liberty, Limestone, Matagorda, Montgomery, Newton, Polk, Refugio, Robertson, Sabine, San Augustine, San Saba, Shelby, Trinity, Victoria, and Wharton Counties.

Preferred nesting habitat in Texas is undisturbed coastal

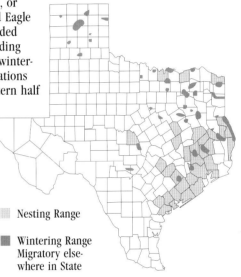

Nesting Range

Wintering Range
Migratory elsewhere in State

regions, or along river systems or lake shores with large, tall (40-120 ft.) trees for nesting and roosting. Nests are usually located within 1 to 2 miles of large bodies of water, such as lakes, reservoirs or rivers, and are often located in the ecotone or edge between forest and marsh or water. Bald Eagles often build their nests in the tallest trees in an area, providing an unobstructed flight path to the nest. Nests are built in a variety of tree species. In east Texas eagles nest primarily in loblolly pine. Throughout the rest of the breeding range in Texas, nests are found in a variety of trees, including bald cypress, water oak, live oak, American elm, cottonwood, sycamore, and pecan. Open water or wetland areas located within approximately one mile of nesting habitat are needed to provide feeding areas.

Most of the Bald Eagles seen in Texas breed in the northern states and spend the winter (December through March) in Texas. Wintering populations may occur statewide, but generally are found near large lakes and reservoirs, such as Lake Meredith, Buffalo Lake, Lake Texoma, Wright-Patman Lake,

Lake O' the Pines, Lake Fork, Lake Tawakoni, Lake Whitney, Lake Fairfield, Toledo Bend Reservoir, Sam Rayburn Reservoir, Lake Livingston, Lake Conroe, Lake Buchanan, Lake Cooper, Lake Palestine, Lake Pat Mayse, Lake Warren, and Palo Duro Lake.

Bald Eagle wintering habitat is characterized by abundant, readily available food sources. Most wintering areas are associated with open water, where eagles feed on fish or waterfowl. Wintering populations are also found on rangelands of the Davis Mountains, western Edwards Plateau, and the Panhandle, where eagles may take rabbits and feed on carrion.

The availability of night roost sites is often an important characteristic of wintering habitat. Bald Eagles may roost singly or in groups, and the same roosts are used from year to year. Roost trees are usually the oldest and largest trees in an area, and most have large horizontal limbs and open branching that allows plenty of room for takeoff and landing. Eagles generally choose roosts that allow unobstructed visibility to the surrounding areas, with a minimum of human activity in the immediate vicinity. Roost sites are often located near water, but eagles also roost on windbreaks and in secluded canyons well away from water.

Life History

Bald Eagles are opportunistic predators. They feed primarily on fish, but also eat a variety of waterfowl and other birds, small mammals, and turtles, when these foods are readily available. Carrion is also common in the diet, particularly in younger birds during the winter. Bottom-dwelling fish tend to occur more frequently in the diet. It is thought that the downward visual orientation of bottom-feeding fish makes them more vulnerable to eagle attacks than surface sight-feeders, which are more aware of movements from above. Eagles capture fish by extending their talons a few inches below the water's surface. Therefore, live fish are vulnerable only when near the surface or in shallows. Studies in Texas have shown that eagles commonly

eat coots, catfish, roughfish, and soft-shell turtles.

In Texas, Bald Eagles nest from October to July. Nests are constructed primarily by the female, with the male assisting. The typical nest is constructed of large sticks, with softer materials such as leaves, grass, and spanish moss used as nest lining. Nests are typically used for a number of years, with the birds adding nest material every year. Bald Eagle nests are often very large, measuring up to 6 feet in width and weighing hundreds of pounds. Eagles often have one or more alternative nests within their territories.

Peak egg-laying occurs in December, with hatching primarily in January. The female lays a clutch of 1 to 3 eggs, but the usual clutch is 2 eggs. A second clutch may be laid if the first is lost. Incubation begins when the first egg is laid and usually lasts 34 to 36 days. The young generally fledge (fly from the nest) in 11 to 12 weeks, but the adults continue to feed them for another 4 to 6 weeks while they learn to hunt. When they are on their own, young Bald Eagles migrate northward out of Texas, returning by September or October.

Nest surveys in Texas from 1981-1991 have shown that 64% of the nests successfully produced young, with production averaging 1 young per active nest found. Studies show that at least 70% of the juveniles survive their first year. Causes of first year mortality include disease, lack of food, inclement weather, and human interference.

Bald Eagles reach sexual maturity at 4 to 6 years of age; however, they have been known to successfully breed at 3 years. They are monogamous and are believed to mate for life; however, if one of the pair dies, the surviving bird will accept another mate. Bald Eagles are believed to live up to 30 years or more in the wild.

Threats and Reasons for Decline

Habitat loss over the past 200 years is the factor most consistently associated with declines in Bald Eagle populations. Unfortunately for eagles, people also like to live and

Mature Bald Eagles
© USFWS

spend their leisure time near water. In recent decades, the accelerated pace of development along the coast and near inland rivers and waterways is a primary cause of habitat loss. There are, however, encouraging signs in Texas that a significant amount of new habitat has been created in the form of man-made reservoirs. Reservoirs primarily provide habitat for wintering birds, but they are gradually receiving more use by nesting eagles. Hopefully, if human disturbance is kept to a minimum, a redistribution of nesting to reser-

Young eagles in nest
© TPWD Jim Whitcomb

voirs may offset some habitat loss in other areas.

Shooting has long been recognized as a major human-caused factor in the decline of Bald Eagles. Although primarily fish and carrion eaters, eagles were thought to be a major threat to chickens, livestock, and game animals. As a consequence, many were killed by farm-

Bald Eagle nest
© TPWD Leroy Williamson

ers, ranchers, and hunters. In 1940, Congress passed the Bald Eagle Protection Act, which made it illegal to shoot or harass eagles. In 1969, Bald Eagles gained further legal protection under federal endangered species laws. With heightened public awareness and sensitivity to the plight of the Bald Eagle, coupled with strict laws,

Juvenile Bald Eagles
© TPWD Mark Mitchell

shooting mortality has declined from 62% of total reported deaths from 1961-1965 to 18% from 1975-1981. Although this downward trend is encouraging, shooting mortality could still be a limiting factor, particularly in remote areas.

Human disturbance can also be a cause of population decline.

Activities such as logging, construction, and recreational activity certainly do disturb eagles in some instances. However, the impact of these disturbances is highly variable, depending on the activity, its frequency and duration, its proximity to areas used by eagles, the extent to which the activity modifies the habitat or its use, and timing in relation to the reproductive cycle. Also, some birds are more tolerant of disturbance than others, with adults generally less tolerant than immatures. Despite this variability, disturbance near nests has caused nesting failures.

Finally, the most dramatic declines in Bald Eagle populations nationwide resulted from environmental contaminants. Beginning in 1947, reproductive success in many areas of the country declined sharply, and remained at very low levels through the early 1970's. After several years of study, the low reproduction of Bald Eagles and many other birds was linked to widespread use of the insecticides DDT and Dieldren. These insecticides were used extensively in agriculture and forestry beginning in 1947. As DDT entered watersheds, it became part of the aquatic food chain, and was stored as DDE in the fatty tissue of fish and waterfowl. As eagles and other birds of prey fed on these animals, they accumulated DDE in their systems.

Although occasionally causing death, DDE mainly affected reproduction. Some birds affected by the chemical failed to lay eggs, and many produced thin eggshells that broke during incubation. Eggs that did not break were often addled or contained dead embryos, and the young that hatched often died. Dieldren killed eagles directly rather than causing thin eggshells, but compared to DDT, Dieldren was probably not as important in overall Bald Eagle declines. In 1972, the EPA banned the use of DDT in the United States. Since the ban, DDE residues in Bald Eagle eggshells have dropped significantly, and a slow recovery of eagle productivity has occurred. Most populations appear to be producing chicks at the expected rate.

Of more recent concern is evidence that lead poisoning may be a

significant cause of death in eagles. Chronic low levels of lead can produce nervous system disorders, affect behavior and learning, cause anemia, and increase susceptibility to disease. As laws requiring the use of steel shot to hunt waterfowl become effective, accumulation of lead in the food chain is expected to decline.

Since 1981, Texas Parks and Wildlife Department has conducted extensive aerial surveys to monitor active Bald Eagle nests. The 1995 survey identified 40 active nests. Twenty-eight of the active nests fledged 45 young. This compares with only 7 known nest sites in 1971. Midwinter Bald Eagle counts coordinated by TPWD and conducted by birding enthusiasts throughout the state reported 303 eagles in 1995. From 1986-1989, midwinter counts averaged less than 15 Bald Eagles per survey site. Since 1990, the average number of eagles per survey site has increased to 18. These numbers show encouraging trends for Texas. With continued vigilance, protection, and informed management, today's Texans can insure that future generations will have the opportunity to enjoy the sight of our majestic national symbol - the only eagle unique to North America.

Recovery Efforts

During the 1970's and 1980's, major efforts were directed toward captive breeding and reintroducing young birds into the wild. A total of 124 Bald Eagles were hatched at the Patuxent Wildlife Research Center in Maryland from 1976-1988. These captive-hatched eaglets were an important source for restocking wild populations. One successful reintroduction program placed young eaglets in the nests of adults whose own eggs were infertile or failed to hatch. The "foster" parents readily adopted the chicks and raised them as their own. Another method, called "hacking" places young birds on man-made towers in suitable habitat where populations are low. The nestlings are kept in an enclosure and fed by humans that stay out of sight. When they are able to fly, the enclosure is opened and the birds are free to leave. Food is still provided at the release site until no longer used or needed by the young birds. Hacking has been used very successfully in at least 11 states.

In Texas, the greatest challenge for the future will be to prevent further destruction of habitat. The Texas Parks and Wildlife Department, in cooperation with other agencies and conservation groups, is continuing to monitor Bald Eagle breeding and wintering populations and nesting success. Monitoring of nesting success is particularly important in detecting any problems associated with contaminants in the environment.

Finally, appropriate management of nesting, feeding, loafing, and wintering habitat must be a priority if we are to maintain the current upward trend in Bald Eagle numbers in Texas.

Where To See Bald Eagles

There are a number of State Parks where visitors have the opportunity to see and learn more about Bald Eagles. These include Lake Brownwood, Lake Livingston, Lake Texana, Lake Whitney, and Possum Kingdom State Parks. The Vanishing Texas Rivers Cruise, a privately operated excursion boat, also provides visitors with excellent opportunities to see wintering eagles on Lake Buchanan in Burnet and Llano Counties.

Because the Bald Eagle is a protected species and sensitive to human disturbance, birders and other observers should carefully follow certain viewing ethics. Recorded calls of prey species should not be used to attract birds. Also, observers should be careful not to approach too closely or otherwise disturb or stress birds.

How You Can Help

If you see a Bald Eagle nest, remember that eagles are vulnerable to disturbance throughout the nesting period (October to July in Texas), and are easily disturbed particularly during the first 12 weeks of nesting activity. Observers should remain a safe distance away from the nest (at least 750 feet) and keep noise and other human impacts to a minimum. Private landowners are encouraged to report new Bald Eagle nests to Texas Parks and Wildlife Department.

You can be involved in the conservation of Texas' nongame wildlife resources by supporting the Special Nongame and Endangered Species Conservation Fund. Special nongame stamps and decals are available at Texas Parks and Wildlife Department (TPWD) Field Offices, most State Parks, and the License Branch of TPWD headquarters in Austin. Conservation Passports, available from Texas Parks and Wildlife, are valid for one year and allow unlimited access to most State Parks, State Natural Areas, and Wildlife Management Areas. Part of the proceeds from the sale of these items is used to provide information to park visitors and the public concerning endangered species. Conservation organizations in Texas also welcome your participation and support. Finally, you can encourage and support private landowners who are minimizing nest disturbance and managing their land to protect Bald Eagle habitat.

For More Information Contact

Texas Parks and Wildlife Department
Endangered Resources Branch
4200 Smith School Road
Austin, Texas 78744
(512) 912-7011 or (800) 792-1112
or
U.S. Fish and Wildlife Service
Ecological Services Field Office
10711 Burnet Road, Suite 200
Austin, Texas 78758
(512) 490-0057

Management guidelines are available from Texas Parks and Wildlife Department or the U.S. Fish and Wildlife Service for landowners wishing to protect and manage Bald Eagle habitat.

Placing wing tags on Bald Eagles
© TPWD Leroy Williamson

References

Green, N. 1985. *The Bald Eagle*. The Audubon Wildlife Report 1985:508-531. National Audubon Society.

Hunt, W.G., J.M. Jenkins, R.E. Jackman, C.G. Thelander, and A.T. Gerstell. 1992. *Foraging Ecology of Bald Eagles on a Regulated River*. J. Raptor Research 26(4):243-256.

Mabie, D.W. 1992. *Bald Eagle Post-Fledgling Survival and Dispersal*. Texas Parks and Wildlife Department, Fed. Aid Project No. W-125-R-3, Job. No. 59. 14 pp.

Mabie, D.W., M.T. Merendino, and D.H. Reid. 1994. *Dispersal of Bald Eagles Fledged in Texas*. J. Raptor Research (in press).

Mitchell, M.R. 1992. *Bald Eagle Nest Survey and Management*. Texas Parks and Wildlife Department, Fed. Aid Project No. W-125-R-3, Job No. 30. 10 pp.

Porteous, P.L. 1992. "Eagles on the Rise." *National Geographic Magazine*, November, 1992. National Geographic Society.

U.S. Fish and Wildlife Service. 1989. *Southeastern States Bald Eagle Recovery Plan*. Atlanta Regional Office. 122 pp.

U.S. Fish and Wildlife Service. 1991. *Bald Eagle (*Haliaeetus leucocephalus*)*. Biologue Series.

Funds for the production of this leaflet were provided by the U.S. Fish and Wildlife Service, under Section 6 of the Endangered Species Act.

Habitat Management Guidelines for Bald Eagles in Texas

The following guidelines were developed to help landowners and managers maintain or improve their land for the benefit of the Bald Eagle. Information is also provided so that landowners may recognize and avoid or minimize human-related disturbance to eagles, particularly nesting pairs.

Nesting Habitat

The protection of an actual nest is important, but so is protection of the nest area and all the surrounding habitat factors that attracted the nesting pair to the area. Once the eagles establish a suitable breeding territory, they will return to the same area year after year, often using several nests within the territory during different years. When a given nest or the tree that it is in falls, a pair generally returns to the same territory to begin another nest. If one member of a pair dies, the nest may go unused for several years and then be recolonized by the surviving member returning with a new mate. Nesting territories can even be inherited by offspring. Therefore, protection of nesting territories should apply to "abandoned" nests for at least five consecutive years of documented nonuse.

The following habitat management guidelines are based on two management zones surrounding each nest site, with certain restrictions recommended for each zone.

Primary Management Zone For Nest Sites

This zone includes an area extending 750 to 1,500 feet outward in all directions from the nest site. It is recommended that the following activities not occur within this zone:

1. Habitat alteration or change in land use, such as would result from residential, commercial, or industrial development; construction projects; or mining operations.
2. Tree cutting, logging, or removal of trees, either living or dead.
3. Use of chemicals labeled as toxic to fish and wildlife.
4. Placement of above-ground electrical transmission or distribution lines. Since collision with powerlines and electrocution on powerline structures remain an important cause of death, placement of underground lines is recommended near Bald Eagle nests and winter concentration sites.
5. Helicopter or fixed-wing aircraft operation within 500 feet vertical distance or 1,000 feet horizontal distance of the nest site during the nesting season (October-July).
6. Activities which create minimal disturbance, such as hiking, fishing, camping, and bird-watching can be carried out safely during the non-nesting season if there is no physical alteration of the habitat within the zone. Traditional farming, ranching, and hunting activites which are existing practices and have occurred historically on the site can be carried out safely during the non-nesting season as long as habitat alteration is avoided.

Human presence within this zone should be minimized during the nesting season, especially during the early nesting period from October-April. Traditional agricultural activities and low impact recreational activities are generally not a problem even during the nesting season as long as they do not appear to be adversely affecting nesting success, there is no increase in the level of disturbance from historic levels, and physical alteration of the habitat is avoided. However, activities of any kind should be stopped if it becomes apparent that the birds are suffering from disturbance. The key point is whether the activities keep the breeding birds away from the nest, eggs, or young for extended periods of time. If they do, they are harmful. In general, it is important to protect the nest from human disturbance during very hot or very cold weather, since the parents' absence at these times can be particularly deadly for the eggs or young.

Secondary Management Zone For Nest Sites

This zone encompasses an area extending outward from the primary zone an additional 750 feet to 1 mile. Recommended restrictions in this zone are intended to protect the integrity of the primary zone and to protect important feeding areas, including the eagle's access to these areas. The following activities are likely to be detrimental to Bald Eagles at any time, and in most cases should be avoided within the secondary zone:

1. Development of new commercial or industrial sites.
2. Construction of multi-story buildings or high-density housing developments between the nest and the eagle's feeding area.
3. Placement of electrical transmission or distribution lines between the nest site and the eagle's feeding area.
4. Construction of new roads, trails, canals, or rights-of-way which would tend to facilitate human access to the eagle nest.
5. Use of chemicals labeled as toxic to wildlife.

Certain activities that involve only minimal alteration or disturbance to the habitat can be carried out safely in the secondary zone during the non-nesting season. Examples of these activities include: minor logging or land clearing, minor construction, seismographic exploration employing explosives, oil well drilling, and low-level aircraft operation. However, these activites should avoid major alteration or loss of Bald Eagle habitat as much as possible.

If logging is done, it is best to retain as many large trees as possible for roost and perch trees. Retention of at least 10 to 15 live trees per acre is suggested. Ideally, the trees left uncut should be the largest in the stand, preferably those with open crowns and stout lateral limbs. Selective forestry practices such as seedtree, shelterwood, and single tree selection are recommended over clear-cutting.

Minimal disturbance recreational activities (hiking, fishing, camping, picnicking, bird-watching, hunting) and everyday farming and ranching activities that cause no new alteration of habitat can be safely carried out in the secondary zone at any time.

Feeding Areas

The use of toxic chemicals in watersheds and rivers where Bald Eagles feed should be avoided as much as possible. Where agricultural herbicides and pesticides are used within the watershed, label directions should be strictly followed, including those describing proper disposal of rinse water and containers.

Alteration of natural shorelines where Bald Eagles feed should be avoided or minimized as much as possible. Degraded or eroded shorelines should be revegetated whenever possible.

Winter Roost Concentration Areas

Logging or land clearing activity should be avoided within 1,500 feet of a roosting concentration area. Disruptive, noisy, or out-of-the-ordinary land use activities should be avoided near communal roost sites. Normal agricultural activites which have occurred traditionally on the land are generally acceptable near these roost sites as long as they do not appear to be affecting roosting eagles. However, it is best to avoid even normal activities during evening, night, and early morning hours.

For More Information

Landowners and managers can contact the Texas Parks and Wildlife Department, U.S. Fish and Wildlife Service, U.S. Natural Resources Conservation Service (formerly Soil Conservation Service), or Texas Agricultural Extension Service for technical assistance in managing habitat and protecting Bald Eagle nest sites.

Funds for the production of this leaflet were provided by the U.S. Fish and Wildlife Service, under Section 6 of the Endangered Species Act.

Peregrine Falcon

Scientific Name: *Falco peregrinus*

Federal Status and State Status: the American Peregrine Falcon (*Falco peregrinus anatum*) is endangered and the Arctic Peregrine Falcon (*Falco peregrinus tundrius*) is threatened. Both of these subspecies occur in Texas.

Description

The use of falcons for hunting was developed around 2,000 B.C. in central Asia. By the twelfth century A.D., falconry was widely practiced throughout Europe. Once reserved only for nobility, the falcon's intelligence, strength, and amazing aerial performance made it a highly prized hunting bird.

A spectacular bird of prey, Peregrine Falcons are 16 to 19 inches long, have a wingspan of 39 to 42 inches, yet weigh only about 2 pounds. Females are

Peregrine Falcon
© USFWS

slightly larger than males. Their wings are long and pointed. Adult Peregrines are slate gray to bluish-gray above. With a black crown and nape and a black wedge extending below the eye, the birds appear to be wearing a black helmet. The throat and underparts are white to shades of buff, with fine black barring. The ends of the tail feathers are tipped in light yellow brown. The beak is slate blue, the legs and feet are yellow, and the talons are blue-black.

Immature birds have a dark brown head and neck with sandy streaking. The upper parts are dark brown with light amber-brown feather edging. They are white to sandy underneath and heavily marked with dark brown vertical streaks. The legs and feet are bluish-gray to greenish-yellow.

The Arctic Peregrine tends to be smaller than the American Peregrine and is lighter in color. Immature Arctic Peregrines have a lighter colored forehead and a thinner wedge on each side of the face.

Peregrine Falcons can be distinguished from similar Prairie Falcons by the black "helmet" and, when in flight, by the lack of contrasting dark and light feathers on the underside or "armpit" of the wing.

Distribution and Habitat

The Peregrine Falcon is noted for having a wide and diverse distribution. The American Peregrine currently nests in the western United States, Canada, and Mexico. These birds spend the nonbreeding season near their breeding areas or move only moderately southward. In Texas, they are found primarily in the Trans-Pecos region, including Big Bend National Park, and the Chisos, Davis, and Guadalupe mountain ranges.

The Arctic Peregrine nests in the arctic islands and the tundra regions of Alaska, Canada, and Greenland. They are highly migratory, flying over the United States to winter mostly in South America. The Texas coastline plays an important role in the survival of migrating peregrines. During each migration, falcons assemble on the Texas coast, especially on Padre Island, and accumulate stores of fat to continue their flight. They take advantage of the abundant prey along the open coastline and tidal flats. Some individuals have stayed for as long as a month during either spring or fall.

The Peregrine Falcon nests on coasts, mountains, and canyons of most climatic zones, wherever it locates a suitable high cliff ledge for its eyrie (nest site). Peregrines do avoid some extremes for nesting, however, such as very arid desert regions.

Arctic Peregrine Falcon Wintering Range (migratory elsewhere in state)

American Peregrine Falcon Present Nesting Range (migratory elsewhere in state)

American Peregrines in the Rocky Mountain and Southwest region nest on mountain cliffs and river gorges. Occupied eyries often exist on dominant cliffs which generally exceed 200 feet in height. Nests are situated on open ledges or potholes. South facing cliffs are preferred in the more northerly latitudes. In Alaska, arctic Canada, and Greenland, Arctic Peregrines nest on cliffs in mountainous regions, and along rivers and coastlines.

In the western United States, Peregrines nest from near sea level to over 9,000 feet. Prey abundance and diversity is thought to be a major factor in eyrie selection.

Nest sites are often adjacent to water courses and impoundments because of the abundance of avian prey attracted to these areas.

Before 1950, a healthy but small population of American Peregrines nested in the eastern United States and Canada. The population centers were generally located in the mountainous regions of the East Coast and along major waterways such as the Mississippi, Hudson, Susquehanna, and Connecticut Rivers. Nest sites were generally located on the ledge of a rock cliff or escarpment that provided a clear view of the surrounding area. Despite sharp population declines during the 1950's and 1960's, efforts over the past 15 years to reintroduce Peregrines into former eastern nesting habitats are now paying off. Peregrines are once again occupying cliffs in the eastern mountains and along the coast where they have been absent for 30 years or more.

Western and eastern populations of the American Peregrine are considered relatively nonmigratory, moving short distances as compared to the Arctic Peregrine. Some western falcons can be seen in the vicinity of their eyries throughout the year. Others move short distances to winter near large rivers or marshes where prey is abundant. There is also evidence that some birds move farther south to winter in Mexico.

As in the west, movements of eastern populations are probably determined by the availability of prey. Movements of eastern falcons are frequently east or west, from the mountains to the coast.

In Texas, American Peregrines once nested in suitable habitat throughout the Trans-Pecos region and part of the Edwards Plateau. Although they no longer nest on the Edwards Plateau, there are reports in the literature (1941 and 1950) of Peregrine Falcons preying on bats emerging from a cave in south-central Texas.

Life History
With a flight speed in excess of 60 mph, Peregrines can hunt large areas with little effort. Preferred hunting habitats such as meadows, riverbottoms, cropland, marshes, and lakes attract abundant bird life. Peregrines capture a wide variety of birds, including blackbirds, jays, swifts, doves, shorebirds, and songbirds. Falcons usually strike their prey from above at great speed. The prey is either struck to the ground or killed instantly by the blow from the falcon's talons. Prey species try to evade the falcon's attack by quick aerobatic maneuvers or by diving to cover. If the prey manages to stay above the falcon or reaches cover, it will usually escape. Peregrines are excellent flyers, and rely on maneuverability and surprise as well as speed to capture prey.

American Peregrines nesting at lower latitudes are usually present on nesting cliffs by March, while Arctic Peregrines arrive at their nesting locations by late April or May. The male or female may arrive at a suitable cliff site. While waiting for a member of the opposite sex to appear, the birds drive away all other falcons of the same sex. Quiet perching of the pair in close proximity to each other is an early indication of successful pairing. The falcons soon begin to hunt together, with one bird flushing prey for the other to capture.

The courtship flights of Peregrines are spectacular aerial displays of rapid climbing, spirals, and steep precision dives where the birds sometimes touch in mid-air. On the cliff, courtship behavior includes touching beaks, nibbling at the beak or feet of the mate, and mutual preening. During courtship, the male offers food to the female, both at the cliff and when the pair is in flight. When the female is receptive, she will accept the prey and mating soon follows.

In the United States and much of Canada, a clutch of three or four eggs is laid in April. In Arctic latitudes, Peregrines lay eggs from late May through late June. The female does most of the incubating and all of the brooding, while the male does most of the hunting. Incubation lasts about 33 days. The young remain in the nest for five to six weeks, being fed and cared for by the adults. After they leave the nest, the adults continue to feed

Young Peregrine Falcons
© USFWS

and defend their young for several weeks.

Scientists estimate that about 20 to 25 percent of adult Peregrines and 55 to 60 percent of juveniles die each year of natural causes. The average life expectancy for those young that fledge is probably about 4 years, although maximum life spans of 13 and 17 years have been recorded. In captivity, Peregrines have reached 20 years of age. Peregrines do not normally breed until at least 2 years of age.

Threats and Reasons for Decline
Although habitat loss, human disturbance, indiscriminant shooting, and illegal collection have been identified as contributing to local declines in Peregrine Falcon populations, worldwide declines have been attributed to reproductive failure caused by the widespread use of the pesticide DDT.

The decline of the Peregrine Falcon began in the late 1940's, coinciding with the introduction of DDT in 1947. The decline was first noticed in the northeastern United States, with Peregrine Falcon productivity dropping sharply between 1947 and 1955. Along the Hudson River, which formerly supported one of the healthiest Peregrine populations known, productivity essentially ceased by 1950, and most nest sites were abandoned by the mid-1950's. Surveys in the early 1960's showed that Peregrine productivity in the northeastern United States was near zero.

By the 1950's, it was apparent that declines were also underway in many other parts of North America. Biologists reported widespread reproductive failure and eventual disappearance of breeding pairs. The decline appeared first in the southern parts of the range and moved north. In the more remote

Peregrine Falcon nesting habitat at Black Gap WMA
© Glen Mills

Banding Peregrine Falcons
© TPWD Frank Aquilar

Peregrine populations of Alaska and arctic Canada, a more gradual decline took place. Although the loss of breeding pairs in these regions probably began in the 1950's, a dramatic collapse did not occur until 1970.

By 1969, the Peregrine was essentially gone east of the Mississippi River in both the United States and Canada south of the boreal forest, and only 33 percent of all known nest sites in the Rocky Mountains were still occupied. In the southwestern United States, pre-1947 populations were largely unknown, but similar declines probably occurred.

The lowest point in most North American populations was reached in the mid-1970's. By 1975, only 324 nesting pairs of Peregrines could be confirmed on the continent. After several years of study,

the low reproduction of Peregrine Falcons and other birds of prey was linked to widespread use of insecticides such as DDT and Dieldren. These insecticides were used extensively in agriculture and forestry beginning in 1947. As DDT entered the environment, it became part of the food chain, and was stored as DDE in the fatty tissue of animals. As Peregrine Falcons and other birds of prey fed on these animals, they accumulated DDE in their systems. Although occasionally causing death, DDE mainly affected reproduction. Some birds affected by the chemical failed to lay eggs, or produced thin eggshells that broke during incubation. Eggs that did not break were often addled (rotten) or contained dead embryos, and the young that hatched often died. Abnormal or inattentive behavior by adults sometimes resulted in nest abandonment or loss of young. In 1972, the EPA banned the use of DDT in the United States. Since the ban, DDE residues in Peregrine Falcon eggshells have dropped significantly, and a slow recovery of falcon productivity has occurred. Although most populations in the United States now appear to be producing chicks at a healthy rate, falcons in west Texas are still reproducing at relatively low levels. There is concern that high pesticide levels continue to affect Peregrine Falcon reproduction in west Texas.

Prior to the mid-1940's, it is estimated that the North American continent contained 7000 to 10,000 Peregrine nesting territories, of which probably 80 to 90% were occupied in any given year. Although never common when compared with other birds of prey breeding in North America, Peregrine Falcons were much more numerous historically than they are today.

Recent surveys have confirmed the existence of at least 1,153 breeding pairs on the continent, and many more probably exist in unsurveyed portions of Alaska and northern Canada. The 1992 breeding season estimates for Arizona, California, Colorado, Idaho, Montana, Nevada, New Mexico, Oregon, Texas, Utah, Washington, and Wyoming show a total of 591 breeding pairs. Although

Peregrines are recovering well in many areas, they are still largely absent from most of Canada south of the boreal forest, the Rocky Mountains of the northern United States, the southern half of California, and the northern Pacific coast of Baja California.

Recovery Efforts

Throughout the United States, scientists are conducting breeding and population surveys to determine occupancy of eyries and reproductive success. Eggshells are being collected and tested for thickness, and contaminant levels are being assessed. Continued research on population dynamics, movements, and contamination will provide wildlife managers with the information needed to assist the Peregrine Falcon on its road to recovery.

Since human disturbance can be a serious threat to reproductive success, parks such as Big Bend National Park have visitor use restrictions during the nesting season. Activities such as rock-climbing can be particularly disturbing to nesting Peregrines.

The Peregrine Fund, Inc. in cooperation with the U.S. Fish and Wildlife Service and state wildlife agencies, has released captive-reared chicks into suitable unoccupied habitat. A technique called "hacking" places young birds on man-made towers in suitable habitat where populations are low. The nestlings are kept in an enclosure and fed by humans that stay out of sight. When they are able to fly, the enclosure is opened and the birds are free to leave. Food is still provided at the release site until no longer used or needed by the young birds. Hacking has been used successfully in many areas, primarily in the eastern United States, to increase Peregrine numbers.

In Texas, the greatest challenge for the future will be to protect breeding habitat in the western part of the state, and coastal habitat which is so important to migrating Peregrines. Texas Parks and Wildlife Department, in cooperation with the National Park Service and U.S. Fish and Wildlife Service, is continuing to monitor Peregrine

Falcon populations and nesting success. Monitoring of nesting success is particularly important in detecting any problems associated with contaminants in the environment.

Finally, appropriate management of nesting and feeding habitat must be a priority if we are to achieve and maintain an upward trend in Peregrine Falcon numbers in Texas.

Where To See Peregrine Falcons

The best place to see Peregrine Falcons is along the Texas coast during the spring or fall migrations of Arctic Peregrines. Mustang Island State Park and Padre Island National Seashore, in particular, are good places to see Peregrines. The birds arrive by the hundreds, taking time to feed and rest before continuing their lengthy migration. In fact, the Texas Gulf Coast is the only known spring staging area for Peregrine migration in the Western Hemisphere.

How You Can Help

If you see a Peregrine Falcon or its nest, remember that they are vulnerable to disturbance, particularly when nesting or hunting. Observers should remain a safe distance away from the nest or perch (100 to 300 yards, depending on the sensitivity of the individual bird) and keep noise and other human impacts to a minimum. Landowners and others are encouraged to report sightings or nests of Peregrine Falcons to Texas Parks and Wildlife Department or the U.S. Fish and Wildlife Service at the numbers listed below. Since nesting in Texas is still quite rare, it is important to note the location (county and approximate distance and direction to nearest town), habitat type, behavior, and take a photograph if possible. Well-documented observations will help experts verify your sighting.

You can be involved in the conservation of Texas' nongame wildlife resources by supporting the Special Nongame and Endangered Species Conservation Fund. Special nongame stamps and decals are available at Texas Parks and

Wildlife Department (TPWD) Field Offices, most State Parks, and the License Branch of TPWD headquarters in Austin. Part of the proceeds from the sale of these items are used for endangered species habitat management and public information. Conservation organizations in Texas also welcome your participation and support.

History has taught a sobering lesson concerning the effects of pesticide contamination on wildlife. You can help by doing your part to insure that household and agricultural chemicals are used, and the containers and rinse water disposed of, in accordance with label directions.

Finally, you can encourage and support private landowners who are managing their land to protect habitat for Peregrine Falcons and other birds of prey.

For More Information Contact

Texas Parks and Wildlife Department
Endangered Resources Branch
4200 Smith School Road
Austin, Texas 78744
(512) 912-7011 or (800) 792-1112
or
U.S. Fish and Wildlife Service
Ecological Services Field Office
10711 Burnet Road, Suite 200
Austin, Texas 78758
(512) 490-0057

Immature Peregrine Falcon feeding along the Texas coast
© USFWS

Immature Peregrine Falcon
© D. Keddy-Hector

References

Burnham, W. (Ed.). 1989. *The Peregrine Fund, Inc. Operation Report.* World Center for Birds of Prey, Boise, ID. 229 pp.

Cade, T.J., J.H. Enderson, C.G. Thelander, and C.M. White (Ed.). 1988. *Peregrine Falcon Populations - Their Management and Recovery.* The Peregrine Fund, Inc. Boise, ID. 949 pp.

Maechtle, T.L. 1989. "Peregrine Sojourn." *Texas Parks and Wildlife,* Vol. 47, No. 11, p. 4-13.

Paredes, M., R. Skiles, and D. Neighbor. 1991. *Peregrine Falcon Monitoring Program Report - Big Bend National Park and Rio Grande Wild and Scenic River.* National Park Service, Big Bend National Park, Texas.

U.S. Fish and Wildlife Service. 1984. *American Peregrine Falcon Recovery Plan (Rocky Mountain/Southwest Population).* Prepared in cooperation with the American Peregrine Falcon Recovery Team. USFWS, Denver, CO. 105 pp.

U.S. Fish and Wildlife Service. 1993. *Draft Addendum to the Pacific Coast and Rocky Mountain/Southwest American Peregrine Falcon Recovery Plans.* Portland, Oregon. 20 pp.

Funds for the production of this leaflet were provided by the U.S. Fish and Wildlife Service, under Section 6 of the Endangered Species Act.

Northern Aplomado Falcon

Scientific Name: *Falco femoralis septentrionalis*

Federal Status: Endangered, 2/26/86 • State Status: Endangered

Description

The Aplomado Falcon is a medium-sized falcon, smaller than the Peregrine and Prairie Falcon, but larger than the Kestrel and Merlin. Its total length is about 15 to 18 inches, with a wingspan of about 32 to 36 inches. The name aplomado means "steel gray" in Spanish and describes the color of the adult's back and outer wings. Distinguishing fieldmarks include a dark "cummerbund" or belly band often marked with narrow, horizon-

Aplomado Falcon
© TPWD Glen Mills

tal white bars; a long blackish tail with 6 to 8 white crossbars; and a distinctive facial pattern. The upper breast and throat are white or buff-colored, and sometimes covered with scattered thin dark streaks. The abdomen, thighs and undertail are a cinnamon color, and the fleshy eye ring and legs are brilliant yellow. Compared to adult females, adult males are noticeably smaller, with more pronounced white barring on the cummerbund and less streaking on the upper breast.

Juveniles differ from adults in that the upper breast and throat is a deep cinnamon color rather than white or buff-colored. Also, broad, dark streaks (as opposed to thin streaks in some adults) cover most of the upper breast. Finally, the legs and eye ring are bluish-green, not yellow.

In flight, the Aplomado Falcon can be distinguished from larger falcons (Prairie and Peregrine) and the Merlin by its longer tail and wings that are relatively narrow near the body. The Aplomado's flight profile is most similar to the American Kestrel or Mississippi Kite, but the Aplomado has a slightly longer tail and narrower wings, and is larger than the kestrel.

Distribution and Habitat

The northern subspecies of the Aplomado Falcon once inhabited grassland, savannah, and desert scrub areas throughout parts of southern Texas, New Mexico, and Arizona, and southward through Mexico to the western coast of Guatemala. In the United States, the Aplomado Falcon was regularly seen on the coastal prairies of south Texas. Historical records also exist for the river valleys, desert marshes, and grasslands of Trans-Pecos Texas, southern New Mexico and southeastern Arizona.

Aplomado Falcon habitat consists of open grassland with scattered trees or shrubs. In Arizona, New Mexico, Trans-Pecos Texas, and central plateau of Mexico, Aplomados inhabit semi-desert grassland with scattered mesquite and yucca. In the past, Aplomados were most abundant in the coastal grasslands of south Texas and the savannah grasslands of eastern Mexico. These birds also inhabited coastal dunes and tidal flats, and margins of inland marshes and riparian woodlands. In Mexico, Aplomados nest in savannah grasslands with scattered tropical live oak, lowland pine, or acacia trees, dry tropical

deciduous woodlands, cutover rainforest, and, at higher elevations, stands of tree yuccas and open pine-oak woodlands. Occupied habitat has been described as having tree densities of about 19 trees per 100 acres, an average distance between trees of about 100 feet, and average tree height of 30 feet.

Scientists believe that before the turn of the century, Aplomado Falcons were quite common in the grasslands of southern and western Texas, New Mexico, and Arizona.

Several pioneer naturalists wrote that they frequently saw this species in their travels (Merrill, 1878; Bendire, 1892; Smith, 1910). They described the Aplomado as "quite common," "fairly common," or "frequently encountered."

By the 1930's, the Aplomado Falcon had become very rare in the United States. The last nesting pair reported in Texas was in Brooks County in 1941, and the last confirmed nest within the United States was in New Mexico in 1952. On the King Ranch in south Texas in 1949, Val Lehmann collected the last Aplomado Falcon specimen from the United States. He continued to see Aplomados in this area until the 1950's. Between 1950 and 1960, several Aplomados may have been observed in Big Bend National Park and on the southern Texas coast. More recent sightings include one on the Texas coast in 1963, and one in El Paso County in 1968. During the 1970's, Aplomados were occasionally reported from southern and western Texas, southwestern New Mexico, and southeastern Arizona.

Because of population declines during the the early 1900's, the Aplomado Falcon is exceedingly rare in the United States today. Between 1986 and 1993, The Peregrine Fund released 46 Aplomado Falcons on the Laguna Atascosa National Wildlife Refuge on the southern Texas Gulf Coast. Scattered sightings have been recorded since that time on the refuge and in other parts of south Texas. The Refuge and some private land on its borders are the only areas in Texas where Aplomado Falcons are regularly sighted.

Within the last two years, authenticated sightings have been made at the White Sands Missile Range in New Mexico and in the Trans-Pecos near Marfa, Texas. Also, nesting birds have been discovered in northern Mexico. These recent sightings, coupled with the fact that scattered unconfirmed sightings have been reported since the 1950's from the grasslands surrounding the Davis Mountains of Texas and the Guadalupe Mountains of New Mexico, are cause for hope that Aplomados may be slowly recolonizing their former range in the United States west of the Pecos River. In Mexico, Aplomado Falcons are known to nest in the states of Chihuahua, Tamaulipas, Veracruz, Chiapas, Campeche, San Luis Potosi, and Tabasco.

Life History

Most often seen in pairs, Aplomado Falcons hunt together, often soar together, perch near one another, and even feed together outside the breeding season. During the spring of their second year, pair bonds are formed. Courtship

behavior includes display soaring, feeding, and nest displays. Like other falcons, Aplomados do not construct their own nests. Instead, they use the stick platforms built by other birds. In Mexico and the United States, nests of the Chihuahuan Raven, Swainson's Hawk, Crested Caracara, Roadside Hawk, Brown Jay, White-tailed Kite, Gray Hawk, and Lesser Black Hawk may be used by Aplomado Falcons. Stick nests used by Aplomados generally average about 1 to 3 feet in diameter.

Aplomado Falcons usually lay 2 to 3 eggs. Although both parents share incubation, the female spends more time at the nest than the male. Sometimes the parent incubating eggs leaves the nest temporarily to assist its partner with hunting or nest defense activities. Aplomados actively defend the area surrounding the nest by attacking any intruder perceived to be a threat.

The eggs hatch in about 32 days, and the nestlings are covered with light gray down. Newly hatched nestlings are closely brooded by the female, and this may be the only time of year when mated males typically hunt alone. The young are fed primarily by the female, although sometimes the male assists with the feeding. Nestlings fledge at 32 to 40 days, but parents continue to feed them for about another 4 weeks. In eastern Mexico, Aplomado Falcons nest during the dry season (January-June). They nest only once per year. Although Aplomados have not nested in the United States since the early 1950's, records from the early part of this century show that most nesting occurred in April and May.

As the young grow, the hunting activity of adults increases. The young are fed 6 or more times each day, which represents perhaps 25 to 30 hunting attempts. Aplomado Falcons hunt primarily birds, but also eat insects, small snakes, lizards, and rodents. Favorite avian prey includes doves, cuckoos, quail, woodpeckers, blackbirds, flycatchers, thrushes, meadowlarks, and sparrows. Aplomados typically chase small birds and insects during horizontal flights initiated from

Aplomado Falcon chicks
© Frid Fridrickson

Male falcon providing food
© Noel Synder

a perch. They are extremely fast in level flight, and are capable of outflying species such as Mourning Doves, Rock Doves, and Killdeer. Aplomados readily continue the chase on foot when prey animals try to escape by entering crowns of trees, small shrubs, or dense grass. Agile on foot, Aplomados often run down ground birds. Insects are generally captured and often eaten during flight. Larger insects and birds are taken to favorite perches to be plucked and consumed. Food not immediately eaten is stored in caches placed in the crooks of branches, in small shrubs, or in clumps of grass. Cache sites, with or without stored food, are actively defended by the falcons from other predators.

When hunting small birds, the male and female often work together. In general, the male ranges more widely from the nest site to locate food. When he finds suitable prey within sight of the female, he calls her to help drive the prey from cover or join in the pursuit as it takes flight. For example, a typical hunt starts when the male spots prey perched in trees or feeding on the ground. He flies slowly to a position overhead and

Aplomado Falcon habitat in South Texas
© USFWS Marie Fernandez

Adult Aplomado Falcon
© D. P. Keddy-Hector

hovers, while chipping repeatedly. The female then glides directly to the male, lands, and chases the bird on foot until she captures it or it takes flight, at which point she joins her mate in pursuit. Most hunting activity occurs within view of the nest when nestlings are present, although males do occasionally hunt at more distant locations, particularly after several unsuccessful hunting attempts close to the nest.

Little is known regarding the seasonal movements of Aplomado Falcons. There is no evidence that these falcons are migratory, either in the United States or Mexico, and mated pairs remain on their territories year-round.

Threats and Reasons for Decline

Although it is somewhat of a mystery why the Aplomado Falcon is so rare in the United States today, habitat loss and the bird's sensitivity to pesticide contamination are likely reasons. Loss of habitat probably caused its disappearance from formerly occupied areas, while pesticide contamination may have kept falcon numbers low enough so they did not recolonize portions of their former range.

Brush encroachment resulting from uncontrolled livestock grazing and fire suppression has altered much of the grassland habitat once inhabited by Aplomado Falcons in Texas. Continuous heavy grazing pressure, which reduces plant diversity and leads to declines in range condition and brush invasion, affects Aplomado Falcons by reducing habitat for prey species. Aplomado Falcons tend to abandon nesting territories where grass ground cover gives way to brush.

Well-planned brush management and periodic prescribed burning are management practices that can be used to maintain open rangelands with scattered mottes of brush and trees, which is preferred habitat for Aplomado Falcons. Management for these falcons is therefore very compatible with practices that maintain and restore healthy rangelands. In fact, the presence of Aplomado Falcons often reflects good rangeland management. Well-managed pastures with a diversity of perennial plants and substantial ground cover are likely areas for these falcons. Grazing management (moderate stocking, rotational grazing), selective brush control, range seeding, and prescribed fire can be used to maintain diverse and productive rangelands able to support abundant prey for Aplomado Falcons.

Conversion of rangeland to cropland has also contributed to habitat loss. Since the early 1900's, much of the Lower Rio Grande Valley and gulf coastal plain of Texas and Mexico have been converted to citrus, sorghum, beans and cotton. River floodplains of the middle Rio Grande, the Pecos and the Gila in New Mexico and Arizona have also been altered with some conversion to farmland. Degradation of stream habitats and the loss of seasonally wet playas throughout the desert southwest probably also contributed to the Aplomado's decline because of their importance in supporting avian prey.

Pesticide contamination may have further reduced habitat quality for the Aplomados remaining in the United States at the beginning of the DDT era (1947-1972). As with other birds of prey at the top of the food chain, such as the Peregrine Falcon and Bald Eagle, the Aplomado Falcon is sensitive to pesticide-induced reproductive problems. Studies have shown that falcons affected by chemicals such as DDT failed to lay eggs, and many produced thin eggshells that broke during incubation. Eggs that did not break were often rotten or contained dead embryos, and the young that hatched often died. One study in eastern Mexico showed that Aplomado eggs collected after 1947 were 25% thinner than eggs collected prior to the introduction of DDT. Since DDT and related pesticides were banned in the United States in 1972, species such as the Bald Eagle, Peregrine Falcon, and Eastern Brown Pelican have steadily increased in numbers. Although levels have declined in the United States, pesticide contamination remains a concern, particularly in foreign countries where the use of DDT is still legal. Residual pesticide levels are still relatively high in parts of south Texas. Periodic monitoring of pesticide levels is needed, particularly in grassland habitats that are relatively close to farming areas. Desert grasslands remote from agriculture are unlikely to have residual pesticide contamination.

Recovery Efforts

In 1984, with leadership from The Peregrine Fund, Inc., a non-profit organization dedicated to preventing the extinction of endangered and threatened birds of prey through research and restoration programs, and the U.S. Fish and Wildlife Service, efforts began to re-establish the Northern Aplomado Falcon as a breeding species in the United States. The Aplomado Falcon Restoration Project is based on techniques developed by The Peregrine Fund for the successful restoration of the Peregrine Falcon (*Falco peregrinus*) in the contiguous United States. This involves captive breeding and monitored releases of young into suitable habitat.

The first captive breeding of the Aplomado Falcon was accomplished at the Chihuahuan Desert

Research Institute in 1982. Captive breeding experiments were conducted on the Aplomado Falcon at the Santa Cruz Predatory Bird Research Group facility and World Center for Birds of Prey between 1984 and 1990. These efforts produced 36 falcons and yielded important breeding and management information. Experimental releases of captive-bred Aplomados were conducted at the Laguna Atascosa National Wildlife Refuge (Cameron County) from 1986 through 1989, producing important information on release techniques. During 1991 and 1992, emphasis was placed on enhancing reproduction of captive falcons and establishing a captive population capable of producing at least 50 young each year. Beginning in 1993, program emphasis shifted to production and release of maximum numbers of falcons and monitoring of certain representative individuals.

Reintroduction efforts have already started to pay off. In May, 1995, an Aplomado hatchling was discovered in a nest atop a 65-foot utility pole on a remote tract owned by the Port of Brownsville. By June, this history-making Aplomado Falcon had made its first flight and was learning to hunt. The young bird is the first known Aplomado Falcon to be hatched in the American wild in 43 years.

The success of the Aplomado Falcon Restoration Project depends on cooperation between government, private organizations, and landowners. The amount of public land in Texas is insufficient to maintain a self-sustaining population of Aplomado Falcons, so the cooperation of private landowners will be critical. Landowners with large acreages of rangeland in south and southwest Texas have the opportunity to play a vital role in the recovery of this beautiful falcon. Those interested in cooperating in the restoration effort should contact Texas Parks and Wildlife Department or the U.S. Fish and Wildlife Service.

Biologists from various agencies and groups are increasing their efforts to survey and monitor breeding Aplomados in northern Mexico. It is hoped that these populations will continue to grow and that birds will gradually move north into the United States.

Where To See Aplomado Falcons

The only place in the United States where Aplomado Falcons can be consistently seen is the vicinity of the Peregrine Fund's southern Texas reintroduction project at the Laguna Atascosa National Wildlife Refuge near Rio Hondo, Texas. Recent sightings near the Davis Mountains of Texas are cause for hope that Aplomados from northern Mexico are slowly recolonizing southwestern Texas.

To search for Aplomado Falcons in Texas, the best strategy is to search grassland and savannah habitats in the southern and southwestern portions of the state. Areas with an abundance of small birds and stick nests built by ravens and other raptors should receive special attention. During March through June, all large stick nests should be examined from a distance for signs of adults incubating eggs or brooding chicks. Females often sit quietly on the nest, and the long tail can sometimes be seen protruding over the nest rim. Observers should also carefully search low perch sites such as fenceposts, plowed fields, and the inner branches of trees and shrubs; conduct spotting scope surveys of the sky and distant perches; watch for hawks and falcons attracted to evening bat flights, grassfires, or colonies of swallows, doves, or pigeons; and look closely at any raptors seen near tightly-bunched, erratically moving flocks of small birds.

How You Can Help

If you see an Aplomado Falcon or its nest, remember that they are vulnerable to disturbance, particularly during the nesting period. Observers should remain a safe distance away from the nest or perch (100 to 300 yards, depending on the sensitivity of the individual bird) and keep noise and other human impacts to a minimum.

Aplomado Falcon landing
© TPWD Glen Mills

Landowners and others are encouraged to report sightings or nests of Aplomado Falcons to Texas Parks and Wildlife Department, Endangered Resources Branch. Since this falcon is extremely rare in Texas, it is important to note the location (county and approximate distance and direction to nearest town), habitat type, behavior, and take a photograph if possible. Well-documented observations will help experts verify the sighting.

Owners and managers of large ranches in Texas can do a lot to enhance the recovery of the Aplomado Falcon. Well-planned brush management and periodic prescribed burning are management practices that can be used to maintain open rangelands and a vegetation structure favorable for these birds. Good grazing management practices, such as moderate stocking and rotational grazing will help to maintain productive rangelands able to support Aplomado Falcons.

You can be involved in the conservation of Texas' nongame wildlife resources by supporting the Special Nongame and Endangered Species Conservation Fund. Special nongame stamps and decals are available at Texas Parks and Wildlife Department (TPWD) Field Offices, most State Parks, and the License Branch of TPWD headquarters in Austin. Conservation Passports, available from Texas Parks and Wildlife are valid for one year and allow unlimited access to most State Parks, State Natural Areas, and Wildlife Management Areas. Part of the proceeds from the sale of these items are used to purchase endangered species habitat and to provide information to park visitors and the public concerning endangered species. Conservation organizations also welcome your participation and support. Finally, you can encourage and support private landowners who are managing their land to protect habitat for birds of prey.

For More Information Contact

Texas Parks and Wildlife Department
Endangered Resources Branch
4200 Smith School Road
Austin, Texas 78744
(512) 912-7011 or (800) 792-1112
        or
U.S. Fish and Wildlife Service
Ecological Services Field Office
10711 Burnet Road, Suite 200
Austin, Texas 78758
(512) 490-0057
        or
Laguna Atascosa National Wildlife
    Refuge
P.O. Box 450
Rio Hondo, Texas 78583
(512) 748-3607

References

Hector, D.P. 1980. "Our Rare Falcon of the Desert Grassland." *Birding*, Vol. XII, Number 3, p. 93-102.

Hector, D.P. 1985. "The Diet of the Aplomado Falcon (*Falco femoralis*) in Eastern Mexico." *The Condor* 87:336-342.

Hector, D.P. 1986. "Cooperative Hunting and its Relationship to Foraging Success and Prey Size in an Avian Predator." *Ethology* 73:247-257.

Hector, D.P. 1987. "The Decline of the Aplomado Falcon in the United States." *American Birds* 41(3):381-389.

Hunt, W.G. 1983. "Rare Aplomado May Return to Texas." *Texas Parks & Wildlife*, July, 1983, p. 10-13.

Keddy-Hector, D.P. 1993. "Aplomado Falcon (*Falco femoralis septentrionalis*)." In: *Raptors of Arizona*, R.L. Glinski editor.

Palmer, R.S. (editor). 1988. *Handbook of North American Birds, Volume 5, Diurnal Raptors (Part 2)*. Yale University Press, New Haven, CT. 465 pp.

U.S. Fish and Wildlife Service. 1990. *Northern Aplomado Falcon Recovery Plan*. U.S. Fish and Wildlife Service. Albuquerque, New Mexico. 56 pp.

Funds for the production of this leaflet were provided by the U.S. Fish and Wildlife Service, under Section 6 of the Endangered Species Act.

Mexican Spotted Owl

Scientific Name: *Strix occidentalis lucida*

Federal Status: Threatened, 3/16/93 • State Status: Threatened

Description

The Mexican Spotted Owl is a medium-sized owl, reaching a length of nearly 17 inches. It has dark eyes and white spotting on the head, back, and underparts. It is somewhat similar to the Barred Owl, but with spots on the breast rather than barring and streaking. The Mexican Spotted Owl is one of three spotted owl subspecies occurring in North America. It is distinguished from the California and Northern Spotted Owls primarily by

Mexican Spotted Owl
© F. R. Gehlbach

geographic distribution and plumage. Although the background coloration of the Mexican Spotted Owl is darker brown than the other two subspecies, its spots are larger, more numerous, and whiter in color, giving it a lighter color overall.

The owl's call is usually four-noted and rarely three-noted. The owl also utters what has been described as a series of 3 or 4 hesitant, doglike barks and cries. Calls are most frequently heard throughout the breeding season (February-August). Like most other owls,

Mexican Spotted Owls are usually seen singly or in paris.

Distribution and Habitat

The Mexican Spotted Owl has the largest geographic range of the three spotted owl subspecies. Its range extends from the southern Rocky Mountains in Colorado and southern Utah, southward through Arizona, New Mexico and Trans-Pecos, Texas, to the Sierra Madre Occidental and Oriental mountains in Mexico. Although there are no estimates of the owl's historic population size, its historic range is thought to be similar to its present distribution. The 1990 population estimate of Mexican Spotted Owls in the southwestern United States was 806 pairs and 548 singles for a total of about 2,160 birds. An estimated 91% of Mexican Spotted Owls known to exist in the southwest at the end of 1990 occurred on national forests; the other 9% occurred on Indian reservations (4%), national parks (4%), BLM lands (1%), and private lands (less than 1%).

In Texas, the Mexican Spotted Owl occurs in the Guadalupe Mountains near the New Mexico border. An owl was first observed in these mountains in 1901. One to about 10 owls regularly occupy this habitat. It is possible that Mexican Spotted Owls exist in other mountain ranges of west Texas where suitable habitat occurs.

Characteristics of Mexican Spotted Owl habitat include a canopy cover of mature trees. The owls prefer areas with a multi-layered canopy resulting from trees of different ages. Other habitat characteristics, typical of old-growth stands, include downed logs and snags. Much of the owl's habitat is characterized by steep slopes and canyons with rocky cliffs.

The vegetation in Mexican Spotted Owl habitat can be described as mixed-conifer forests with overstory trees such as white pine, Douglas fir, and ponderosa pine. Understory trees and shrubs include oaks, junipers, and maples. Mountain streams along canyon bot-toms, that support vegetation such as box elder, cottonwood, and walnut also provide important habitat.

Habitat use by Mexican Spotted Owls appears to vary according to activity. The owls roost and nest primarily in closed canopy forests with large trees, snags and many big logs, or in cliff crevaces adjacent to such vegetation. In a recent study in northern Arizona, all the owls monitored roosted primarily in virgin mixed-conifer forests. Foraging owls appear to use a wider variety of habitats, including mature mixed-conifer and ponderosa pine forests. Mature forests likely provide abundant habitat for foraging, nesting, and breeding activities of the owls, including ample perches and numerous downed logs. These habitat features, present in many foraging areas, may be important in providing homes and protective cover for the small mammals on which the owls prey.

Mexican Spotted Owls nest on stick platforms made by other birds (like hawks or ravens), in tree cavities, and, especially in Texas, on cliff ledges. Nest trees selected by owls are of moderate to large diameter and height for their species. Nest trees in Arizona are often located on moderate to steep slopes at elevations ranging from 6,000 to 8,000 feet. Most nest trees occur on northern or eastern facing slopes, indicating a preference for the cooler part of the habitat. Cliff nests in Texas are at 5,000 to 7,000 feet elevation in deep, cool canyons.

Life History

Limited information is available on the reproductive biology of the Mexican Spotted Owl. Generally, spotted owls lay a clutch of 1 to 3 white, unmarked eggs during March and April. The female incubates the eggs for about 30 days, and most eggs hatch by the end of May. Broods generally contain 1 or 2 owlets, although nests with 3 young have been found. Males provide food for the female and young until the owlets are about 2 weeks old. After this, the females assists in capturing food for the young. Reproductive success of Mexican Spotted Owls is widely variable between years. Variation in rainfall and thus prey species abundance are factors affecting reproductive success. In some years when food is scarce, the birds do not nest.

Female owls roost at the nest until 3 to 6 days before the owlets leave the nest. Most owlets fledge (leave the nest) in June, about 35 days after hatching. Owlets are unable to fly when they first leave the nest, but become increasingly better at flight throughout the summer. By early October, the young are fully independent.

Mexican Spotted Owls in northern Arizona were found to occupy areas (home ranges) varying in size from 702 to 2,386 acres. The combined home ranges occupied by pairs averaged 2,092 acres. Within this large home range, the owls appeared to have core areas or centers of activity that were consistently occupied. Core areas of individuals averaged 336 acres, and core areas for pairs averaged 398 acres. The owls tended to favor areas with steep slopes. Most owls remained within their summer home range throughout the year.

Mexican Spotted Owls eat a variety of mammals, birds, reptiles, and insects, although rodents make up the bulk of the diet. The owls hunt at night, capturing primarily rats (especially woodrats), mice, and pocket gophers. They hunt mainly by moving from tree to tree, pausing for a few seconds to minutes, watching and listening for prey. Spotted owls launch their attack at relatively short distances from their prey, so multi-layered forests with many potential perches are advantageous to owls hunting prey.

Goshawks and other hawks, along with Golden Eagles and Great-horned Owls, are potential predators of Mexican Spotted Owls. Although Great-horned Owls occur most often in flatter, more open habitat, there is some overlap between the two species. Young owls are particularly vulnerable as nestlings and after fledging.

Threats and Reasons for Decline

As an inhabitant of closed canopy, uneven-aged mature forests and canyons, the Mexican Spotted Owl is threatened by destruction and modification of its habitat. Harvest of old-growth timber stands, even-aged timber harvest systems, wildfires, and increased predation associated with habitat fragmentation are reasons for the owl's decline.

In Texas, sightings have occurred in or near Guadalupe Mountains National Park, and there is at least some evidence that the owls could exist in other mountainous areas of west Texas. With increased awareness of habitat requirements, public and private land managers in Texas can help to insure the continued existence of the Mexican Spotted Owl.

Recovery Efforts

Research is underway to answer questions concerning habitat use, home range, reproductive biology, and population dynamics of the Mexican Spotted Owl. Population monitoring will continue to provide information concerning the owl's status. Research is needed to better understand the structural features needed by Mexican Spotted Owls and how these features might be retained in managed forest stands. Efforts to inform land managers and the public about the habitat requirements and biology of the Mexican Spotted Owl are an important part of the recovery process.

How You Can Help

Landowners in the Guadalupe Mountains and other mountain ranges of west Texas can help by protecting old-growth forest habitat, particularly areas associated with steep slopes and moist, cool canyons. Landowners and park visitors are encouraged to report sightings of Mexican Spotted Owls to the Texas Parks and Wildlife Department, U.S. Fish and Wildlife Service, or the National Park Service. Be sure to record notes concerning appearance, behavior, habitat being used, and location. Take a photograph if possible, or record the owl's call. Observations should be made without disturbing the birds.

You can be involved in the conservation of Texas' nongame wildlife resources by supporting the Special Nongame and Endangered Species Conservation Fund. Special nongame stamps and decals are available at Texas Parks and Wildlife Department (TPWD) Field Offices, most State Parks, and the License Branch of TPWD headquarters in Austin. Part of the proceeds from the sale of these items are used for endangered species habitat management and public information. Conservation organizations also welcome your participation and support. Finally, you can encourage and support efforts to conserve old-growth forests of the southwestern United States.

For More Information Contact

Texas Parks and Wildlife Department
Endangered Resources Branch
4200 Smith School Road
Austin, Texas 78744
(512) 912-7011 or (800) 792-1112
or
U.S. Fish and Wildlife Service
Ecological Services Field Office
10711 Burnet Road, Suite 200
Austin, Texas 78758
(512) 490-0057

References

Ganey, J.L., and R.P. Balda. 1994. "Habitat Selection By Mexican Spotted Owls in Northern Arizona." *The Auk* 111(1):162-169.

Ganey, J.L., and R.P. Balda. 1989. "Home Range Characteristics of Spotted Owls in Northern Arizona." *J. Wildl. Manage.* 53:1159-1165.

Ganey, J.L. 1990. "Calling Behavior of Spotted Owls in Northern Arizona." *Condor* 92:485-490.

Gehlbach, F.R. (in press). "Biogeographic controls of avifaunal richness in isolated coniferous forests of the Borderlands." In: *Storm Over a Mountain Island: Conservation Biology and the Mount Graham Affair.* C. Istock and R. Hoffman, eds. University of Arizona Press, Tucson.

U.S. Fish and Wildlife Service. 1993. "Endangered and Threatened Wildlife and Plants; Final Rule to List the Mexican Spotted Owl as a Threatened Species." *Federal Register* 58(49):14248-14271.

Funds for the production of this leaflet were provided by the U.S. Fish and Wildlife Service, under Section 6 of the Endangered Species Act.

Kemp's Ridley Sea Turtle

Scientific Name: *Lepidochelys kempii*

Federal Status: Endangered, 12/2/70 • State Status: Endangered

Description

The Kemp's ridley is the smallest member of the sea turtle family Cheloniidae. Adults have a carapace (upper shell) length of up to 28 inches and can weigh 75 to 100 pounds. Juvenile Kemp's ridleys have broad, heart-shaped, keeled carapaces that are serrated along the trailing edge. In adults, the carapace is round and can be wider than it is long. Hatchlings and juveniles have a dark-charcoal

Kemp's Ridley turtle
© TPWD Bill Reaves

Kemp's Ridley hatchling
© TPWD Mary E. Candee

colored carapace, but as they age this color changes to olive-green or gray. The lower shell (plastron) is a light cream color. Adult males often have a concave plastron and long tails that extend beyond the rear of the carapace. Kemp's ridleys have large, somewhat triangular heads and powerful, massive jaws.

Distribution and Range

Kemp's ridley adults are generally only found in the Gulf of Mexico. Juveniles have been reported most commonly in the northern Gulf of Mexico between Texas and Florida. Juveniles are also found along the eastern seaboard of the United States as far north as Nova Scotia, Canada. Apparently, drifting hatchlings and juveniles from the western Gulf enter the eastern Gulf Loop Current and are carried by the Florida Current and the Gulf Stream up the eastern coast of the United States. Some researchers have speculated that these young turtles are "waifs" and possibly lost to the population. Other scientists have shown that young turtles along Florida's east coast move south as temperatures drop in the winter, and therefore have the capability to move back into the Gulf of Mexico. At present, the numbers returning from the north to breed in the Gulf of Mexico are unknown.

Habitat

Shallow waters are preferred habitat for juvenile and adult Kemp's ridleys. Satellite-tracked females migrating away from the nesting beach at Rancho Nuevo, Mexico remained in nearshore waters less than 165 feet deep, and spent less than an hour each day at the surface. It is thought that juvenile and adult Kemp's ridleys feed primarily near the bottom.

Hatchlings spend many months as surface drifters in the open ocean (pelagic phase). Recent evidence suggests that they may be found in surface water areas where drifting material, such as floating marine vegetation and debris, accumulate. These areas are called convergence zones or drift lines. Little is known regarding how long they drift, what they eat, or how they get back to the coast. Studies have shown that, after the pelagic phase,

body size of Kemp's ridley is related to water depth. For example, the smallest juveniles are found in shallow waters of bays or lagoons, often foraging in less than 3 feet of water, whereas larger juveniles and adults are found in deeper water.

Juvenile Kemp's ridleys studied in the Chesapeake Bay area used the estuary for summer feeding. They occupied shallow foraging areas over extensive seagrass beds

and fed mostly on blue crabs. In Texas, Kemp's ridley and loggerhead sea turtles are thought to partition food resources: the ridleys forage on relatively fast blue and spotted crabs, whereas the loggerheads feed on seapens and slow-moving crabs.

The nesting beach at Rancho Nuevo, in the Mexican State of Tamaulipas, is the primary land habitat (used only for nesting) for Kemp's ridley. This remote stretch of beach along the Gulf of Mexico is located about 100 miles north of Tampico, Mexico. It is the only known major nesting beach for this species in the world. No substantial nesting has ever been reported at any other beach.

Life History

The diet of juvenile and adult Kemp's ridley turtles consists primarily of crabs, shrimp, snails, bivalves, sea urchins, jellyfish, sea stars, fish, and occasionally marine plants. Crabs are a preferred food and several species are eaten. In some regions, the blue crab is the most common food item. Although feeding habits of hatchlings have not been observed in the wild, they are presumed to eat swimming and floating animal matter located at or near the surface of the open Gulf of Mexico and Atlantic Ocean.

Reproduction in Kemp's ridley differs from that of other sea turtles in four important ways. First, most female Kemp's ridleys, along with their sister species Olive ridleys (*Lepidochelys olivacea*), arrive at nesting beaches in large groups. These nesting events are called "arribazones." Many females gather in the waters near the nesting beach and emerge to nest simultaneously over a period of several hours or days. Second, Kemp's ridleys nest mainly during the daytime, whereas other sea turtles usually nest at night. Third, almost all nesting occurs on one stretch of beach, which is unique for sea turtles. Occasionally, Kemp's ridleys nest along the Texas coast. There are also records of four single recent nests in Florida, North Carolina, and South Carolina; and a small colony between Tuxpan and Tecolutla, Veracruz. Fourth, Kemp's ridley females nest every 1 to 2 years, whereas other sea turtles nest about every 2 to 3 years.

During the breeding season, male and female Kemp's ridleys migrate toward the nesting beach. Courtship and mating occur in nearby offshore waters several weeks prior to and during the nesting period. Nesting usually occurs during April, May, and June, although it can occur in July and August if cool spring weather delays the onset of the reproductive period.

A well-defined and elevated dune area, above the tidal zone, is preferred for nesting. The female digs a hole in the sand, deposits her eggs, and returns to the sea, a process which takes about 45 minutes. Females generally deposit one to three clutches per season, laying an average of about 100 soft, leathery, white eggs per clutch. After about 50 to 55 days of incubation in the sand, the eggs hatch. The temperature of the incubating eggs during the middle third of the incubation period determines the gender of the developing embryo. Warmer temperatures produce primarily females and colder temperatures primarily males.

To escape a variety of land predators, hatchlings move quickly from the beach through the surf zone and into open waters of the Gulf of Mexico. Scientists think the baby turtles may remember or "imprint" on the particular smell, chemical make-up, or magnetic location of the beach where they hatched. Other predators await them in the water. At sexual maturity, adults return to the shallow waters of the western Gulf of Mexico, the females returning to nest at the same beach where they hatched. Although it is not known how many years wild Kemp's ridleys require to reach sexual maturity, it may be as long as 10 to 20 years.

Threats and Reasons for Decline

The Kemp's ridley population crash that occurred between 1947 and the early 1970's was probably a result of the combination of intensive annual harvest of eggs and mortality of juveniles and adults in shrimp trawl nets.

Kemp's ridley eggs were (and still are in many places) considered a delicacy. Between about 1947 and 1966 people dug up truckloads of eggs and sold them in the towns and cities of Texas and Mexico. Since many of the eggs were either taken by people or eaten by predators, there was a drastic decline in the turtle population. Also, prior to its being listed as endangered by the U.S. Fish and Wildlife Service in 1970, Kemp's ridleys, along with green and loggerhead turtles, were taken for meat by commercial fishermen in the northern and northeastern Gulf of Mexico. Human consumption of turtle eggs and meat has declined with national and international protection. Although nesting turtles and nests

Nesting female
© NPS D. J. Shaver

Marine debris ingested by Kemp's Ridley turtle
© NPS R. W. Wilder

are protected at Rancho Nuevo, the harvest of eggs and slaughter of animals continue to be potential problems in other areas.

Because the Kemp's ridley sea turtle is a shallow water inhabitant, it is frequently caught in shrimp trawl nets that may drown or exhaust the turtle. There is strong evidence that shrimp trawling is the primary agent for sea turtle mortality today. The National Marine Fisheries Service estimated that, prior to the 1990 law requiring Turtle Excluder Devices (TEDs), about 12,000 sea turtles drowned each year in nets. The National Research Council's Committee on Sea Turtle Conservation estimated in 1990 that 86% of the human caused deaths of juvenile and adult loggerheads and Kemp's ridleys resulted from shrimp trawling.

Trash discarded at sea is another serious problem facing this species and other marine animals. Some of this debris never makes it to shore because it is eaten by fishes, sea turtles, birds, and marine mammals that mistake it for food. Postmortem examinations of sea turtles found stranded on the south Texas coast from 1986 through 1988 revealed 54% (60 of

Releasing "headstarted" Kemp's Ridley turtles
© TPWD Mario Gonzalez

National Park Service biologists with a nesting Kemp's Ridley turtle
© NPS P. Eubank

the 111 examined) of the sea turtles had eaten some type of marine debris. Plastic materials were most frequently ingested, and included pieces of plastic bags, styrofoam, plastic pellets, balloons, rope, and fishing line. Non-plastic debris such as glass, tar, and aluminum foil were also ingested by the sea turtles examined. Much of this debris comes from offshore oil rigs, cargo ships, commercial and recreational fishing boats, research vessels, naval ships, and other vessels operating in the Gulf of Mexico. Laws enacted during the late-1980's

prohibit the disposal of all types of plastics, and regulates the distance from shore that non-plastic debris may be discarded. However, enforcement of these laws is difficult over vast areas of water. In addition to trash, pollution from heavy spills of oil or waste products pose additional threats.

Other sources of human-caused mortality include dredging, entanglement in drift and gill nets, collisions with boats, explosives used to remove oil rigs, and entrapment in coastal power plant intake pipes. These sources account for an estimated 5 to 65 Kemp's ridley deaths per year.

Less than 50 years ago, Kemp's ridley was a very abundant sea turtle in the Gulf of Mexico. The most reliable measure of Kemp's ridley population size has been the annual count of adult nesting females at Rancho Nuevo. A film taken by a Mexican businessman in 1947, and discovered by scientists in 1961, shows an estimated 40,000 females nesting in one day on the single known nesting beach on the northeastern coast of Mexico. Today, with fewer than 1,000 adult females, all conservation efforts are desperately needed.

Recovery Efforts

Since the principal nesting beach is in Mexico, the continued, long-term cooperation of two nations is necessary to recover the species. A joint United States-Mexican management program is underway which includes nesting beach protection and incubation of eggs. The U.S. Fish and Wildlife Service has provided assistance at the Rancho Nuevo nesting beach since 1978. Continued assistance to Mexico is needed to ensure long-term protection of the major nesting beach, including protection of adult turtles and enhanced production and survival of hatchlings. Various conservation organizations support the joint U.S.-Mexican efforts to patrol the nesting beaches. Some produce educational materials concerning turtle conservation for American and Mexican children. It is hoped that through education of children, the conservation message will be spread throughout local communities. In the United States, the U.S. Fish and Wildlife Service, National

Marine Fisheries Service, National Park Service, and Sea Grant conduct programs to educate the public about sea turtle conservation.

Research is underway to fill in gaps in knowledge that will result in better management of these sea turtles. Research priorities include determining distribution and habitat use for all life stages, migration routes and foraging areas of adults, critical mating and reproductive behaviors and physiology, and survivorship of hatchlings.

Regulations went into effect in the United States in 1990 and in Mexico in 1993 which require commercial trawlers to install Turtle Excluder Devices (TEDs) on their boats. This device guides turtles and other large objects out of the net through a trap door. Hopefully, widespread use of these devices in the Gulf of Mexico by the shrimp fleets of the United States and Mexico will substantially reduce mortality associated with net entanglement.

Finally, during each summer from 1978 to 1988, approximately 2000 Kemp's ridley eggs were shipped to Padre Island National Seashore from Rancho Nuevo, Mexico in an experimental attempt to establish a secondary breeding colony of this species through "artificial imprinting." Eggs were incubated by the National Park Service at Padre Island National Seashore. Hatchlings that emerged from these eggs were transferred to the National Marine Fisheries Laboratory in Galveston and held for 9 to 11 months before being released into the Gulf of Mexico. It was hoped that the larger size of the turtles after "headstarting" would increase survival in the wild, and that imprinting on Padre Island beaches would establish a nesting colony at some time in the future. Entry of headstarted turtles into the nesting population has not yet been documented. However, it is unknown how many survived after release and if any have reached sexual maturity. We do know that some headstarted turtles are surviving, since about 14% of live caught turtles on the Texas coast were headstarted. Attempts to search for nesting of these turtles at Padre Island and Rancho Nuevo will continue. Now in Phase II, the Kemp's ridley headstart project is looking for evidence that headstarted turtles are reproducing. The project has produced useful information on sea turtle behavior, husbandry, and physiology. However, until the results of this experiment are better known, it is not yet considered to be a long-term management technique for species recovery.

How You Can Help

Visit Padre Island National Seashore or the Texas State Aquarium in Corpus Christi to learn more about sea turtles. You can also contact the National Marine Fisheries Service office in Galveston (409-766-3500) or the Texas A&M Marine Advisory Service in Galveston (409-762-9800).

If you see a sea turtle or its nest on the beach, do not disturb it. Report beach sightings of live or dead turtles to the National Marine Fisheries Service (beeper no. 409-943-1531 for the upper coast), the University of Texas Marine Science Institute (512-749-6720 for Mustang Island), Padre Island National Seashore (512-949-8173 for the lower coast), your local game warden, Extension Service representative, or the Texas Parks and Wildlife Department (512-993-4492 in Corpus Christi or 800-792-1112 in Austin). Nesting turtles and nests should be reported immediately so that they can be protected and documented as quickly as possible.

Do not discard trash of any type, especially plastics, in the bays or Gulf. If you catch a sea turtle on a hook and line, contact one of the agencies listed above and wait for a representative to pick up the turtle. If you can't call or wait, remove the hook if you can, or cut the line as close to the hook as possible, since ingested fishing line and hooks are often deadly to sea turtles.

Commercial fisherman can contact the National Marine Fisheries Service or the Texas A&M Marine Advisory Service for technical assistance with design and use of TEDs.

For More Information Contact

Texas Parks and Wildlife Department
Endangered Resources Branch
4200 Smith School Road
Austin, Texas 78744
(512) 912-7011 or (800) 792-1112
        or
U.S. Fish and Wildlife Service
Ecological Services Field Office
10711 Burnet Road, Suite 200
Austin, Texas 78758
(512) 490-0057
        or
U.S. Fish and Wildlife Service
Corpus Christi Field Office
CCSU, Campus Box 338
Corpus Christi, Texas 78412
(512) 994-9005

Nesting habitat
© TPWD Glen Mills

References

Conant, R. 1975. *A Field Guide to Reptiles and Amphibians of Eastern and Central North America*. Houghton Mifflin Co., Boston.

Dean, R., and D.W. Steinbach. 1981. *Endangered Marine Turtles of the Gulf Coast*. Texas Agri. Extension Service Pub. L-1867.

Marquez-M., R. 1990. *An Annotated and Illustrated Catalogue of Sea Turtle Species Known To Date*. FAO Fisheries Synopsis Vol. 11, No. 125. FAO, Rome. 81 pp.

National Research Council. 1990. *Decline of the Sea Turtles, Causes and Prevention*. National Academy Press, Washington, D.C. 259 pp.

U.S. Fish and Wildlife Service. 1980. *Selected Vertebrate Endangered Species of the Seacoast of United States - Kemp's (Atlantic) Ridley Sea Turtle*. FWS/OBS-80/01.30. Gainesville, FL. 9 pp.

U.S. Fish and Wildlife Service and National Marine Fisheries Service. 1992. *Recovery Plan for the Kemp's Ridley Sea Turtle (*Lepidochelys kempii*)*. National Marine Fisheries Service, St. Petersburg, Florida.

Funds for the production of this leaflet were provided by the U.S. Fish and Wildlife Service, under Section 6 of the Endangered Species Act.

Concho Water Snake

Scientific Name: *Nerodia paucimaculata*

Federal Status: Threatened, 9/3/86 State Status: Endangered

Description

The Concho Water Snake is small compared to most other water snakes, with adults rarely exceeding 3 feet in total length. This nonvenomous snake has four rows of alternating dark brown spots or blotches on its back, two rows on each side. The coloration on its back is similar to a checkerboard of dark brown spots on a gray, brown, or reddish-brown color. The Concho Water Snake has a light pinkish or orange belly that is unmarked or has somewhat indistinct spots along the sides.

Concho Water Snake
© TPWD Martin Whiting

Two other water snakes occur within the range of the Concho Water Snake. Both the Diamond-back Water Snake (*Nerodia rhombifer rhombifer*) and the Blotched Water Snake (*Nerodia erythrogaster transversa*) have dark markings on the back. However, adult Diamondback and Blotched Water Snakes may be distinguished from Concho Water Snakes by their larger size. The Diamondback Water Snake has a distinct black chain-like pattern on its back. The Blotched Water Snake has three rows of large squarish blotches on the back, which are especially prominent in juveniles. As Blotched Water Snakes age, they become darker in color and may appear to lack markings.

The cottonmouth is another large aquatic snake that can be confused with the Concho Water Snake. The cottonmouth, a poisonous snake, is usually uniformly black or dark brown with little or no trace of a pattern. Cottonmouths vibrate their tails when excited, whereas water snakes do not. Also, an aroused cottonmouth will often stand its ground, throw its head upward and backward, and hold its mouth wide open, revealing a white "cotton-like" interior.

Distribution

Historically, the Concho Water Snake occurred over about 276 river miles of the Colorado and Concho Rivers in central Texas. The snake was first collected from the South Concho River and Dove Creek, which are tributaries to the Concho River west of San Angelo, Texas. When the subspecies was described in 1961, these records and one other on the Colorado River south of Robert Lee in Coke County were the only known localities for this snake. The Concho Water Snake is endemic to Texas, which means it lives nowhere else in the world. It has one of the smallest distributions of any North American snake.

The Concho Water Snake may once have been more widely distributed, but the E.V. Spence Reservoir upstream and Lake Buchanan downstream have inundated many miles of river habitat at both ends of the current range. Scientists have estimated the historic range of the subspecies based on museum records, unpublished records, and county records supported by specimens. The probable historic range of this snake is estimated to include, at a minimum, the Colorado River from Spence Reservoir downstream to the vicinity of Lake Buchanan, Elm, Bluff, and Coyote Creeks (Runnels County), and the entire Concho River (Tom Green and Concho Counties) and its headwater tributaries, Dove Creek, Spring Creek, and the South Concho River (Irion and Tom Green Counties).

Today, the Concho Water Snake occupies a restricted geographic range in the Concho and Colorado River Basins. The current distribution includes relatively continuous occupation of riverine habitat of the Colorado River below the town of Bronte (Coke County), of Elm, Coyote, and Bluff creeks below Winters (Runnels County), and of the Concho River from San Angelo (Tom Green County) downstream to its confluence with the Colorado River, and then downstream to the FM 45 bridge over the Colorado River (Mills and San Saba Counties). This is a distance of about 233 river-miles.

Apparently isolated lake populations have been found in E.V. Spence Reservoir and Ballinger Municipal

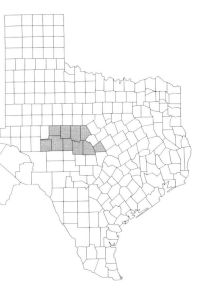

Lake (formerly Lake Moonen). Concho Water Snakes have also been found at a number of sites in O.H. Ivie Reservoir, and there are indications that this population is reproducing. Scattered river populations occur along the Colorado River above Lake Buchanan, near the towns of Regency, Harmony Ridge, Adams, and Bend. Recently, Concho Water Snakes have been found at all six artificial riffles (fast-flowing, shallow water over a rocky bottom) constructed in 1989 in the 17-mile stretch of the Colorado River between the Robert Lee Dam and Bronte.

Although the Concho River has been dammed and channelized within the City of San Angelo, a population of Concho Water Snakes persists just below the Bell Street bridge. They have also been found about 4 river-miles downstream from Bell Street Dam. From this point they are present in all suitable habitat to the confluence with Ivie Reservoir, a distance of about 43 river-miles.

Habitat

Optimal habitat for the Concho Water Snake consists of free-flowing streams over rocky substrates, abundant rock debris and crevices for shelter, and shallow riffles. Periodic scouring by floods is important in providing relatively sediment free rock rubble and open banks.

Riffles, considered critical to juvenile survival, are characterized by shallow, fast-flowing water connecting deeper areas of quiet water. Riffles begin when the upper pool overflows at a change in slope and forms rapids. They end when the rapids enter the next downstream pool. Riffles often contain bars, shoals, or islands separated by flowing water.

Limestone bedrock shelves in and along the stream channel seem to support the largest snake populations. The snakes forage and seek cover among the numerous splits, crevices, cracks, and jumbled stream cobble of shelf rock. Other rock, such as limestone boulders, can also provide suitable habitat.

Juvenile snakes are generally restricted to rocky riffles. Neonates (newborn snakes) are most often found in gravel bars or along the shoreline in areas where rocks range in size from small cobbles to small boulders. However, some habitats with thriving populations lack typical gravel bars. In these areas, juveniles use boulders and shelf rock for cover. During their second year, snakes begin to use larger rocks, usually medium to large boulders.

Mature snakes use a much wider range of habitats than juveniles. Although adults forage in riffles, they are known to use a variety of cover sites for resting, including exposed bedrock, thick herbaceous vegetation, debris piles, and crayfish burrows. During the latter stages of gestation, gravid females occupy dense patches of vegetation and brush piles.

In lake habitats, Concho Water Snakes occupy areas of broken rock along the shoreline. Although they seem to prefer the shallower areas, they are occasionally found on steeper shorelines where rock is present. As in river habitats, first-year snakes use smaller rocks for cover, while mature snakes use medium to large rocks. When available, dead shrubs and trees killed by fluctuating water levels are used as basking sites by juveniles and adults. At Spence Reservoir, where there are almost no dead trees or shrubs, snakes bask on the ground among the protection of rocks.

Bank and shoreline vegetation is important in providing cover and basking sites for Concho Water Snakes. Although the type of vegetation does not appear to be important, its use depends on vegetation density and orientation. For example, pregnant females seek basking sites protected by thick vegetation. Larger trees and shrubs, such as pecan, cedar elm, and willow, with limbs that hang over water, provide basking sites for juveniles and adults. Common bank and shoreline vegetation used for cover and basking sites include switchgrass, spiny aster, greenbriar, poison ivy, willow, salt cedar, button bush, hackberry, pecan, cedar elm, and mesquite.

Concho Water Snakes hibernate during the winter, either singly or in small groups. Adults use a variety of sites for hibernation, including crayfish burrows, rock ledges, debris piles, and concrete low water crossings. These sites are usually within 20 feet of the water. Newborn snakes have been found hibernating in areas of loose rock and moist soil.

Life History

Concho Water Snakes are active primarily from March through October. Adult activity gradually decreases during June and remains low until mid-September. Activity levels increase again during late September and October. The snakes enter the hibernation site during late October, although they are occasionally seen on warm winter days basking outside the hibernacula. Newborn Concho Water Snakes, born in August and September, are commonly found under rocks in late summer and early fall. In the heat of the summer, Concho

Concho Water Snake river habitat
© USFWS Pat Connor

Habitat along the shoreline of Spence Reservoir
© UWFWS Alisa Shull

Water Snakes are active primarily in the early morning and evening until about 9 p.m.

Research indicates that adult males move an average of 141 to 325 ft/day. Pregnant females move less, averaging 62 to 131 ft/day, with distances decreasing as parturition approaches, and increasing again after the young are born. Linear distances of river habitat occupied by individual snakes range from 689 to 1,542 feet.

Long range movements of 3.1 and 4.5 miles have been recorded for juvenile snakes dispersing from their birthplace. In one instance, a snake moved 12 river-miles over a four-year period.

The diet of the Concho Water Snake is composed almost entirely of fish. In river habitats, minnows are most often consumed. Neonates (newborn snakes) feed

Habitat on the Concho River
© USFWS Alisa Shull

Artificial riffle habitat
© USFWS Pat Connor

almost exclusively on minnows, particularly the red shiner and bullhead minnow. Their diet becomes more varied as their body size increases. In addition to minnows, large snakes consume mosquitofish, channel catfish, flathead catfish, gizzard shad, and several species of sunfish. The bigscale logperch was found to be the dominant prey in the diet of neonates and juveniles in Ballinger Municipal Lake.

Concho Water Snakes catch prey by remaining stationary near fish concentrations or by actively searching under and around rocks in riffles. Juveniles are most often seen using the "sit-and-wait" strategy.

Mating occurs predominantly in April and early May, and sometimes again in October. Litter sizes average 10 embryos per female, and births occur from late July through September. As females increase in size, their litter size also increases.

Concho Water Snakes grow rapidly and mature early, at about 11 to 12 months of age. Females produce their first litters at 2 or 3 years of age. Females grow more rapidly and mature at larger sizes than males, with adult females reaching a length on average 30% greater than adult males. Differences in growth rates and mature

sizes have been observed between populations, suggesting differences in food availability.

Survivorship of Concho Water Snakes is directly related to age. Only about 20% of Concho Water Snakes survive their first year. The adult survival rate is estimated to be about 50 percent. Population studies have shown that most adults are less than 4 years old, and only one snake in 100 exceeds 5 years of age. Predation is considered to be a significant source of mortality. Major natural predators include kingsnakes, Coachwhip Snakes, racers, Raccoons, Great Blue Herons, and various hawks and owls.

Threats and Reasons for Decline

Habitat loss and degradation has been identified as the greatest general threat to Concho Water Snake populations. Reservoir construction has flooded many miles of former stream habitat above the dams. Below the dams, restriction of streamflow and prevention of floodwater scouring have resulted in siltation of rocky streambeds, encroaching vegetation, and loss of riffle habitat required by young snakes. Loss of adequate instream flow due to natural and/or man-made conditions is also a concern.

Pollution and degradation of water quality in the Concho and Colorado Rivers or their tributaries is another potential threat in certain portions of the snake's range. Non-point source pollution in the vicinity of San Angelo, petroleum production, refining, and transportation in the watershed, treated sewage disposal, pesticide use, and feedlot activities have been identified as water quality concerns that could affect habitat. These same water quality issues affect municipal water supplies and recreational use of lakes and rivers. Keeping the water clean benefits people as well as the Concho Water Snake and other wildlife.

Finally, fragmentation and isolation of populations following various habitat alterations remain a concern. The full effects of recent habitat modifications and natural events are unknown.

Recovery Efforts

Several ongoing and recently completed studies are leading to a better understanding of the habitat

requirements, life history, and genetic structure of Concho Water Snake populations. Future studies concerning the management of Ivie Reservoir are planned. Although the number of Concho Water Snakes killed by people is negligible, conservation education that provides information and raises public awareness is also important.

Since 1987, the Colorado River Municipal Water District (CRMWD) has monitored Concho Water Snake populations at 15 sites three times each year. Physical aspects of the habitat are also recorded and changes noted. Fish populations are surveyed at the monitoring sites each fall. In addition, potential habitat along the shoreline of Ivie Reservoir has been characterized, and researchers are documenting the reservoir's Concho Water Snake distribution.

The CRMWD is releasing water from both Spence and Ivie Reservoirs according to a schedule which scientists hope will maintain suitable habitat for the Concho Water Snake. These water releases include both continuous daily flows and flushing flows designed to maintain stream channels.

The Conservation Reserve Program (CRP) of the U.S. Department of Agriculture provides incentives to set aside highly erodible lands and establishing these areas to perennial native vegetation. The program benefits the Concho Water Snake by reducing soil erosion and contributing to maintenance of high quality surface waters. Enrollment in the CRP of the primary areas contributing to sedimentation in the watershed may significantly reduce the threat of sedimentation of riffle habitat.

Finally, in an effort to restore former habitat heavily degraded by siltation and vegetation encroachment, six artificial riffles were built in 1989 in an unoccupied stretch of the Colorado River below Spence Reservoir. Though this area once contained excellent habitat and dense populations of Concho Water Snakes, none were found in surveys done in the late 1980's. In 1991, four of the artificial riffles were found to be occupied by Concho Water Snakes, and by 1992, all six were occupied. Future restoration efforts will likely involve construction of more riffles in river habitat. The use of various man-made structures by Concho Water Snakes indicates high potential for success with habitat enhancement.

The Concho Water Snake controversy provides a good example of an effective compromise between human resource needs and endangered species management; objectives which are not necessarily mutually exclusive. Efforts by numerous individuals representing various universities and local, state, and federal agencies, serve as a model of cooperation and compromise. The future of the Concho Water Snake is not as bleak as once thought. If habitat conditions remain stable and adequate instream flows are maintained, the Concho Water Snake will remain a part of the diversity of Texas for many years to come.

Where To See Concho Water Snakes

Concho Water Snakes can sometimes be found along rocky shorelines of Ivie and Spence Reservoirs and Ballinger Municipal Lake. They may also be seen on the Concho and Colorado Rivers. If you see one of these snakes, remember that they are protected by federal and state laws. Do not disturb them or the surrounding area in any way.

How You Can Help

You can encourage and support private landowners who are managing their land to protect the rivers, streams, and lakes that serve as habitat for the Concho Water Snake. If you are a landowner along one of the rivers or streams that serve as habitat, we encourage you to learn about the habitat requirements of the Concho Water Snake and other species that depend on these waterways. Landowners can help by maintaining clear free-flowing streams over rocks, rock debris and crevices for shelter, shallow riffle areas, and basking sites, and by being careful with pesticides and other potential pollutants. Alternatives such as integrated pest management, organic gardening, and the use and management of native plants can help reduce reliance on chemicals and can often save money.

Do what you can as an individual to conserve water, particularly during drought periods. In the home, you can save water by installing fixtures, appliances, and toilets designed to use less water, repairing leaky faucets, and turning off the tap while brushing teeth or doing dishes. Landscaping with native, drought tolerant plants, watering lawns in the early morning or evening to reduce evaporation, and installing a rainwater collection system for your home are other effective ways to conserve water. By protecting the natural beauty, flow, and water quality of the Colorado and Concho Rivers, landowners can play a role in assuring that future generations of Texans have the chance to enjoy the rich diversity of life these rivers support.

If you are a fisherman, boater, or enjoy swimming in the Concho or Colorado Rivers and their tributaries, remember that your actions, especially when multiplied by thousands of other recreational users, can have an immense impact on the rivers. Responsible recreational use should include proper disposal of trash and other potential pollutants, respect for private property rights, preventing harm to plants and wildlife, and generally keeping human impacts to a minimum.

Finally, you can be involved in the conservation of Texas' nongame wildlife resources by supporting the Special Nongame and Endangered Species Conservation Fund. Special nongame stamps are available at

Concho Water Snake moving over rocky streambed
© TPWD Martin Whiting

Texas Parks and Wildlife Department (TPWD) field offices, most state parks, and the License Branch of TPWD headquarters in Austin. Contributions to this fund help TPWD conduct research, manage habitat and develop informational materials and programs for the benefit of nongame and endangered wildlife. Conservation Passports, available from Texas Parks and Wildlife, are valid for one year and allow unlimited access to most State Parks, State Natural Areas, and Wildlife Management Areas. Conservation organizations in Texas also welcome your participation and support.

For More Information Contact

Texas Parks and Wildlife Department
Endangered Resources Branch
4200 Smith School Road
Austin, Texas 78744
(512) 912-7011 or (800) 792-1112
or
U.S. Fish and Wildlife Service
Ecological Services Field Office
10711 Burnet Road, Suite 200
Austin, Texas 78758
(512) 490-0057

References

Dixon, J.R. 1987. *Amphibians and Reptiles of Texas*. Texas A&M University Press, College Station. 434 pp.

Greene, B.D. 1993. *Life History and Ecology of the Concho Water*, Nerodia harteri paucimaculata. Unpublished Ph.D. dissertation. Texas A&M University. 128 pp.

Scott, Jr., N.J., T.C. Maxwell, O.W. Thornton, Jr., L.A. Fitzgerald, and J.W. Flury. 1989. "Distribution, Habitat, and Future of Harter's Water Snake, *Nerodia harteri*, in Texas." *Journal of Herpetology* 23:373-389.

U.S. Fish and Wildlife Service. 1993. *Concho Water Snake Recovery Plan*. Albuquerque, New Mexico. 66 pp.

Whiting, M.J. 1993. *Population Ecology of the Concho Water Snake*, Nerodia harteri paucimaculata, *in artificial habitats*. Unpublished M.S. thesis. Texas A&M University. 137 pp.

Funds for the production of this leaflet were provided by the U.S. Fish and Wildlife Service, under Section 6 of the Endangered Species Act.

Edwards Aquifer Species

Scientific Name: San Marcos Salamander – *Eurycea nana*, Texas Blind Salamander – *Eurycea rathbuni*, San Marcos Gambusia – *Gambusia georgei*, Foundatin Darter – *Etheostoma fonticola*

Federal Status: Endangered except for the San Marcos Salamander, which is listed as Threatened •
State Status: Endangered except for the San Marcos Salamander, which is listed as Threatened

San Marcos Salamander
© Danal Tern

Texas Blind Salamander
© Glenn Longley

San Marcos Gambusias
© Bob Edwards

Fountain Darters
© Glenn Longley

Description of Species, Habitats and Life History

The **San Marcos Salamander** is small and slender, with a total length of about 2.5 inches. It is uniformly light brown to golden brown, with small yellow flecks along each side of the back. The underside of its body is yellowish-white. A member of the brook salamander group, the San Marcos Salamander has external gills, which are retained throughout life. It has relatively short slender legs, with four toes on the fore feet and five on the hind feet. It has a slender tail with a well developed dorsal or top fin.

The San Marcos Salamander occurs only in Spring Lake and an adjacent downstream portion of the upper San Marcos River. They are often found in spring areas with a substrate of sand and gravel interspersed with large limestone boulders. These boulders in shallow water support a lush growth of aquatic moss. Interspersed with the moss and covering the shallow sandy substrate are thick mats of coarse filamentous blue-green algae. The dark reddish-brown color of this algae almost perfectly matches the dark dorsal color of the San Marcos salamander. Vegetative cover is important for protection and for providing habitat for living organisms that serve as food for the salamander. This species does not inhabit areas with a sandy bottom devoid of vegetation, nor do they occur where the bottom is muddy, whether or not vegetation is present. Clean, clear, flowing water of constant temperature is required for suitable habitat.

San Marcos Salamanders feed on amphipods (tiny aquatic crustaceans), aquatic insects, and small aquatic snails. Breeding is thought to occur throughout the year with a possible peak in May and June.

The **Texas Blind Salamander** occurs only in the subterranean waters of the Edwards Aquifer near San Marcos, Texas. Because it is adapted to living in a subterranean environment, it lacks eyes and has little skin pigment. It is all white, with blood-red external gills and toothpick-like legs. The head and snout of this salamander are strongly flattened, with two small

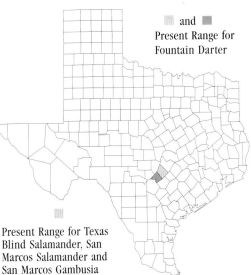

and ▓
Present Range for
Fountain Darter

Present Range for Texas
Blind Salamander, San
Marcos Salamander and
San Marcos Gambusia

black dots representing vestigial eyes beneath the skin. Its total length is about 5 inches.

This salamander is entirely aquatic, and lives in the water-filled caverns in the San Marcos Pool of the Edwards Aquifer. It requires clean water of relatively constant temperature.

The Texas Blind Salamander feeds on a variety of small subterranean aquatic organisms, including tiny snails, amphipods, and shrimp. When feeding, the salamanders probe the bottom using lateral movements of the head. When anything living is encountered, the mouth quickly opens and the food item is immediately sucked into the mouth. Numerous sharp teeth prevent the prey from escaping. It is thought that sensitivity to water vibrations also helps these salamanders locate food.

Although courtship and reproductive behavior have been observed and recorded for captive specimens, little information exists regarding reproduction of the Texas Blind Salamander in its natural habitat. Females with eggs and juveniles have been observed throughout the year, so it is thought that reproduction occurs year-round.

One of the rarest animals of the San Marcos River, and one which may already be extinct, is the **San Marcos Gambusia**. Last collected in the wild in 1983, this fish is a member of a genus having more than 30 species of livebearing freshwater fishes. It is a small fish, about 1 inch in length, known only from the San Marcos River. This species is plainly marked and similar in appearance to the mosquitofish (*Gambusia affinis*). It has a prominant dark stripe along the upper edges of the dorsal fin. The unpaired fins tend to be yellow or yellowish-orange. A bluish sheen is evident near the head, especially in more darkly pigmented adult females. The anal fin of *Gambusia* males is modified into a tube-like structure called a gonopodium. The gonopodium is used to transfer sperm from the male to the female.

The San Marcos Gambusia prefers shallow, quiet waters adjacent to sections of flowing water. Constant water temperature is also very important. This fish prefers a muddy, but not silted, bottom. Partial shade from bridges or overhanging vegetation also seems to be an important habitat factor.

There is little information on the food habits or reproduction of this species. It is thought that insect larvae and other invertebrates comprise most of the diet.

The **Fountain Darter** is a small fish, usually about 1-2 inches in length, found only in the San Marcos and Comal River headwaters. It is reddish-brown with fine specks in the dorsal region. A series of horizontal stitch-like dark lines occur along the middle of the sides, forming an interrupted lateral streak. There are three small dark spots on the base of the tail, and one on the opercle (flap covering the gills). Dark bars appear in front of, below, and behind the eye. The lower half of the dorsal fin is black, above this is a broad red band, and above this the fin is edged in black.

The Fountain Darter prefers vegetated stream-floor habitats with a constant water temperature. The fish are most often found in mats of filamentous green algae and other aquatic plants. They are occasionally found in areas lacking vegetation. Young Fountain Darters are found in heavily vegetated, backwater areas of the San Marcos and Comal Rivers where there are low water velocities. Adults occur in all suitable habitats, including riffles.

Fountain Darters feed on copepods (tiny aquatic crustaceans) and mayfly larvae. They feed primarily during the day, and show selective feeding behavior. Observations suggest that darters feed on small moving aquatic animals, while ignoring immobile ones.

Threats and Reasons for Decline

Both the San Marcos and Comal Rivers originate from springs fed by the Edwards Aquifer. Because the flow of these springs is intimately tied to water usage over the entire Edwards Aquifer region, human population growth and increased use of groundwater resources throughout the region are likely to decrease spring flow. Relatively constant water temperatures and flows are requirements for these listed species. The danger of reduced spring flow is the most serious threat to the continued existence of the San Marcos and Comal Rivers and their endemic plants and animals.

The effects of periodic drought coupled with increased groundwater use is a serious threat. For example, a severe drought from 1950-1956 greatly reduced the aquifer level and spring discharges.

San Marcos River
© TPWD Leroy Williamson

San Marcos River
© Leroy Williamson

During 1956, Comal Springs ceased to flow for five months. Less severe droughts in 1984 and 1990 resulted in minimum daily flows at Comal Springs of 24 cfs (cubic feet per second) and 46 cfs, respectively, compared to the mean spring flow discharge (1933-1990) of 293 cfs.

Other threats associated with increased urbanization include increased flooding and erosion, pollution, siltation, and storm water runoff. All of these factors can adversely affect the listed species and their habitats. Also, exotic species pose a threat because they may destroy aquatic vegetation, prey on these endangered animals, or compete with them for resources.

Urban development along the San Marcos River
© TPWD Leroy Williamson

River pollution
© TPWD Bill Reaves

Sampling Fountain Darters in the Comal River
© TPWD

Recovery Efforts

Monitoring existing populations and habitats is important in understanding the factors affecting the listed species and their habitats. Basic biological research addressing habitat requirements and aspects of life history, such as food habits, reproduction, diseases and parasites, and predation and competition, is currently underway to better understand the survival needs of each species.

The U.S. Fish and Wildlife Service, Texas Parks and Wildlife Department and other cooperators are engaged in a multi-year study to assess spring flow and stream flow needs of the threatened and endangered species of the Comal and San Marcos springs ecosystems. The U.S. Fish and Wildlife Service is also working with the City of New Braunfels to insure that the management of city properties such as parks is compatible with the conservation of the Comal Springs/River Ecosystem and the endangered species it supports.

Finally, providing information to the public regarding protection of the San Marcos and Comal River ecosystems, and the unique plant and animal species dependent on them, also is vital to the recovery of the listed species.

How You Can Help

Support conservation efforts to protect the San Marcos and Comal River ecosystems and their associated native species. Conservation of these spring ecosystems will result in the continued ability to use water in areas downstream from their habitats. Stay informed about conservation issues relating to the quality and quantity of groundwater and surface water in the Edwards Aquifer region. Do your part to conserve water, prevent pollution and introduction of exotic species, and preserve streambed vegetation so that Texans can continue to enjoy the clean, flowing waters and diversity of plant and animal life of the San Marcos and Comal River ecosystems.

For More Information Contact

Texas Parks and Wildlife Department
Endangered Resources Branch
4200 Smith School Road
Austin, Texas 78744
(512) 912-7011 or (800) 792-1112
    or
U.S. Fish and Wildlife Service
Ecological Services Field Office
10711 Burnet Road, Suite 200
Austin, Texas 78758
(512) 490-0057

Management guidelines are available from the Texas Parks and Wildlife Department and U.S. Fish and Wildlife Service for landowners and managers wishing to protect the Edwards Aquifer waters and their associated endemic species.

References

Edwards, R.J., E. Marsh, and C. Hubbs. 1980. *The San Marcos Gambusia Status Report.* Endangered Species Report 9. U.S. Fish and Wildlife Service, Albuquerque, NM. 34 pp.

Longley, G. 1978. *Status of the Texas Blind Salamander.* Endangered Species Report 2. U.S. Fish and Wildlife Service, Albuquerque, NM. 45 pp.

Linam G.W., Mayes, K., Saunders, K., Linam, L.A.J., and D.R. Hernandez. 1993. *Conservation of the Upper San Marcos and Comal Ecosystems.* Endangered Species Section 6 Project No. E-1-4, Job No. 2.5. Texas Parks and Wildlife Dept. 34 pp.

Thurow, T.L., W.H. Blackburn, and C.A. Taylor, Jr. 1986. "Hydrologic Characteristics of Vegetation Types as Affected by Livestock Grazing Systems, Edwards Plateau, Texas." *J. Range Manage.* 39(6):505-509.

U.S. Fish and Wildlife Service. 1984. *San Marcos River Recovery Plan.* U.S. Fish and Wildlife Service, Albuquerque, N.M. 109 pp.

Welch, T.G., R.W. Knight, D. Caudle, A. Garza, and J.M. Sweeten. 1991. *Impact of Grazing Management on Nonpoint Source Pollution.* Texas Agr. Extension Service Pub. L-5002. 4 pp.

Funds for the production of this leaflet were provided by the U.S. Fish and Wildlife Service, under Section 6 of the Endangered Species Act.

Management Guidelines for Endangered and Threatened Species of the Edwards Aquifer

Conserve Water

Do what you can as an individual to conserve water, particularly during drought periods. In the home, you can save water by installing fixtures, appliances, and toilets designed to use less water, repairing leaky faucets, and turning off the tap while brushing teeth or doing dishes. Landscaping with native, drought tolerant plants (xeriscaping), watering lawns in the early morning or evening to reduce evaporation, and installing a rainwater collection system for your home are other effective ways to conserve water.

Texas wild-rice in the San Marcos River
© Jackie M. Poole

Prevent Water Pollution

Some herbicides, insecticides, and other chemicals can impact water quality and adversely affect the listed species. Alternatives, such as integrated pest management, organic gardening, and the use and proper management of native vegetation reduce reliance on chemicals. These practices reduce the risks of environmental contamination and can often save money. When insecticide or herbicide treatments must be used, label directions should be carefully followed. Avoid contamination of rivers, streams, and other natural wetlands by limiting use of these products near them. Dispose of rinse water and empty containers in strict accordance with label directions. Contact the Texas Department of Agriculture or the U.S. Natural Resources Conservation Service (formerly Soil Conservation Service) for guidance on ways to minimize the environmental effects of agricultural chemicals.

If you graze livestock on your property, keep them out of creeks and streams by providing permanent, clean water sources away from natural waterways. This not only prevents water pollution but can also improve animal health and management. If you have caves or sinkholes on your property or in your neighborhood, protect them from development, dumping and vandalism. Remember that these areas harbor sensitive underground species and are direct conduits to your water supply.

Urban and suburban homeowners can help prevent water pollution by reducing the use of chemicals in lawn and landscape care. Landscaping with native plants requires much less water and little or no fertilizers or pesticides. Using native plants saves you money on water bills and lawn chemicals, and fewer chemicals means a healthier home environment for children, pets, and backyard wildlife. Contact a native plant nursery or organic gardening center near you for more information on chemical-free lawn and garden care.

Motor oil, gasoline, and radiator and brake fluids all contain toxic compounds. These compounds tend to stick to porous limestone, releasing polluting chemicals over a long period of time. Many common household items such as paints, paint thinners, cleaning fluids, drain cleaners, tires, and batteries also contain hazardous compounds which can pollute the aquifer if disposed of improperly. Never dump these materials down the drain or on the ground. Used automotive fluids and hazardous household wastes should be stored until they can be recycled or disposed of properly. Most service stations and auto maintenance businesses will take used motor oil to be recycled. Many cities and towns have designated collection facilities for hazardous waste products. Residents in the Austin area can contact the Household Hazardous Waste Collection Facility at 416-8998 for more information. For additional information on ways to prevent water pollution, call the Clean Texas 2000 Hotline of the Texas Natural Resources Conservation Commission at 1-800-64-TEXAS, or the Lower Colorado River Authority (LCRA) at 1-800-776-5272. Also, contact the Texas Water Development Board (512) 463-7847 for water conservation tips or the Edwards Underground Water District 1-800-292-1047 for specific information concerning the Edwards Aquifer.

Prevent Damage To Streambed Vegetation or Bottom Substrates

The Fountain Darter and San Marcos Salamander, in particular, are dependent on bottom vegetation to provide food and protection from predators. Do not pull up or otherwise damage streambed vegetation. You could be damaging the endangered Texas wild-rice.

The type of substrate is also an important habitat component. For example, the San Marcos Gambusia prefers mud but not silt, whereas the San Marcos Salamander inhabits vegetated areas of sand and gravel. Avoid any activity that alters the bottom sediments, such as removing or adding fill material, or scraping/trampling the bottom.

Avoid Introduction of Non-native Plants or Animals

Because of similarities in habitat and diet, predatory effects, and habitat modifications, exotic species pose a significant threat to the listed species. Do not release snails, fish, or other aquatic animals or plants into our lakes, creeks, or rivers.

Manage Surface Vegetation to Prevent Erosion and Runoff

Siltation and pollution from urban and rural runoff is a serious threat to water quality and a healthy aquatic ecosystem. On agricultural land, management of surface vegetation is the key to preventing soil erosion and runoff, and encouraging rainfall infiltration and aquifer recharge. Vegetation cover is important in preventing nonpoint source pollution because of its impact on falling raindrops and surface runoff. Raindrops falling on the soil surface dislodge soil particles and can move them a considerable distance. This splash erosion creates a suspension of soil and water which is moved in surface runoff. Suspended soil particles also plug soil pores, reducing the downward movement of water into the soil (infiltration). Standing vegetation and mulch on the soil surface intercept raindrops and reduce their splash effect.

Proper grazing management, which includes moderate stocking and rotational grazing, maintains rangelands with good vegetative cover and soil surface conditions, thus minimizing erosion and runoff. Research has shown that central Texas rangelands with abundant cover of deep-rooted tall and mid-height bunchgrasses, such as little bluestem, indiangrass and sideoats grama, are better able to absorb rainfall and hold soil than rangelands dominated by shallow-rooted shortgrasses, such as common curlymesquite and buffalograss.

Funds for the production of this leaflet were provided by the U.S. Fish and Wildlife Service, under Section 6 of the Endangered Species Act.

Houston Toad

Scientific Name: *Bufo houstonensis*

Federal Status: Endangered, 10/13/70 • State Status: Endangered

Description

The Houston Toad is 2 to 3.5 inches long and similar in appearance to Woodhouse's Toad (*Bufo woodhousei*), but smaller. General coloration varies from light brown to gray or purplish gray, sometimes with green patches. The pale ventral (underneath) surfaces often have small, dark spots. Males have a dark throat, which appears bluish when distended.

Houston Toad
© Bruce G. Stewart

Habitat

The Houston Toad is a terrestrial amphibian associated with deep sandy soils within the Post Oak Savannah vegetational area of east central Texas. Since Houston Toads are poor burrowers, loose friable soils are required for burrowing. The toads burrow into the sand for protection from cold weather in the winter (hibernation) and hot, dry conditions in the summer (aestivation). Large areas of predominantly sandy soils greater than 40 inches deep are considered preferred habitat. The vegetation type of currently known Houston Toad sites can typically be described as pine or oak woodland or savannah, with native bunchgrasses and forbs (flowering plants) present in open areas. Plants that are often present in Houston Toad habitat include loblolly pine, post oak, bluejack or sandjack oak, yaupon, and little bluestem.

For breeding, including egg and tadpole development, Houston Toads also require still or slow-flowing bodies of water that persist for at least 30 days. These water sources may include ephemeral (temporary) rain pools, flooded fields, blocked drainages of upper creek reaches, wet areas associated with seeps or springs, or more permanent ponds containing shallow water. The source of ephemeral or permanent water should be located within one-half to three-quarters mile of the toad's hibernation/foraging habitat (deep sands supporting woodland or savannah). The toads do best in ponds without predatory fish.

Life History

The Houston Toad is a year-round resident where found, although its presence can most easily be detected during the breeding season, when males may be heard calling. Males usually call in or near shallow water or from small mounds of soil or grass surrounded by water. Males occasionally call from wooded habitat located within about a 100-yard radius of breeding ponds. The call is a high clear trill that lasts an average of 14 seconds. The call is much like that of the American Toad (*Bufo americanus*), but usually slightly higher in pitch. The American Toad occurs in Texas, but north of the range of the Houston Toad.

Houston Toads may call from December through June. Most breeding activity takes place in February and March, and is stimulated by warm evenings and high humidity. Toads emerge from hibernation to breed only if moisture and temperature conditions are favorable. Females, responding to calling males, move toward the water to mate. The female lays her eggs as long strings in the water, where they are fertilized by the male as they are laid. The eggs hatch within seven days and tadpoles metamorphose (turn into toadlets) between 15 and 100 days, depending on the water temperature. Young toadlets are about one-half inch long when they complete metamorphosis. They then leave the pond and spend their time feeding and growing in preparation for the next breeding season. Males generally breed when they are a year old, but females may not breed until they are two years old.

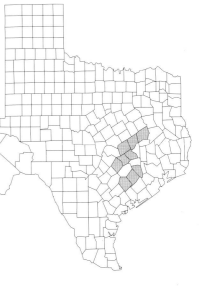

Houston Toads, especially first-year toadlets and juveniles, are active year round under suitable temperature and moisture conditions. Their diet consists mainly of insects and other invertebrates.

Threats and Reasons for Decline

Habitat loss and alteration are the most serious threats facing the Houston Toad. Alteration of ephemeral and permanent natural wetlands for urban and agricultural uses eliminates breeding sites. Draining a wetland, or converting an ephemeral wetland to a permanent pond, can eventually cause the Houston toad to decline or be eliminated entirely. Conversion to permanent water not only makes them more vulnerable to predation by snakes, fish, and other predators; but also increases competition and hybridization with closely related species.

Periodic drought is also a threat, particularly long-term drought such as that experienced during the 1950's. Drought may result in the loss or reduction of breeding sites as well as enhanced mortality of toadlets and adults.

Extensive clearing of native vegetation near breeding ponds and on the uplands adjacent to these ponds reduces the quality of breeding, foraging, and resting habitat, and increases the chances of predation and hybridization. Conversion of native grassland and woodland savannah to sod-forming introduced grasses, such as bermudagrass and bahiagrass, eliminates habitat because grass growth is generally too dense for the toad to move freely. Dense sod also inhibits burrowing.

High traffic roads are a barrier to Houston Toad movement, and toads are sometimes killed on roads. Other linear features such as pipelines and transmission lines can create barriers between foraging, hibernating, and breeding sites, especially if native vegetation has been removed.

Continuous grazing (not rotating cattle), heavy stocking rates, and long term fire suppression have caused loss of habitat in a significant part of the toad's range. Historically, periodic fire played an important role in maintaining native bunchgrass communities in loblolly pine and post oak savannah. Due to poor grazing management practices and fire suppression since the arrival of European man, much of the former savannah grasslands of the Post Oak region has grown into brush thickets devoid of herbaceous vegetation. Houston Toads need the herbaceous layer of bunchgrasses for cover and foraging habitat.

Although the toad is believed to be adapted to fire regimes, prescribed burning may result in toad mortality. Frequent and/or severe burns may be detrimental to the toad, particularly for small, fragmented populations. However, increased fuel loads due to prolonged periods of fire prevention may result in very hot wildfires. Additional research is needed to determine the effects of prescribed burning programs.

The invasion of the Red Imported Fire Ant makes it harder to ensure the long-term survival of the Houston Toad. These toads occur in small, scattered populations, and may be more seriously affected by fire ants than species that are more common and widespread. Fire ants kill young toadlets (less than 7-10 days old) moving out of the breeding pond into the surrounding land habitat. Current research shows that fire ants have a devastating impact on local arthropod communities, and thus may also limit the toad's food supply.

There is no specific information on the effects of various chemicals on the Houston Toad, but it is known that amphibians in general are very sensitive to many pollutants, including pesticides and other organic compounds. These chemicals may affect the toad directly, particularly in the tadpole stage, or indirectly by lowering the abundance and diversity of its food supply. Widespread use of pesticides and herbicides from about 1950 to 1975 may also have contributed to declining populations. During this period, DDT and similar non-specific chemicals accumulated in the environment, affecting a wide variety of animal life. Although threats from persistent, non-specific chemicals are not as serious today as in the past, the use of pesticides and herbicides for agricultural and residential purposes may still pose a danger for the Houston Toad.

Although Houston Toad populations are inherently separated because they exist only in areas of deep sandy soil, further fragmentation of habitat due to human activity can be a problem. Widely scattered parcels of habitat may not easily be re-colonized by distant Houston Toads if extensive areas of unsuitable habitat occur between

Calling male
© Bruce G. Stewart

Toads in amplexus
© Jim Godwin

populations, or human impacts eliminate a population.

Recovery Efforts
Research is continuing into the life history, habitat requirements, and land management practices affecting the Houston Toad. Population surveys are being conducted in areas where toads have been found and in potential habitat areas. Efforts to provide information and educational opportunities to the general public and landowners regarding life history and habitat requirements of the toad are a vital part of the recovery process.

Where To See The Houston Toad
The best place to visit if you want to see and learn about the Houston Toad is Bastrop State Park near Bastrop, Texas. The largest known population of the toad exists within the park. For more information, contact Bastrop State Park at (512) 321-2101.

Breeding pond in Milam County
© TPWD Andrew Price

*Breeding pond in
Bastrop State Park*
© TPWD Andrew Price

thoughtful and effective compromises between human resource needs and habitat management will allow for the continued survival and recovery of the Houston Toad.

You can be involved with the conservation of Texas' nongame wildlife resources by supporting the Special Nongame and Endangered Species Conservation Fund. Special nongame stamps and decals are available at Texas Parks and Wildlife Department (TPWD) field offices, most state parks, and the License Branch of TPWD headquarters in Austin. Conservation organizations in Texas also welcome your participation and support.

How You Can Help

You can help by protecting pond habitat. Conservation and wise management of native vegetation is important in preserving Houston Toad habitat. You can also help by landscaping with native plants to reduce water and pesticide use, and by proper storage and disposal of household, gardening, and agricultural chemicals. Hopefully,

For More Information Contact

Texas Parks and Wildlife Department
Endangered Resources Branch
4200 Smith School Road
Austin, Texas 78744
(512) 912-7011 or (800) 792-1112
or
U.S. Fish and Wildlife Service
Ecological Services Field Office
10711 Burnet Road, Suite 200
Austin, Texas 78758
(512) 490-0057

Management guidelines are available from the Texas Parks and Wildlife Department and U.S. Fish and Wildlife Service for landowners and managers wishing to protect and improve habitat for the Houston Toad.

References

Garrett, J. and D.G. Barker. 1987. *A Field Guide to the Reptiles and Amphibians of Texas*. Texas Monthly Press, Austin, TX. 225pp.

Hatch, S.L., K.N. Gandhi, and L.E. Brown. 1990. *Checklist of the Vascular Plants of Texas*. Texas Agr. Exp. Station Pub. MP-1655. Texas A&M Univ., College Station, TX. 158 pp..

Price, A. 1990. *Houston Toad Status Report*. Prepared for U.S. Fish and Wildlife Service, Albuquerque, NM.

U.S. Fish and Wildlife Service (USFWS). 1984. *Houston Toad Recovery Plan*. USFWS, Endangered Species Office, Albuquerque, NM.

Funds for the production of this leaflet were provided by the U.S. Fish and Wildlife Service, under Section 6 of the Endangered Species Act.

Management Guidelines for the Houston Toad

The following guidelines address land management practices that can be used to maintain existing Houston Toad habitat or enhance degraded habitat. They are intended primarily to serve as general guidance for landowners and managers in Texas. The guidelines are based on our current understanding of the biology of this species.

Post Oak Savannah vegetation on deep sandy soil
© NRCS Mike Stellbauer

Protect Pond Habitat

Avoid modification or disturbance of temporary wet-weather ponds and other small natural ponds located within one-half mile of deep sandy soils supporting post oak or loblolly pine woodland or savannah. These small ephemeral wetlands are prime breeding habitat for the Houston Toad. Extensive clearing of native vegetation and alteration of drainage patterns should be avoided in and around these ponds.

Because predators and other toad species live in and near permanent ponds, it is important that these ponds be located away from breeding ponds. To reduce predation and hybridization between Houston Toads and other toads, permanent ponds for livestock water should be located as far as possible from any existing temporary or natural pond. Also, permanent ponds should not impound ephemeral ponds or wetlands, in order to discourage predation and hybridization. Alternatives for livestock water, such as pipelines and windmills, should be considered in lieu of disturbing natural ponds and seeps that could serve as breeding habitat.

Since predation can be an important factor in reducing Houston Toad populations, predatory fish should not be introduced into breeding ponds. In addition, a fungus commonly found in hatchery raised fish has been shown to be harmful to the eggs of other toad species and could be a potential problem.

Conserve and Manage Existing Post Oak or Loblolly Pine Woodland and Savannah and the Associated Native Plant Communities

Conservation and wise management of rangeland and native grassland pasture in the Post Oak Savannah region are the keys to preserving Houston Toad habitat. Preventing overuse by livestock is important. Maintaining and improving range condition through moderate stocking, rotational grazing, and prescribed burning, will help restore the plant communities with which the Houston Toad evolved and is dependent. Good range management practices such as these will also benefit livestock, deer, and other wildlife.

Prescribed burning is an important management tool for maintaining the open woodland savannah preferred by the Houston Toad. Periodic burning (every 3 to 5 years) will stimulate native bunchgrasses, improve plant diversity, and reduce excessive mulch buildup. Prescribed burning also improves forage quality and availability for livestock and enhances habitat for deer, quail, turkey and other wildlife. Generally, prescribed burning should be done during cold, dry periods when toads are most likely to be hibernating in burrows. Burning prior to February 1 is recommended to avoid the breeding season. The timing of prescribed burning may vary from year to year depending on how weather conditions affect the toad's activity and the vegetation.

At this time, little is known concerning the effects of prescribed burning on Houston Toads. During the next five years, studies will be conducted to address questions concerning how prescribed burning affects Houston Toads and their habitat. Because prescribed burning could result in the death or injury of individual toads, landowners are advised to contact the Texas Parks and Wildlife Department or U.S. Fish and Wildlife Service for further information concerning prescribed burning in Houston Toad habitat.

Clearing of trees and brush should be limited to reducing woody canopy enough to allow sufficient sunlight to reach the ground for herbaceous plant production. Initial brush management can then be followed by prescribed burning to maintain a more open savannah grassland.

Reduce Loss of Habitat Due to Pasture Establishment

The introduction of sod-forming grasses, such as bermudagrass and bahiagrass, on deep sandy soils has reduced habitat for the Houston Toad in the Post Oak Savannah region. Ideally, areas of potential habitat should be managed as native rangeland pasture for the production of native bunchgrasses and forbs. If improved forage production through pasture establishment is an objective, it is better to plant high quality native bunchgrasses that are adapted to local conditions and sandy soils, such as indiangrass and little bluestem.

Use Safe, Effective Alternatives to Chemicals Whenever Possible

Amphibians such as the Houston Toad are susceptible to chemical contamination. The toads can be affected either directly, or through reduction in their food supply. Some pesticides can impact water quality and adversely affect the Houston Toad and other species. Alternatives, such as integrated pest management, organic gardening, and the use and proper management of native vegetation reduce reliance on chemicals and can improve cost effectiveness.

When insecticide or herbicide treatments must be used, label directions should be carefully followed. Avoid contamination of temporary ponds and other natural wetlands by limiting use of these products near them. Dispose of rinse water and empty containers in strict accordance with label directions. Contact the Texas Department of Agriculture or the U.S. Natural Resources Conservation Service (formerly Soil Conservation Service) for guidance on ways to minimize the environmental effects of agricultural chemicals.

Control Fire Ants

Although the full impact of fire ants on the Houston Toad is not known, fire ants are believed to be a serious and increasingly important threat. You can help control fire ant infestations by limiting soil disturbance, inspecting imported soil and nursery products thoroughly for fire ants, and properly disposing of trash. Controlling heavy fire ant infestations in Houston Toad habitat may help minimize their impact.

Where fire ant control is needed, the U.S. Fish and Wildlife Service recommends treatment of individual fire ant mounds with commercial fire ant bait. Bait should be placed only near fire ant mounds and not near the mounds of native ant species. To avoid affects on non-target species apply bait when ants are actively foraging and prevent accumulations of excess bait.

For More Information

Technical assistance in range and wildlife management, including management for endangered species, is available to landowners and managers by contacting the Texas Parks and Wildlife Department (TPWD), U.S. Natural Resources Conservation Service, or Texas Agricultural Extension Service. Further guidance and specific questions concerning landowner responsibilities under the Endangered Species Act, should be directed to the U.S. Fish and Wildlife Service.

Funds for the production of this leaflet were provided by the U.S. Fish and Wildlife Service, under Section 6 of the Endangered Species Act.

Clear Creek Gambusia

Scientific Name: *Gambusia heterochir*

Federal Status: Endangered, 3/11/67 • State Status: Endangered

Description

The Clear Creek Gambusia is a small, stocky fish, about 1.2 to 1.3 inches in length, with a metallic sheen. Scattered dark markings on some scales form distinctive crescent-shaped patterns. Unlike some other Gambusia species, this fish has no speckling on the tail or yellow pigment on the dorsal or anal fins. Females have a pronounced anal spot, especially when pregnant, and males have a deep notch at the top of the pectoral fin. Like other live-bearers, the male's anal fin is modified into a tube-like structure called a gonopodium for transferring sperm to the female.

Clear Creek Gambusia
© TPWD Glen Mills

Habitat

The Clear Creek Gambusia is restricted to the springfed headwaters of Clear Creek, a tributary of the San Saba River in Menard County in central Texas. This fish was first discovered in February, 1953. Upper Clear Creek consists of a series of limestone springs (Wilkinson Springs) originating from the Edwards Trinity Aquifer. Prior to 1890, a low, earthen-concrete dam was built about 80 yards downstream from the headsprings. In the 1930's, three additional dams were built downstream from the original dam, ponding water to the base of each dam. Extensive collecting of fish in 1956 and 1957 showed that the Clear Creek Gambusia was restricted to the springfed uppermost pool. This area, about 2.5 acres in size, provides clear spring water of constant temperature and low pH (slightly acidic), with abundant aquatic vegetation. Below the first dam, the habitat changes abruptly, with higher pH (more alkaline), different vegetation, and greater temperature fluctuations. This habitat is less suitable for the spring-dwelling Clear Creek Gambusia, and more suitable for the Western Mosquitofish (*Gambusia affinis*), a major competitor.

Life History

The Clear Creek Gambusia is viviparous (bears living young). Once fertilized, females can store sperm for several months, and they may produce several broods of young from March through September. Factors such as day length, temperature, and food availability have been shown to influence reproductive success.

The Clear Creek Gambusia is closely associated with coontail (*Ceratophyllum* sp.), an aquatic plant, and an endemic amphipod (small crustacean), *Hyalella texana*. The plant supports the amphipod, which in turn serves as a primary food source for the fish.

Other species inhabiting the upper pool include the Roundnose Minnow and the Greenthroat Darter. These small fishes do not compete with the Clear Creek Gambusia because of different food preferences and feeding locations. Maintenance of submerged aquatic plants, which provide protective cover from predators such as bass and sunfish, is important for both the Clear Creek Gambusia and its prey.

Threats and Reasons for Decline

Originally, Clear Creek was a clear springrun that flowed freely for about 3 miles to its confluence with the San Saba River. Most or all of the creek was probably inhabited by springrun species such as the Clear Creek Gambusia and associated plants and animals. A series of dams, the first one built in the 1880's and the others during the 1930's, were constructed to provide irrigation to cultivated fields. The resulting changes in habitat encouraged population buildup of plants and animals more tolerant of a wide range of water temperatures. These eurythermal (wide temperature tolerance) organisms soon overwhelmed the springrun animals that were not isolated upstream from the first dam (Dam 1).

Since the only habitat for the Clear Creek Gambusia exists upstream from Dam 1, this dam is vital for protecting an environment isolated from invasion by the Western Mosquitofish. In 1979, Dam 1 was in serious disrepair due to age, the effects of tunnelling by nutria (a large introduced rodent), and the expansion of root systems of

trees. Hybridization between the Clear Creek Gambusia and Western Mosquitofish had occurred in the vicinity of the dam. This hybridization problem was the result of mosquitofish juvenile females moving to the upper pool through damaged portions of the dam. If allowed to continue, hybridization and competition from the Western Mosquitofish would have eliminated the Clear Creek Gambusia. In the summer of 1979, Dam 1 was rebuilt, securing the upper pool habitat for the Clear Creek Gambusia.

In 1985, researchers found an increased number of Clear Creek Gambusia downstream from the reconstructed dam. Apparently, soon after the dam was rebuilt, Rainwater Killifish (*Lucania parva*) were found in Clear Creek below the dam. This fish is not native to the Edwards Plateau and may have been released into Clear Creek by someone discarding leftover bait. Rainwater Killifish and Western Mosquitofish, although not closely related, are very similar with respect to food habits, habitat preferences, and tendency to move seasonally to areas of warmer water. Thus, Rainwater Killifish compete directly with Western Mosquitofish. Reduction in the numbers of mosquitofish allowed the Clear Creek Gambusia to survive in greater numbers below the upper dam.

Finally, the continued existence of the Clear Creek Gambusia depends on continued flow of Wilkinson Springs. Protection of the Edwards-Trinity recharge zone is essential. Any changes which reduce water flow or deteriorate water quality in Wilkinson Springs could have disastrous consequences for the Clear Creek Gambusia.

Recovery Efforts

Continuous monitoring is underway to detect factors that may affect the Clear Creek gambusia population. Research also is underway to better understand habitat requirements, life history, and limiting factors affecting the species. The owners of Wilkinson Springs have been instrumental in protecting the species' habitat. Providing information to landowners and the general public concerning habitat requirements for rare and endangered fishes is an important part of the recovery process.

How You Can Help

Area landowners can help by protecting the groundwater of the Edwards-Trinity Aquifer. Do what you can as an individual to conserve water and prevent pollutants from entering the aquifer. Care should be taken to avoid reduction in recharge to the aquifer. Limestone aquifers are vulnerable to pol-

lution and measures to prevent aquifer contamination are urged. Land managers can help by implementing sound range management practices designed to protect vegetative cover, improve range condition, and prevent soil erosion and runoff. Good vegetation management will help to ensure optimum aquifer recharge and the continuous flow of Wilkinson Springs and others like it. Management guidelines are available for other endangered species that occur in central Texas, such as the Black-capped Vireo. Contact Texas Parks and Wildlife Department or the U.S. Fish and Wildlife Service for more information.

Since competition and/or hybridization with closely related or introduced species is a major threat to endangered fishes, never release fish into natural waters from which they didn't originate. Although an exception occurred in the case of the Rainwater Killifish at Clear Creek, beneficial impacts resulting from introductions of exotic species are the exception and not the rule.

Finally, you can support the Special Nongame and Endangered Species Conservation Fund by purchasing a stamp, available at the Texas Parks and Wildlife Department (TPWD) headquarters in Austin or at most State Parks. Conservation Passports, available from TPWD, are valid for one year and allow free access to most State Parks, State Natural Areas, and Wildlife Management Areas. Part of the proceeds from the sale of these items are used to conserve habitat and provide information concerning rare and endangered species.

Clear Creek spring
© Gary Garrett

Biologists using a seine net to sample fish
© Gary Garrett

For More Information Contact

Texas Parks and Wildlife Department
Endangered Resources Branch
4200 Smith School Road
Austin, Texas 78744
(512) 912-7011 or (800) 792-1112
or
U.S. Fish and Wildlife Service
Ecological Services Field Office
10711 Burnet Road, Suite 200
Austin, Texas 78758
(512) 490-0057

References

Edwards, R.J., and C. Hubbs. 1985. *Temporal Changes in the* Gambusia heterochir x G. affinis *Hybrid Swarm Following Dam Reconstruction.* USFWS, Albuquerque, New Mexico. 31 pp.

U.S. Fish and Wildlife Service. 1980. *Clear Creek Gambusia* (Gambusia heterochir) *Recovery Plan.* USFWS, Albuquerque, New Mexico. 29 pp.

Funds for the production of this leaflet were provided by the U.S. Fish and Wildlife Service, under Section 6 of the Endangered Species Act.

Desert Spring Fishes

Scientific Name: Comanche Springs Pupfish – *Cyprinodon elegans,* Leon Springs Pupfish – *Cyprinodon bovinus,* Pecos Gambusia – *Gambusia nobilis,* Big Bend Gambusia – *Gambusia gaigei*

Federal Status: All Endangered; 3/11/67, 8/15/80, 10/13/70, and 3/11/67, respectively •
State Status: All Endangered

Description of Species, Habitats, and Life History

Comanche Springs Pupfish

The Comanche Springs Pupfish seldom exceeds 2 inches in total length. It is gray-green above and pale yellow to white below, with clear to light orange fins. The sides are silvery white with blue-black blotches forming a "stripe" along the side (often faint on the male). Males have black speckling on the side and a black edge on the caudal (tail) fin. In contrast to other *Cyprinodon* species, this pupfish has a slender body and lacks vertical bars.

Comanche Springs Pupfish
© Dave Schleser

Leon Springs Pupfish
© TPWD

Historically, this pupfish occurred in two separate spring systems of the Pecos River drainage. One was Comanche Springs, with headwaters (now almost always dry) within the city limits of Ft. Stockton, Texas, and the other was a group of springs near Balmorhea. The pupfish population at Comanche Springs were extirpated (lost) when the springs first went dry in 1955. At present, the species occurs primarily in aquatic habitat fed by springflow from Phantom Lake, Giffin, and San Solomon springs near Balmorhea, Texas. Habitat consists mostly of a system of concrete and earthen irrigation canals. The pupfish are often abundant in earthen ditches and concrete flumes 4 inches or more deep with bottoms covered with debris and vegetation, such as muskgrass (*Chara* spp.). They are rarely found in concrete flumes where water depth is less than 4 inches and/or the bottom is scoured of debris.

The Comanche Springs Pupfish is known only from freshwater to slightly saline habitats. The springs near Balmorhea have low salinities, as did the now dry Comanche Springs. Other species of pupfish in the Pecos River system inhabit more saline waters. Breeding is thought to occur during most months of the year, and spawning (egg-laying) occurs in areas of flowing water as well as in stagnant pools. In irrigation canals, the pupfish prefer shallow areas with low current velocities. Although they feed mostly on the bottom, they also feed at the surface and at other levels in the water column.

Leon Springs Pupfish

The Leon Springs Pupfish is a small (about 2 inches), robust pupfish, with a wider head and body than most pupfish. Breeding males are powdery blue-gray with fins of varying shades of yellow edged with black. Females are grayish-yellow or grayish-brown on top, and lighter below.

The Leon Springs Pupfish was first discovered in 1851 by members of the U.S. and Mexican Boundary Survey. The fish was originally found at Leon Springs, a spring system that once flowed in the Leon Creek drainage about 6 miles west of Fort Stockton in Pecos County. Its historic range probably included all permanent waters within Leon Creek and the associated springs. In 1918, the area where the fish was first collected was inundated by Lake Leon, an irrigation and fishing impoundment. By 1938, the Leon Springs Pupfish could no longer be found in the area where it was first discovered. Although Leon Springs once produced a flow of about 20 cfs (cubic feet per second), the springs produced no measurable flow by 1958 due to groundwater pumping in excess of aquifer recharge.

From 1958 until 1965, the Leon Springs Pupfish was thought to be extinct. The fish were rediscovered in 1965, when they were collected from Diamond-Y Spring, located about 10 miles north of Fort Stockton. The fish have since been found in Leon Creek, downstream from Diamond-Y Spring in waters that are quite saline. The recent localities are about 15 miles

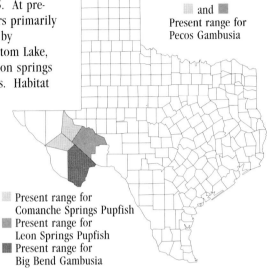

and ▨
Present range for
Pecos Gambusia

▨ Present range for
Comanche Springs Pupfish
▨ Present range for
Leon Springs Pupfish
▨ Present range for
Big Bend Gambusia

downstream from where the fish was originally found.

The Leon Springs Pupfish presently occurs within two 3-mile spring-fed segments of Leon Creek and Diamond-Y Spring. Diamond-Y draw is a tributary to Leon Creek. These spring-fed segments are separated by about one mile of usually dry stream bed. The fish prefer slow-flowing stretches of water, with a substrate of mud and aquatic plant roots. They are also abundant in natural spring-fed marshes (cienegas), channels, and pools along this watercourse.

The Leon Springs Pupfish feeds primarily on the bottom, ingesting large amounts of detritus (decomposed organic material) and mud. Food items include diatoms, algae, and small invertebrates. "Pit digging" has been observed, where the fish (mostly males) rest on the bottom of the pool and undulate their bodies to churn up the substrate. This behavior is thought to be associated with locating buried food items.

The Leon Springs Pupfish spawns throughout the year, with females laying up to 10 eggs per day. Spawning occurs on the bottom substrate in territories aggressively defended by individual males. Shallow shelf areas with slow currents, warmer than the deeper channels, are preferred for spawning. This species is known to tolerate an unusually wide range of salinities and temperatures. However, studies suggest that the temperature range required for successful reproduction may be quite narrow. The extended breeding season, wide salinity and temperature tolerances, and broad food habits suggest that the Leon Springs Pupfish is a generalist that does best in simple communities with few competing species.

Pecos Gambusia

The Pecos Gambusia is a small (2 inches long), live-bearing fish with a dark lateral stripe and a metallic gray-blue color. Females have a black area on the abdomen that surrounds the anal fin and anus. The anal fin of males is mod-

ified into a gonopodium, a tube-like structure used in fertilization of the female.

Historically, the Pecos Gambusia was restricted to the Pecos River basin in southeastern New Mexico and western Texas. The species occurred from as far south as Fort Stockton, Texas to as far north as Fort Sumner, New Mexico. The populations of Pecos Gambusia that once existed at Leon Springs and Comanche Springs were lost when these springs went dry during the mid-1950's. Presently in Texas, populations of the Pecos Gambusia occur near Balmorhea in aquatic habitat supported by springflow from Phantom Lake, Giffin, San Solomon, and East Sandia Springs. A substantial population also occurs in Leon Creek and in Diamond-Y Spring outflow north of Fort Stockton. The species also occurs in a limited number of locations in New Mexico.

The Pecos Gambusia occurs abundantly in spring-fed pools, spring runs, and downstream areas having relatively constant temperatures, abundant overhead cover, sedge-covered marshes, and in gypsum sinkholes with no surface flow. It is capable of occupying a variety of habitats if factors such as temperature and salinity are suitable.

The closest relatives of the Pecos Gambusia are found in south Texas and Mexico, so the species has a long history of adaptation to warmer climates. The fish does not occur even in spring-fed waters at higher elevations, presumably because water temperatures are too cold. Maximum temperature is also important in determining suitable habitat. The Pecos Gambusia seems to be less tolerant of higher temperatures than the Western Mosquitofish (*Gambusia affinis*), a major competitor. Studies indicate that the Pecos Gambusia is more abundant in spring-fed waters, but it may also do well in less spring-like waters if there is enough cover from above to buffer temperature changes.

Predation by Green Sunfish (*Lepomis cyanellus*) and Largemouth Bass (*Micropterus salmoides*) can become a major limiting factor in areas where there is no submerged vegetation or shal-

Pecos Gambusia
© Dave Schleser

Big Bend Gambusia
© TPWD

low water to provide protection from predators. Females produce up to 40 young every 4 to 5 days.

The Pecos Gambusia is an opportunistic feeder. Primarily a surface feeder, major food items include insects, other small invertebrates, and some filamentous algae.

Competition with other Gambusia species is important in determining the relative abundance of the Pecos Gambusia. Studies have shown that, over a period of years, the Western Mosquitofish outcompetes the Pecos Gambusia in isolated pools and downstream waters well removed from spring influence. Salinity seems to be important in determining the influence of an introduced competitor, the Largespring Gambusia (*Gambusia geiseri*). Since the Pecos Gambusia is tolerant of a wide range of salinities, it can outcompete the Largespring Gambusia in the saline waters of Leon Creek, while the Largespring Gambusia seems competitively superior in the freshwaters of the Balmorhea area.

Big Bend Gambusia

The Big Bend Gambusia (*Gambusia gaigei*) is a small, live-bearing fish which reaches a maximum length of about 2 inches. The fish is yellowish in color, with a faint lateral stripe and orange to yellow dorsal and anal fins. Other markings include a bar beneath the eye, and a faint, dark chin bar. Males are smaller than females, and as with other gambusia species, the male's anal fin is modified into a

Diamond-Y Spring
© TPWD

A spring-fed creek in Big Bend Ranch State Park
© Matt Wagner

tube-like gonopodium for fertilizing the female.

The Big Bend Gambusia is known only from spring habitats in the vicinity of Boquillas Crossing and Rio Grande Village in Big Bend National Park. Historically, the fish may have existed in other springs in the vicinity of Rio Grande Village. The population at Boquillas Spring (located about 660 ft. north of Boquillas Crossing) became extinct when spring flow ceased in 1954. The population at the spring located near Rio Grande Village drastically declined between 1954 and 1956, after the spring outflow was altered to provide a fishing pool for the park campground. The Big Bend Gambusia was extirpated from this location by 1960. Two possible factors in

Phantom Lake cienega and spring
© TPWD Andrew Price

the loss of this population include competition with the Western Mosquitofish and predation by the introduced Green Sunfish. All present populations of Big Bend Gambusia consist of descendants of three fish (two males and one female) taken from the declining Rio Grande Village population in 1956. The fish are now being maintained in a refugium pond located in Big Bend National Park. Small populations also exist at the Dexter National Fish Hatchery and Technology Center in New Mexico and at the University of Texas.

The habitats originally occupied by the Big Bend Gambusia were marshes and natural pools, with clear, shallow water fed by warm springs. Dense aquatic vegetation presumably occurred in these areas. Although the present refugium has open water in excess of 3 feet, the Big Bend Gambusia are most abundant among the cattails and muskgrass near the shore.

The Big Bend Gambusia preys on aquatic invertebrates. Little is known concerning factors limiting reproduction in this species, but temperature, daylight hours, and food availability are known to affect reproductive success in related species. Competition with the Western Mosquitofish is thought to be a major factor affecting the survival of the Big Bend Gambusia.

Threats and Reasons for Decline

The major threats to the survival of the desert spring fishes are habitat loss from declining springflows and reduced surface waters, competition with introduced species, and loss of genetic integrity due to hybridization with introduced species.

Introductions of fish and mollusk species from inland rivers, the Gulf Coast, and other sources pose a serious threat to these fishes, which have relatively general ecological requirements. Almost any co-occurring species of fish, either indigenous or introduced, would potentially exert some competitive pressure on populations of these fishes. Competition with introduced species that are ecologically similar poses an especially serious threat.

Large artesian springs, such as those in the Balmorhea area, are diminishing in flow. Phantom Lake Spring, near Balmorhea, is particularly vulnerable because it is at a higher elevation and thus would be the first of these larger springs to stop flowing. In many parts of west Texas, more water is being withdrawn from aquifers by pumping than is being replaced by rainfall. In addition, surface waters are being diverted from aquifer recharge zones. This continued mining of aquifers could eventually cause the demise of spring systems throughout west Texas, and with them the extinction of a whole array of unique fishes and aquatic plants and animals. This would also have serious consequences for Texans of the Trans-Pecos, who would lose a valuable water supply.

Recovery Efforts

Research is underway to better understand the life history, habitat requirements, and limiting factors affecting the endangered fishes of west Texas. Continued monitoring of endangered fish populations and habitat is very important.

A cooperative project is currently underway to create a manmade, but biologically functional desert cienega or marsh at Balmorhea State Park. This project, sponsored by Texas Parks and Wildlife Department, the Educational Foundation of America, and the National Fish and Wildlife Foundation, will not only create habitat for the Comanche Springs Pupfish and the Pecos Gambusia, but will also provide spring-fed habitat for a wide variety of native plants and animals. It will also provide an excellent opportunity for school children and park visitors to learn about this unique ecosystem.

A refugium canal within the Balmorhea State Park supports several thousand Comanche Springs Pupfish and Pecos Gambusia. A similar refugium canal, constructed by the Bureau of Reclamation, was recently completed at Phantom Lake Spring. This canal is expected to support abundant, healthy populations of these fishes.

In 1990, The Nature Conservancy of Texas purchased the land encompassing Diamond-Y Spring, and the portion of Leon Creek designated as critical habitat for the Leon Springs Pupfish. In the 1970's, a portion of Leon Creek was renovated, significantly reducing the problems of competition and hybridization. Future scientific management of this habitat will provide protection for the Pecos Gambusia as well as the Leon Springs Pupfish.

A small population of Comanche Springs Pupfish is held at the National Fish Hatchery in Uvalde, Texas. Likewise, small populations of Big Bend Gambusia and Leon Springs Pupfish are being held at the Dexter National Fish Hatchery in New Mexico. These populations provide an opportunity for researchers to obtain specimens for study without affecting wild populations, and provide stocks for reintroductions in the event of the loss of a population.

Where To See The Desert Spring Fishes

The best places to see and learn more about these fishes are Balmorhea State Park and Big Bend National Park. At Balmorhea State Park, visitors can cool off in the world's largest spring-fed swimming pool, where the Comanche Springs pupfish and the Pecos gambusia can sometimes be seen hiding in the shallow, grassy areas of the pool. Also, the refugium canal at Balmorhea State Park is an excellent place to observe these fish. A refugium pond near the Rio Grande Village Campground in Big Bend National Park offers visitors a chance to see the Big Bend gambusia and its habitat.

How You Can Help

Do what you can as an individual to conserve water. Comanche Springs, Leon Springs and others have gone dry because more water is being used than is replaced by rainfall. When springs dry up, a whole host of plant and animal life disappears with them. The competition for water has taken a toll on the wetland plants and animals of west Texas. The existence of these endangered fishes, and other aquatic animals and plants which share their habitat, depends on the continued flow of the springs near Balmorhea, Leon Creek, and in Big Bend. Conservation of these spring ecosystems will result in the continued ability to use water in areas downstream from their habitats.

Since competition with introduced species is a major threat to these endangered fishes, never release fish into natural waters. Serious problems have resulted from people releasing non-native fishes (especially by emptying bait buckets) into streams and springs, or intentionally releasing fish into state waters in an effort to improve fishing.

Be careful with the application of pesticides (insecticides and herbicides) and other agricultural chemicals. Improper use of chemicals can have devastating effects on aquatic systems. Always follow label precautions carefully, including instructions concerning proper disposal of rinse water and containers. Check with the Texas Department of Agriculture (TDA) for information concerning proper use of herbicides and pesticides and licensing requirements.

Due to the toxicity of some pesticides to aquatic life, special management methods are needed for certain chemicals to help prevent possible harm to protected species. Local representatives of wildlife, agriculture, and conservation groups are working with landowners to develop measures that will allow normal agricultural production to coexist with the desert fishes. Farmers, ranchers, and pesticide applicators can contact their local county extension agent, or Coordinator, Endangered Species Pesticide Protection, Texas Department of Agriculture in Austin (512-463-7476) to find out about current recommendations.

A significant portion of the remaining habitat for the Comanche Springs Pupfish and Pecos Gambusia consists of the irrigation canals in the Balmorhea-Toyahvale area of Reeves and Jeff Davis counties. Conservation of

Phantom Lake canal and refugium
© USFWS Ruth Stanford

Biologists using a seine net to sample fish in Leon Creek
© Gary Garrett

these two endangered fishes can be enhanced by ensuring that water quality in the canals supports a functional aquatic community. Farmers can help by careful handling of all fuels, oils, and hydraulic fluids so that canals are not contaminated. Also, maintaining a water depth greater than 1 foot in canals occupied by these fishes is desirable.

West Texas landowners with springs and associated surface water resources can provide additional protection to various populations of rare fishes by limiting habitat disruption, preventing introduction of exotic species, and implementing conservation measures designed to maintain spring flow and water quality in spring-fed creeks and marshes. These precious water resources provide unique areas of plant and animal life. Their protection is vital to the diversity of life which they support.

Finally, you can support the Special Nongame and Endangered Species Conservation Fund by purchasing a stamp, available at the Texas Parks and Wildlife Department headquarters in Austin or at most state parks. Conservation Passports, available from Texas Parks and Wildlife, are valid for one year and allow free access to most State Parks, State Natural Areas, and Wildlife Management Areas. Part of the proceeds from the sale of these items are used to provide information to park visitors concerning endangered species.

For More Information Contact

Texas Parks and Wildlife Department
Endangered Resources Branch
4200 Smith School Road
Austin, Texas 78744
(512) 912-7011 or (800) 792-1112
    or
U.S. Fish and Wildlife Service
Ecological Services Field Office
10711 Burnet Road, Suite 200
Austin, Texas 78758
(512) 490-0057
    or
Texas Department of Agriculture
P.O. Box 12847
Austin, Texas 78711
(512) 463-7476

References

Hubbs, C., R.J. Edwards, and G.P. Garrett. 1991. *An Annotated Checklist of the Freshwater Fishes of Texas, with Keys to Identification of Species*. The Texas Journal of Science, suppl., Vol. 43, No. 4. 56 pp.

Page, L.M., and B.M. Burr. 1991. *A Field Guide to Freshwater Fishes*. The Peterson Field Guide Series. Houghton Mifflin Company, Boston, MA. 432 pp.

U.S. Fish and Wildlife Service. 1980. *Comanche Springs Pupfish* (Cyprinodon elegans) *Recovery Plan*. USFWS, Albuquerque, New Mexico. 25 pp.

U.S. Fish and Wildlife Service. 1985. *Leon Springs Pupfish* (Cyprinodon bovinus) *Recovery Plan*. USFWS, Albuquerque, New Mexico. 26 pp.

U.S. Fish and Wildlife Service. 1982. *Pecos Gambusia* (Gambusia nobilis) *Recovery Plan*. USFWS, Albuquerque, New Mexico. 41 pp.

U.S. Fish and Wildlife Service. 1984. *Big Bend Gambusia* (Gambusia gaigei) *Recovery Plan*. USFWS, Albuquerque, New Mexico. 43 pp.

Funds for the production of this leaflet were provided by the U.S. Fish and Wildlife Service, under Section 6 of the Endangered Species Act.

Karst Invertebrates

Scientific Name: Bee Creek Cave Harvestman – *Texella reddelli*, Bone Cave Harvestman – *Texella reyesi*, Tooth Cave Pseudoscorpion – *Tartarocreagris texana*, Tooth Cave Spider – *Neoleptoneta myopica*, Tooth Cave Ground Beetle – *Rhadine persephone*, Kretschmarr Cave Mold Beetle – *Texamaurops reddelli*, Coffin Cave Mold Beetle – *Batrisodes texanus*

Federal Status: Endangered, 9/16/88 • State Status: Endangered

Description of Species and Life History

Of these species, three are insects (one ground beetle and two mold beetles) and four are arachnids (one pseudoscorpion, one spider, and two harvestmen). All are troglobites, which are animals that are specially adapted to subterranean existence and spend their entire lives underground. Troglobites usually have small eyes or lack eyes entirely, long appendages, reduced pigmentation and other adaptations to a subterranean environment.

Most of the endangered karst invertebrates are believed to be predators of microarthropods (tiny insects). They also feed on well-decomposed organic matter. Most troglobites eat a variety of foods (food generalists), although some degree of prey specialization probably exists in some species. There is little information on the biology or life cycles of these karst species. Collections made throughout the year suggest that, unlike their surface-dwelling relatives, cave species do not have distinct seasonal cycles.

The **Bee Creek Cave Harvestman**, or daddy-longlegs, has a body about 2 to 3 mm in length and relatively long legs. Its body color is light yellowish-brown, and it has no eyes. It is found under rocks in darkness or in dim light, and preys on tiny, hopping insects called collembolans. This species, like other small harvestmen, tend to walk rather slowly and deliberately, unlike spiders, which tend to move faster.

The **Bone Cave Harvestman** is a long-legged, blind, pale orange harvestman, with a body length of about 1.4 to 2.7 mm. This species is especially sensitive to humidities below saturation. They are most often found under large rocks, but are occasionally seen walking on moist floors. In the hottest part of the summer when small caves warm up and become drier, they can be found only in the coolest, dampest spots.

The **Tooth Cave Pseudoscorpion** grows to about 4 mm and resembles a tiny, tailless scorpion without eyes. Pseudoscorpions use their pinchers to catch prey, and are thought to be predators of microarthropods. Usually found under rocks, this species is quite rare and little is known of its habits.

The **Tooth Cave Spider** is the smallest of the listed invertebrates, about 1.6 mm in length. It is a pale cream-colored spider with relatively long legs. Although it is restricted entirely to caves, it does possess rudimentary eyes. A minute and delicate predator of microarthropods, the Tooth Cave spider is a sedentary aerial spider that hangs from a small tangle or sheet web on long, thin legs.

The **Tooth Cave Ground Beetle** is a slender, reddish-brown beetle with reduced eyes. It attains a length of 7 to 8 mm at maturity. This is the largest, most visible, and

Bone Cave Harvestman
© USFWS Wyman Meinzer

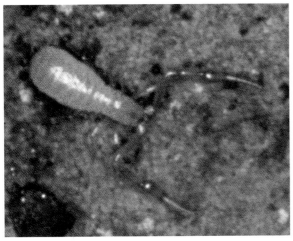

Tooth Cave Pseudoscorpion
© USFWS Wyman Meinzer

Present range for Coffin Cave Mold Beetle

and Present range for Tooth Cave Ground Beetle and Bone Cave Harvestman

Present range for Tooth Cave Pseudoscorpion, Tooth Cave Spider, Kretschmarr Cave Mold Beetle and Bee Creek Cave Harvestman most active of the karst species. It is usually found under rocks, but has been seen walking on damp rocks and silt when conditions are favorable. It runs rapidly as it searches the cave floor for prey. This species appears to be restricted to areas of deep, uncompacted silt, where it digs holes to feed on cave cricket eggs deposited into the silt.

The **Kretschmarr Cave Mold Beetle** has short wings and long legs, and is less than 3 mm long. It is dark brown and eyeless. This mold beetle is found in total darkness under and among rocks and organic debris and buried in silt. Although food preferences are unknown, it is believed to be a predator.

The **Coffin Cave Mold Beetle** is a small, long-legged beetle with short wings. Its body length is about 2.6 to 2.9 mm and it is eyeless. This species is also found in total darkness under rocks. Its food preferences are unknown. The Coffin Cave mold beetle is the only one of the endangered invertebrates found exclusively in Williamson County.

Habitat

"Karst" is a term used by geologists to describe a type of terrain formed when calcium carbonate from limestone bedrock is slowly dissolved by mildly acidic groundwater. This process creates numerous caves, sinkholes, fractures, and interconnections so that in places the bedrock resembles a honeycomb. Many of the karst features occupied by the listed species were formed at or below the water table, and thus were once filled with water. As the water table lowered, these features dried out and are now air-filled. The lowering of the groundwater table led to ceiling collapse in some cavities, forming caves and sinkholes. Some karst features act as important recharge structures to underground streams and aquifers.

During the course of climatic changes during the Pleistocene epoch (2 million to 10 thousand years ago), the ancestors of these animals retreated from the soil surface and mulch into the more stable cave environments. Subsequently, these animals became adapted to cave environments.

Through faulting and downcutting by water in stream channels, the karst terrain along the Balcones Fault Zone became increasingly dissected, creating "islands" of karst that are barriers to dispersal of the troglobites. This led to increasing isolation of troglobite populations and the subsequent evolution of distinct species.

Troglobites require high humidities (near saturation) and are very susceptible to drying. Most also require stable temperatures. Cold, dry air entering a cave causes the animals to retreat to more humid, warmer areas. During these times, some troglobites may be found in small ceiling pockets where the conditions are probably warmer and damper than on the cave floor. During hot, dry periods, these animals may retreat into the cave soil or small cracks and fissures in the walls or ceiling where environmental conditions are more stable.

Because there is little light and limited capacity for photosynthesis by plants, karst ecosystems depend almost entirely on surface plant and animal communities for nutrients and energy. Caves receive nutrients from the surface in the form of leaf mulch, plant roots, and other organic debris that washes or falls into the cave. Cave crickets are especially important because many invertebrates are known to feed on their eggs, feces, nymphs, and dead body parts. Cave crickets roost and lay eggs in caves during the day and leave the cave at night to feed on the surface. Raccoons and other small mammals are also important in many cave communities because their feces provide a rich medium for the growth of fungi and, subsequently, tiny insects that become prey for troglobites.

Most of the caves inhabited by the listed species were not significant bat roosts in the past. Studies indicate that although most karst systems containing the listed ani-

Tooth Cave Spider © USFWS Wyman Meinzer

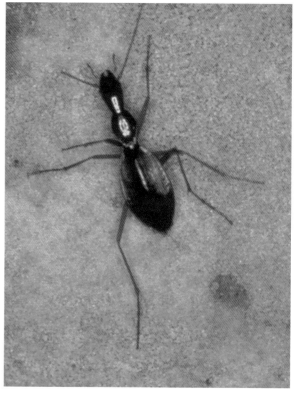

Tooth Cave Ground Beetle © USFWS Wyman Meinzer

Kretschmarr Cave Mold Beetle © USFWS R. W. Mitchell

Cave Cricket © USFWS Wyman Meinzer

Limestone cave in Travis county
© USFWS Wyman Meinzer

Cave formations
© George Veni

mals do not depend on bats for nutrient input, some of these invertebrates can live in caves with small bat colonies and may benefit from the increased input of nutrients found in bat guano.

Surface plant communities around karst features range from pastureland to mature oak-juniper woodland. In addition to providing nutrients to the karst system, maintaining adequate plant cover is important in minimizing temperature fluctuations, drying, and groundwater contamination.

Threats and Reasons for Decline

The primary threat to the listed species is loss of habitat due to urban development. The continued urban expansion in Travis and Williamson counties has negatively impacted numerous caves. Most of the species are located in areas adjacent to or near residential subdivisions, schools, golf courses, roads, and commercial and industrial facilities. Threats from urban development include filling in or collapse of caves, alteration of drainage patterns, alteration of surface plant and animal communities, contamination by pollutants, and detrimental impacts caused by human visitation.

The introduction of non-native predators and competitors also poses a major threat to the karst invertebrates. For example, the Red Imported Fire Ant is an increasingly serious threat. Fires ants eat the invertebrates directly, or impact cave systems by preying on other species that are important for nutrient input.

Recovery Efforts

A number of surveys and research projects are underway to better define the taxonomy and distribution of karst fauna in Travis and Williamson counties. Many of these studies are associated with areas proposed for development. Fire ant control studies have also been conducted to determine the effectiveness of various treatments on fire ants. Efforts are also underway to protect many of the caves known to contain endangered invertebrates.

How You Can Help

Individuals and private groups can support efforts in Travis and Williamson counties to conserve and manage habitat for endangered species, and prevent ground and surface water pollution.

Conservation organizations can provide additional information, and they welcome your support.

For More Information Contact

Texas Parks and Wildlife Department
Endangered Resources Branch
4200 Smith School Road
Austin, Texas 78744
(512) 912-7011 or (800) 792-1112
  or
U.S. Fish and Wildlife Service
Ecological Services Field Office
10711 Burnet Road, Suite 200
Austin, Texas 78758
(512) 490-0057

Management guidelines are available from Texas Parks and Wildlife Department and the U.S. Fish and Wildlife Service for landowners and managers interested in protecting karst ecosystems underlying their property.

References

Slack, Doug et al. 1990. *Austin Regional Habitat Conservation Plan.* Comprehensive Report of the Biological Advisory Team.

U.S. Fish and Wildlife Service. 1993. *Draft Recovery Plan for Endangered Karst Invertebrates in Travis and Williamson Counties, Texas.* 133 pp.

Funds for the production of this leaflet were provided by the U.S. Fish and Wildlife Service, under Section 6 of the Endangered Species Act.

Management Guidelines for
Karst Invertebrates

Preserve Known Cave Sites

The karst features inhabitated by these species and the ecosystems on which they depend have evolved slowly over millions of years. Once destroyed, they cannot be recreated. Protection of these ecosystems will require maintaining moist, humid

Cave entrance
© USFWS Ruth Stanford

Cave entrance
© George Veni

conditions and stable temperatures in the air spaces; maintaining an adequate nutrient supply; preventing contamination of the water entering the system; and preventing or controlling invasion of exotic species, such as fire ants.

Preservation of known caves, fissures, and other karst features is important to maintaining this unique ecosystem and the animals that live there. Building and road construction should be avoided in the vicinity of known caves and cave entrances. These entrances should not be filled because input of nutrients and surface water is important in maintaining the system. Where cave entrances are large enough to pose a hazard to humans or livestock, they can be fenced or gated to restrict access by large animals yet allow movement of raccoons, small mammals, insects, and water into the cave.

Avoid Altering Surface Drainage Patterns

Landowners should avoid altering surface drainage patterns in the vicinity of known caves. Because karst ecosystems depend on air spaces with some water infiltration, diverting water away from a cave could result in drying and death for the cave and for many cave animals. Also, too much water can lead to flooding and loss of air-breathing species. Altering the quantity of water inflow can also result in changes in the nutrient input.

Preserve Native Vegetation

Maintaining native vegetation in areas containing karst features is important. When native vegetation is destroyed or replaced by introduced plants, the overall species diversity declines. Many of these plants and animals may be critical to the nutrient regime of the karst ecosystem, and their loss could lead to nutrient depletion. By maintaining native surface vegetation in the vicinity of karst features, landowners can help minimize temperature

fluctuations, maintain moisture regimes, reduce potential for contamination, and reduce sedimentation from soil erosion.

Prevent Groundwater Contamination

Because karst is highly susceptible to groundwater contamination, the proper use and disposal of chemicals such as pesticides, motor oil, and household chemicals is very important. The use of broadcast pesticides, either liquid or granular, should be avoided in areas near known cave entrances or other karst features.

Restrict Human Visitation

Landowners can protect cave systems by restricting access and thereby reducing human visitation and impacts. Detrimental human impacts include habitat disturbance or loss due to soil compaction, changes in temperature and humidity, vandalism, abandonment of the cave by associated surface animals, and accumulation of toxic trash such as alkaline batteries.

Control Fire Ants

Although the full impact of fire ants on the karst ecosystems is not known, fire ants are believed to be a serious and increasingly important threat to the karst fauna. Controlling fire ants in areas surrounding cave entrances may help minimize their impact on the cave fauna. Effective treatments include hot water and commercial fire ant baits.

At present, there is little information available on the impacts that chemical methods of fire ant control used on the surface have on species that live exclusively underground. Because of this lack of information, the U.S. Fish and Wildlife Service (USFWS) recommends that only boiling water treatments be used on fire ant mounds within 35 feet of the cave entrance. This treatment involves pouring 1 to 4 gallons of hot water directly on the mound. The colony should be drenched with enough liquid so that the mound caves in on top of itself. Drenching is most effective during mid-morning, when the sun has started to warm up the mound. At this time, the colony should be located just under the upper crust on the side of the mound facing the sun. Do not in any way disturb the mound prior to treatment, since this causes the colony to take the queens to safety deep down in the mound or to a satellite mound.

For areas between 35 and 300 feet from the cave opening, the USFWS recommends treatment with boiling water or small amounts of fire ant bait. Since commercial fire ant baits such as Logic and Amdro may be harmful if ingested by other arthropods, they should be applied in a controlled manner to minimize effects on non-target species.

Bait should be placed only near fire ant mounds and not near the mounds of native ant species. The bait should be applied before noon if possible to allow time for the ants to gather most of it before nightfall, when cave crickets come out to forage. Care should be taken to prevent excess bait from remaining on the ground after allowing time for the ants to forage. It is important that the ground be dry (no morning dew) and the weather be clear and dry, with no forecast of rain in the next few hours. Also, bait is more effective if the ants are actively foraging. To test for this, put out a little bit of cheese, tuna fish, or peanut butter, and go back and check it in 15 to 20 minutes. If it is covered with fire ants, they are foraging and it is a good time to treat. By following these recommendations, you can help prevent the active ingredients in fire ant control chemicals from entering the food chain either directly or through cave crickets foraging on the surface at night.

The USFWS recommends the above strategy for treatment of fire ants near endangered species caves. In addition, any significant karst features in the vicinity of a cave with listed species, or that lie over the subterranean extent of a cave with listed species, should be treated according to the above recommendations. The USFWS recognizes that there may be instances where more intensive treatment is needed. Landowners and managers who believe more intensive treatment is necessary should contact the USFWS before proceeding, since permits may be required.

More information concerning management to protect caves and karst systems is available from the Texas Parks and Wildlife Department, U.S. Fish and Wildlife Service, or Texas Cave Management Association.

Funds for the production of this leaflet were provided by the U.S. Fish and Wildlife Service, under Section 6 of the Endangered Species Act.

Appendix 1
The Endangered Species Process

The Listing Process

To list a species, the U.S. Fish and Wildlife Service follows a strict legal process to propose and later to adopt regulations that have the effect of law. The USFWS publishes notices of review that identify U.S. species considered as "candidates" for listing. A priority system (based on degree and immediacy of threat and taxonomic factors) has been developed to direct efforts toward plants and animals with the greatest need for protection.

By law, listing decisions must be based solely on the best available biological data. Generally the USFWS requires information on a species distribution, biology and threats in order to make a listing decision.

In addition to USFWS initiation of listing proposals, such actions may also start as a recommendation or petition from individuals or organizations. Any person may suggest that a species be listed, but adequate information must be presented for the USFWS to make a positive listing decision. As part of the listing process, the USFWS must decide if a species should be proposed for listing as endangered or threatened. An endangered species is one in danger of extinction throughout all or a significant portion of its range. A threatened species is one likely to become endangered within the foreseeable future.

Once a species has been chosen for possible listing, preproposal letters of inquiry are sent to species experts, federal and state agencies, and other interested organizations and individuals. If biological information supports the decision to continue the listing process, a proposed rule is then published in the *Federal Register*. All interested parties are encouraged to comment and provide additional information and submit statements at any public hearings that may be held. The comment period is usually 60 days, and the public has 45 days to request a public hearing.

Within one year of publication of a listing proposal, one of three possible courses of action must be taken:

1) A final listing rule is published;
2) If the available biological information does not support the listing, the proposal is withdrawn; or
3) If, at the end of one year, there is substantial disagreement within the scientific community concerning the biological justification of the listing, the proposal may be extended for a maximum of six months. After that time, a decision must be made on the basis of the best scientific information available.

If approved, the final listing rule generally becomes effective 30 days after publication in the *Federal Register*. After a species is listed, its status is reviewed at least every five years to determine if federal protection is still warranted.

The Consultation Process

Section 7 of the Endangered Species Act requires that all federal agencies consult with the USFWS on endangered and threatened species. This consultation requirement involves all actions authorized, funded, or carried out by federal agencies. There are two categories of consultations – informal and formal.

Informal Consultation Steps

- Federal agency (or designated agent) contacts the USFWS for a list of endangered or threatened species in the project area and/or for information on the species.
- Federal agency (or designated agent) then makes a determination on whether the proposed action "may affect" the listed species. They may prepare a biological assessment to help make this determination.

- If it is determined by the federal agency or agent (and agreed upon by the USFWS) that the action would have no effect on the listed species, then no further consultation is necessary.
- If it is determined that the proposed action may affect listed species, then the federal action agency must initiate formal consultation with the USFWS.

Formal Consultation Steps

- The federal action agency initiates formal consultation with the USFWS in writing, and includes a description of the proposed action, the specific area of the proposed action, any federally listed species that may be affected by the action, how the proposed action may affect the listed species, and any other information available.
- The USFWS has up to 90 days to complete a biological opinion on the effects of the action on listed species. The purpose of the biological opinion is to determine whether or not the project will jeopardize the continued existence of a listed species or adversely modify its critical habitat. Formal consultation concludes at the end of the 90 days, unless the consultation period is extended by mutual agreement with the federal action agency and the USFWS.

The Recovery Process

Recovery is the process by which the decline of an endangered or threatened species is stopped or reversed (and threats to its survival are removed so that its long-term survival in nature can be assured). The primary goal of this process is the maintenance of secure, self-sustaining wild populations of species to the point where they no longer require the protection of the Endangered Species Act.

The steps in the USFWS' recovery program are:

1) Identify those ecosystems and organisms that face the highest degree of threat.
2) Determine tasks necessary to reduce or eliminate the threats.
3) Apply the resources available to the highest recovery tasks.
4) Reclassify and delist the species as appropriate.

The first step in the recovery process is the development of species-specific recovery goals and the identification and ranking of species information and management needs in terms of their relative importance and timing for recovery. This information is usually set forth in a recovery plan for each listed species.

A recovery plan is a broad planning document that outlines the tasks that will contribute to the recovery of the species, including those that (if successful) are likely to permit reclassification or delisting of the species. These recovery plans present an overview of recovery actions needed for a species and associated cost estimates by all cooperating agencies. However, they do not obligate any agency, entity, or persons to implement the various tasks listed in the plan. They serve as a blueprint for private, federal and state interagency cooperation in the implementation of recovery actions.

Coordination among federal, state, and local agencies; academic researchers; conservation organizations; private individuals; and major land users is perhaps the most essential ingredient for the development and implementation of an effective recovery program. In its role as coordinator of the recovery process, the USFWS must emphasize cooperation and teamwork among all involved parties.

The recovery planning process provides opportunities for public participation, since commitments and partnerships from various segments of society are needed in order for the process to succeed.

Appendix 2
State Listed Endangered and Threatened Species

Endangered

Common Name	Scientific Name
American Peregrine Falcon	*Falco peregrinus anatum*
Atlantic Hawksbill Sea Turtle	*Erethmochelys imbricata imbricata*
Attwater's Greater Prairie-Chicken	*Tympanuchus cupido attwateri*
Bald Eagle	*Haliaeetus leucocephalus*
Big Bend Gambusia	*Gambusia gaigei*
Black Bear	*Ursus americanus*
Black Right Whale	*Eubalaena glacialis*
Black-capped Vireo	*Vireo atricapillus*
Black-footed Ferret	*Mustela nigripes*
Black-spotted Newt	*Notophthalmus meridionalis*
Blackfin Goby	*Gobionellus atripinnis*
Blanco Blind Salamander	*Eurycea robusta*
Blotched Gambusia	*Gambusia senilis*
Blue Whale	*Balaenoptera musculus*
Bluntnose Shiner	*Notropis simus*
Brown Pelican	*Pelecanus occidentalis*
Chihuahuan Mud Turtle	*Kinosternon hirtipes murrayi*
Clear Creek Gambusia	*Gambusia heterochir*
Comanche Springs Pupfish	*Cyprinodon elegans*
Concho Water Snake	*Nerodia paucimaculata*
Eskimo Curlew	*Numenius borealis*
Finback Whale	*Balaenoptera physalus*
Fountain Darter	*Etheostoma fonticola*
Golden-cheeked Warbler	*Dendroica chrysoparia*
Gray Wolf	*Canis lupus*
Greater Long-nosed Bat	*Leptonycteris nivalis*
Houston Toad	*Bufo houstonensis*
Interior Least Tern	*Sterna antillarum athalassos*
Ivory-billed Woodpecker	*Campephilus principalis*
Jaguar	*Panthera onca*
Jaguarundi	*Felis yaguarondi cacomitli*
Kemp's Ridley Sea Turtle	*Lepidochelys kempii*
Leatherback Sea Turtle	*Dermochelys coriacea*
Leon Springs Pupfish	*Cyprinodon bovinus*
Loggerhead Sea Turtle	*Caretta caretta*
Louisiana Black Bear	*Ursus americanus luteolus*
Louisiana Pine Snake	*Pituophis melanoleucus ruthveni*
Margay	*Felis wiedii*
Mexican Wolf	*Canis lupus baileyi*
Northern Aplomado Falcon	*Falco femoralis septentrionalis*
Northern Cat-eyed Snake	*Leptodeira septentrionalis septentrionalis*
Ocelot	*Felis pardalis*
Paddlefish	*Polyodon spathula*
Pecos Gambusia	*Gambusia nobilis*
Phantom Shiner	*Notropis orca*
Red Wolf	*Canis rufus*
Red-cockaded Woodpecker	*Picoides borealis*
San Marcos Gambusia	*Gambusia georgei*
Shovelnose Sturgeon	*Scaphirhynchus platorynchus*
Smooth Green Snake	*Liochlorophis vernalis*
South Texas Siren (large form)	*Siren sp.*
Speckled Racer	*Drymobius margaritiferus*

Common Name	Scientific Name
Sperm Whale	*Physeter macrocephalus*
Texas Blind Salamander	*Eurycea rathbuni*
West Indian Manatee	*Trichechus manatus*
White-lipped Frog	*Leptodactylus labialis*
White-nosed Coati	*Nasua narica*
Whooping Crane	*Grus americana*

Threatened

Common Name	Scientific Name
Alligator Snapping Turtle	*Macroclemys temminckii*
American Swallow-tailed Kite	*Elanoides forficatus*
Arctic Peregrine Falcon	*Falco peregrinus tundrius*
Atlantic Spotted Dolphin	*Stenella frontalis*
Bachman's Sparrow	*Aimophila aestivalis*
Big Bend Blackhead Snake	*Tantilla rubra*
Black-striped Snake	*Coniophanes imperialis*
Blackside Darter	*Percina maculata*
Blue Sucker	*Cycleptus elongatus*
Bluehead Shiner	*Notropis hubbsi*
Brazos Water Snake	*Nerodia harteri harteri*
Cactus Ferruginous Pygmy-Owl	*Glaucidium brasilianum cactorum*
Cascade Caverns Salamander	*Eurycea latitans*
Chihuahua Shiner	*Notropis chihuahua*
Comal Blind Salamander	*Eurycea tridentifera*
Common Black-Hawk	*Buteogallus anthracinus*
Conchos Pupfish	*Cyprinodon eximius*
Coues' Rice Rat	*Oryzomys couesi aquaticus*
Creek Chubscuker	*Erimyzon oblongus*
Devils River Minnow	*Dionda diaboli*
Dwarf Sperm Whale	*Kogia simus*
False Killer Whale	*Pseudorca crassidens*
Ferruginous Pygmy-Owl	*Glaucidium brasilianum*
Gervais' Beaked Whale	*Mesoplodon europaeus*
Goose-beaked Whale	*Ziphius cavirostris*
Green Sea Turtle	*Chelonia mydas*
Indigo Snake	*Drymarchon corais*
Killer Whale	*Orcinus orca*
Mexican Burrowing Toad	*Rhinophrynus dorsalis*
Mexican Stoneroller	*Campostoma ornatum*
Mexican Treefrog	*Smilisca baudinii*
Mountain Short-horned Lizard	*Phrynosoma douglasi hernandesi*
Northern Beardless-Tyrannulet	*Camptostoma imberbe*
Northern Gray Hawk	*Buteo nitidus maximus*
Northern Scarlet Snake	*Cemophora coccinea copei*
Opossum Pipefish	*Microphis brachyurus*
Palo Duro Mouse	*Peromyscus truei comanche*
Pecos Pupfish	*Cyprinodon pecosensis*
Piping Plover	*Charadrius melodus*
Proserpine Shiner	*Cyprinella proserpina*
Pygmy Killer Whale	*Feresa attenuata*
Pygmy Sperm Whale	*Kogia breviceps*
Rafinesque's Big-eared Bat	*Corynorhinus* (=Plecotus) *rafinesquii*
Reddish Egret	*Egretta rufescens*
Reticulate Collared Lizard	*Crotaphytus reticulatus*
Reticulated Gecko	*Coleonyx reticulatus*
Rio Grande Chub	*Gila pandora*
Rio Grande Darter	*Etheostoma grahami*
River Goby	*Awaous tajasica*
Rose-throated Becard	*Pachyramphus aglaiae*

Common Name	Scientific Name
Rough-toothed Dolphin	*Steno bredanensis*
San Marcos Salamander	*Eurycea nana*
Sheep Frog	*Hypopachus variolosus*
Short-finned Pilot Whale	*Globicephala macrorhynchus*
Sooty Tern	*Sterna fuscata*
Southern Yellow Bat	*Lasiurus ega*
Spotted Bat	*Euderma maculatum*
Texas Botteri's Sparrow	*Aimophila botterii texana*
Texas Horned Lizard	*Phrynosoma cornutum*
Texas Kangaroo Rat	*Dipodomys elator*
Texas Lyre Snake	*Trimorphodon biscutatus vilkinsoni*
Texas Scarlet Snake	*Cemophora coccinea lineri*
Texas Tortoise	*Gopherus berlandieri*
Timber Rattlesnake	*Crotalus horridus*
Toothless Blindcat	*Trogloglanis pattersoni*
Tropical Parula	*Parula pitiayumi nigrilora*
White-faced Ibis	*Plegadis chihi*
White-tailed Hawk	*Buteo albicaudatus*
Widemouth Blindcat	*Satan eurystomus*
Wood Stork	*Mycteria americana*
Zone-tailed Hawk	*Buteo albonotatus*